The Gathering Storm

A VOLUME IN THE SERIES

THE UNITED STATES IN THE WORLD

Edited by David C. Engerman,
Amy S. Greenberg, and Paul A. Kramer

A list of titles in this series is available at cornellpress.cornell.edu.

The Gathering Storm

Eduardo Frei's Revolution in
Liberty and Chile's Cold War

Sebastián Hurtado-Torres

Cornell University Press
Ithaca and London

First published 2020 by Cornell University Press

Library of Congress Cataloging-in-Publication Data

Names: Hurtado-Torres, Sebastián, 1982– author.
Title: The gathering storm : Eduardo Frei's revolution in liberty and
    Chile's cold war / Sebastián Hurtado-Torres.
Description: Ithaca : Cornell University Press, 2020. | Series: The United
    States in the world | Includes bibliographical references and index.
Identifiers: LCCN 2019025914 (print) | LCCN 2019025915 (ebook) |
    ISBN 9781501747182 (hardcover) | ISBN 9781501747199 (epub) |
    ISBN 9781501747205 (pdf)
Subjects: LCSH: Frei Montalva, Eduardo, 1911–1982. | United
    States—Foreign relations—Chile. | Chile—Foreign relations—
    United States. | Chile—Politics and government—1920–1970.
Classification: LCC E183.8.C4 H87 2020 (print) | LCC E183.8.C4
    (ebook) | DDC 327.73083—dc23
LC record available at https://lccn.loc.gov/2019025914
LC ebook record available at https://lccn.loc.gov/2019025915

To the memory of Macarena Acuña Bardessi

Contents

Acknowledgments

In crafting this book, I have had the fortune of receiving assistance, support, and encouragement from a number of people and institutions, the mention of whose names in this section is only a minimal and insufficient form of acknowledgment and gratitude on my part. First, I must thank, in the names of Drs. John Brobst, Katherine Jellison, Chester Pach, Ingo Trauschweitzer, and Steve Miner, the Department of History and the Contemporary History Institute at Ohio University for invaluable assistance for my research, which included a number of trips I could not have afforded without their generous funding. The rest of the faculty of the Ohio University Department of History taught me to better understand the United States and its foreign policy, thus helping me develop a more nuanced view of the history of the relations between Latin America and its big neighbor of the north. Outside the Department of History, Dr. Brad Jokisch also contributed in this regard. The Office of the Vice President for Research at OU and the Graduate Student Senate also granted me helpful assistance in research for this book. Finally, the administrative staff at the OU Department of History and the Contemporary History Institute, especially Kara Dunfee, Sherry Gillogly, and Brenda Nelson, made my life easier while I was a graduate student by performing their duties with great professionalism, dedication, and care. CONICYT, the Chilean chapter of the Fulbright Foundation, and the Institute of International Education, especially through Zamaly Diaz and Megan Shuck, helped me find and apply to the doctoral program at Ohio University and provided the funding I needed to complete the program and obtain the degree.

As a foreigner in the heartland of the United States, I had the privilege of being warmly welcomed by a number of people who became my friends and made my stay in the beautiful town of Athens, Ohio, one of the happiest times of my life. In one way or another, Patrick Campbell, Meredith Hohe, Tracy Kelly, and Bill King provided me with a helping hand when I needed it, without asking for or expecting anything in return. The same must be said of Anthony Crews, Gerald Goodwin, Joe Venosa, and Ben Wollet, whose friendship and intellectual kinship I value beyond words. Michael Cook, a man of great integrity and a most generous heart, privileged me with his friendship, even though our backgrounds and outlooks are worlds apart. Finally, Berlin, Wisconsin's, one and only Brad Eidahl, by way of our shared interest in Chilean history, satirical humor, and Dr. Pepper, became my closest and most enduring friend; in addition to that, and to make all this pertinent, he gave me his comments on various sections of this book.

In doing research for this book, I had the opportunity to visit a number of archives in Chile and the United States. In all of them, the staff was incredibly helpful and nice to me. By particularly thanking Mr. Roberto Mercado of the Historic Archive of the Chilean Ministry of Foreign Relations, I thank all the people who helped me at the National Archives II, the Archives of the International Monetary Fund, the John F. Kennedy Presidential Library, the Lyndon B. Johnson Presidential Library, the Richard Nixon Presidential Library, the Eduardo Frei Montalva Library and Museum, the National Library of Chile, and the Alden Library at Ohio University. Tomás Croquevielle, for his part, deserves my gratitude for all the assistance he gave me gathering material for this book and in other academic endeavors of mine. The editorial team of Cornell University Press, especially Michael McGandy, has also been helpful in making the publication of this book possible. As is the case with all scholarship, my work would not have been possible without the work of them all.

English is my second language, so I am in great debt to all the people who helped me acquire the skills necessary to write this book. The English teachers at my high school, Instituto Nacional, deserve this symbolic and insufficient display of gratitude at least as much as anyone else. Mmes. Laura Toledo, Isabel Ebensperger, Sonia Landeros, Avelina Valdés, and Jeanette Rojas strived to help us learn a language we had little exposure to, in the challenging and sometimes hostile environment of an all-male public school. At the time I did not recognize that effort properly; today, I must say that, thanks to their dedication, I learned more than just the basics of the English language. Without their work, I wouldn't have been able to study in the United States, let alone write this book. In the same vein, the teachers with the English Program for

Internationals at the University of South Carolina did a great job helping me get ready for the daunting challenge of pursuing a doctoral degree in the United States. Charles Portney, Vanessa Torres, Marit Bobo, Kathie Bledsoe, Lynn Voit, and, especially, Dick Holmes contributed greatly to my ability to put these words on paper.

Two scholars of the highest quality and reputation have taught me most of what I know about being a historian. Dr. Patrick Barr-Melej directed my work as a graduate student at Ohio University with great care and taught me how to properly write a dissertation. What is more, he has been extremely generous in helping me understand the nuts and bolts of U.S. academia. Furthermore, going well beyond his duties as an adviser, he has become a close friend whose counsel and words of encouragement have helped me keep standing in times of great distress and anguish. I have no words to thank him properly for this. Dr. Joaquín Fermandois, one of the greatest historians of Chile, has been my mentor since we first met when I was an undergraduate student at Pontificia Universidad Católica in the early 2000s. He has treated me always with great respect and has helped me at every stage of my career. Moreover, by engaging with my intellectual arguments, in writing or conversation over numerous dinners, he has forced me to think of history and human nature in ways I could probably not have conceived of by myself. My intellectual growth and, consequently, this book are to a large extent the result of Dr. Fermandois' guidance.

My family has been with me, in all the connotations that expression has, all along this process. My mother Patricia and my aunt Marisol have done their best to help me and my siblings become good persons, even though circumstances many times seemed to push us all in a different direction. My sister Sofía has always been a source of inspiration and bliss, while my brother Diego has been a worthy intellectual counterpart and has helped me lighten the burden of my worries by worrying, himself, about things that should in truth be the responsibility of others. In addition, he read the first draft of this book and gave me his insightful comments on it.

I have been fortunate to have made many friends who have also helped me in moments of need and have, therefore, made their contribution to the making of this book. Dr. Cristina Rigo-Righi, Sebastián Figueroa, Mauricio Barraza, José Díaz, and Patricio Delgado literally taught me how to walk again. Without their help, I could not have done anything I have done, for better or worse, in my adult life. Sergio Jorquera and Javier Aravena gave me a hand at a time I needed it with great urgency. Camila Tejo and Francisco Orrego, in addition to their close friendship, provided me with indispensable assistance in moments of great transitions in my life. These words represent barely a fraction of the gratitude I feel toward them. I also have to mention those friends who, over a decade ago, made the effort of throwing a party in my honor and genuinely shared with me a moment of pure happiness. Marcela, Carmen, Macarena, Paz, Felipe, Alejandro, Alfredo, Marcelo, Felipe, María Estela, and, above all, Walter, gave me a pat on the back that I can only partially reciprocate by naming them here. Finally, the greatest acknowledgment of all must go to Susan, the one person who stood by me every single moment of the process of making this book a reality; mentioning her name here is an embarrassingly insufficient way of recognizing her efforts and thanking her for all she ever did for me.

Abbreviations

AID	Agency for International Development
API	*Alianza Popular Independiente*; Popular Independent Alliance
CEPAL	*Comisión Económica para América Latina y el Caribe*; Economic Commission for Latin America and the Caribbean
CUT	*Central Única de Trabajadores*; National Workers' Union
DR	*Democracia Radical*; Radical Democracy
FD	*Frente Democrático*; Democratic Front
FRAP	*Frente de Acción Popular*; Popular Action Front
IMF	International Monetary Fund
INDAP	*Instituto de Desarrollo Agropecuario*; Institute for Agrarian Development
MAPU	*Movimiento de Acción Popular Unitario*; Unitarian Popular Action Movement
MNR	*Movimiento Nacionalista Revolucionario*; National Revolutionary Movement (Bolivia)
OAS	Organization of American States
PADENA	*Partido Democrático Nacional*; Democratic National Party
PC	*Partido Comunista*; Communist Party
PDC	*Partido Democratacristiano*; Christian Democratic Party
PL	*Partido Liberal*; Liberal Party
PN	*Partido Nacional*; National Party
PR	*Partido Radical*; Radical Party
PS	*Partido Socialista*; Socialist Party

UP   *Unidad Popular,* Popular Unity
USOPO   *Unión Socialista Popular,* Popular Socialist Union

The Gathering Storm

Introduction

The United States and Chilean Politics in the Cold War

In 2004, former U.S. ambassador to Chile Ralph Dungan gave an interview to a Chilean newsmagazine during which he spoke freely about the generous financial aid the United States government—and the Central Intelligence Agency (CIA) in particular—provided to the presidential campaign of Christian Democratic leader Eduardo Frei Montalva in 1964.[1] This was anything but fresh news, and Dungan must have assumed as much. The reports of a conspicuous U.S. congressional committee had already unveiled that story in 1975, as had numerous scholars interested in U.S.-Chilean relations during the Cold War.[2] Members of Chile's Christian Democratic Party (PDC), however, reacted to these seemingly insignificant remarks in a truly Orwellian fashion, vehemently denying that the CIA channeled money to the Frei campaign in 1964. Among the emphatic deniers was Andrés Zaldívar, one of the most reputable PDC leaders of the last decades.[3] Zaldívar occupied an important position on Frei's campaign team in 1964 and served as minister of finance from March 1968 to November 1970. In that position, he developed a relatively close and consequential relationship with U.S. Ambassador Edward Korry (who served as ambassador to Chile from 1967 into 1971). Afterward, Zaldívar was a prominent opponent of Popular Unity (UP)—the coalition of Communists, Socialists, Radicals, and former Christian Democrats led by President Salvador Allende—that had governed Chile between 1970 and 1973. In the 1980s, Zaldívar became a leader of the opposition to the military dictatorship, which he and his party had welcomed at first, and endured a few years of exile as a result. After the end of the Augusto Pinochet dictatorship (which ran from

1973 into 1990), Zaldívar served as minister and senator, and later launched an unsuccessful presidential bid in 1999. His remarkable career rested on his refined political acumen, his consistent identification with a moderate strain of reformist politics, and his ability to change course when circumstances required. Consequently, he was widely respected as a politician with significant clout. His credentials, intelligence, and keen political judgment notwithstanding, Zaldívar has adamantly denied that any CIA funding buttressed the Frei campaign in 1964.

The PDC's denials reflect immediate political considerations. In Chile's political culture, marked by a suspiciousness toward the intentions of the United States and, in some cases, by outright anti-Americanism, accepting the truth of U.S. sponsorship of the Frei campaign in 1964 might be akin to accepting complicity with foreign intervention and, more ominously, with the imperialistic designs of the continental hegemon.[4] In addition, men like Zaldívar and other long-standing members of the PDC may very well feel guilty about their own roles on the road toward the destruction of Chilean democracy in 1973. Consequently, they now view their partnership with the United States in a very different light. Since Chilean democracy eroded rapidly from the end of the 1960s and eventually fell to a brutal military coup in 1973, politicians who actively participated in such a process are logically reluctant to embrace actions that may be currently considered conducive to the breakdown. As these retrospective assessments are often visceral and usually expressed in Manichaean terms, a vindication of the partnership between Eduardo Frei's so-called Revolution in Liberty and the United States runs the risk of placing the PDC on the same side of an international hegemonic power that, at least until 1977, supported Augusto Pinochet's dictatorship explicitly.[5] Even worse, such vindication would bring to the fore the fact that the PDC was once a fierce ideological and political adversary of the very same political forces—Socialists, Radicals, and Communists—with which it has established alliances since the return of democracy in 1990.

In this case, however, the PDC's denial of one specific fact—the CIA's patronage—entails the denial of a significant segment of the party's history and, arguably, of its very ideological identity. The PDC became a powerful force in Chilean politics by the end of the 1950s largely because it presented the country with a project for development attuned with Chile's political system and culture. Eduardo Frei Montalva reached the presidency in 1964 because his promise of a Revolution in Liberty—an ambitious attempt at social and economic reform without a significant modification of the existing political structures—resonated with the largest constituency in Chile's electorate:

those opposed to a precarious and unequal socio-economic status quo as well as to the radical project of transformation presented by the Marxist Left.[6]

The PDC's political project in 1964 reflected a strongly anti-Marxist sensibility and a forward-looking reformist program; on either count, it should not be dissociated from its main international sponsor: the United States. Nonetheless, mostly because of the negative images of intervention evoked by the United States as a result of President Richard Nixon's hostile policies toward the Allende government, the PDC has chosen to deny or at least downplay its close association with the administration of President Lyndon B. Johnson between 1964 and 1969, especially at the time of the 1964 election. In Chile's current political culture and memory, Frei's Revolution in Liberty has lost one of the fundamental dimensions it had in the context of the Cold War: its legitimacy as an explicit and even militant alternative to Marxism on the Chilean stage and in the continental and worldwide ideological struggles between two distinctive paths toward modernization.[7] In this regard, the partnership between Frei's Revolution in Liberty and the Johnson administration (1963–1969) should occupy a much more significant place in the narrative of the PDC and, by extension, Chile's political history.

Not that this attitude of denial is exclusive to the Christian Democratic Party. As a result of the trauma inherited from the breakdown of Chilean democracy and the violence of the Pinochet dictatorship, almost all Chilean political forces have developed, more or less successfully, romanticized or sanitized views of their own histories. On the Left, the PDC's posture toward its past finds counterparts in the stubborn convictions of many in Chile and abroad that the United States was directly involved in the 1973 military coup— no record or credible testimony has shown this to be true, even if it is clear that the Nixon administration's covert overt policies toward Chile between 1970 and 1973 aimed at the failure of the UP government—and in the common yet misleading admiration of Allende as the leader of an unquestionably democratic project despite the undeniable fact that all the political models the Chilean Left admired during the Cold War (the USSR, East Germany, Yugoslavia, Cuba, and so forth) were undemocratic and authoritarian. On the Right, even today, a good number of people justify the coup that overthrew Allende and the brutal dictatorship that followed on the basis of a supposedly massive presence in Chile of armed foreigners, mostly Cubans, intent on helping Allende to swiftly and bloodily establish a communist regime. As a consequence, a visible and shocking gap has developed between the current state of our historical understanding of Chilean politics in the 1960s and the narrative about the same period underlying the country's political culture.

The deliberate preference of Chilean politicians for doublethink, if not out-right lying, is appalling and indefensible. Since one of the main functions of scholarship is to shed light—as honestly and rigorously as possible—on contro-versial matters that those with vested interests may want to obscure, I have come to think of this work not only as an academic contribution to the historiogra-phy of U.S.-Chilean relations but also as an intervention in a Chilean political culture that appears to be at odds with a considerable evidentiary base on the subject of the experience of the Cold War in Chile. Hence, one of the main purposes of this book is to emphasize the critical and heretofore elided impor-tance of one of those aspects on which several scholars have written abun-dantly but which Chilean political actors have chosen to overlook or deny: the close relationship between Frei's Revolution in Liberty and the United States, beginning with the partnership they forged during the 1964 Chilean presidential campaign.

The United States and Frei's Revolution in Liberty

This book also offers a fresh contribution to our understanding of the Latin American foreign policy of the United States in the years of the Johnson ad-ministration and, more particularly, the purposes and mechanisms of U.S. in-volvement in Chilean politics since 1964. For the United States foreign policy apparatus, the Christian Democratic Party of Chile—with its commitment to liberal democracy; its reformist zeal; and its capacity to act within a relatively effective and solid political system—appeared to be a model partner in the real-ization of the goals of the Alliance for Progress, the Latin American policy conceived by President John F. Kennedy and continued, though without the same level of enthusiasm and hope, by his successor, Lyndon B. Johnson. In its original conception, Kennedy's Latin American policy had ambitious eco-nomic, social, and political goals. The channeling of aid from the United States to Latin American countries in the 1960s sought to reflect the interplay be-tween those aims, even if the implementation of the Alliance for Progress sorely lacked in consistency and constancy, which to a large extent explains its failure to deliver on the greatest part of its promise. In the case of Chile and Eduardo Frei's Revolution in Liberty, the exceptionally generous provision of aid by the United States went hand in hand with a deep involvement of agents of U.S. foreign policy, especially the political staff of the embassy in Santiago, in the day-to-day functioning of Chilean politics—welcomed and, in many cases, invited by local actors.

By exploring and analyzing the mechanisms of U.S. involvement in Chilean politics, this work offers a comprehensive narrative of the relations between the United States and Chile during the Frei administration, which, rather surprisingly, no scholarly work has done before. Thus, it adds a new layer to a corpus of literature that has concentrated on more particular dimensions of that involvement, such as the undercover operations undertaken in Chile by the CIA or the policymaking process behind the provision of foreign aid.[8] Furthermore, by focusing the narrative on Chilean political developments rather than on the policymaking process in Washington, this book offers a new perspective on the process of erosion of Chilean democracy that began during the Frei administration and on the role played by the United States in that process.

Three major arguments about the character of U.S. involvement in Chilean politics in the years of the Revolution in Liberty underlie the narrative of this book. First, the partnership between the Johnson and Frei administrations stood as much on a shared vision of modernization as it did on their opposition to the Marxist Left. Starting with Ralph Dungan (ambassador to Chile from 1964 into 1967), who embraced the program and spirit of the Revolution in Liberty as much as the most committed Christian Democrat, U.S. diplomatic officials stationed in Chile or dealing with Chilean matters from Washington had a genuine interest in Frei's success as an agent of what they saw as the right kind of modernization, representing the sensibility of the entire U.S. foreign policy apparatus of the Kennedy-Johnson era. As Ambassador Korry put it, the Revolution in Liberty of Chile's Christian Democratic Party was a "noble and necessary experiment," worth supporting generously and enthusiastically.[9] In fact, defeating the Marxist Left—the most urgent objective of the U.S. strategy toward Chile—was itself a function of the deeper ideological convictions underlying the U.S. position in the Cold War. After all, the United States opposed Marxism in Chile, as everywhere else, because it represented a vision for the world irreconcilably different from its own. In the specific case of the partnership between the Johnson administration and Frei's Revolution in Liberty, the ideological views of U.S. liberalism on modernization, and on the long-term promotion of U.S. interests abroad, and the specific mediation of diplomatic agents committed to such vision all served as a strong foundation for an extraordinarily close and warm relationship.[10]

Second, I argue that the U.S. embassy in Santiago, at some points teaming with the CIA, became an informal but empowered actor in Chilean politics. Its staff developed a wide network of relationships with Chilean political figures whose interests converged with those of the United States. Christian Democrats and politicians of other persuasions, moreover, drew U.S. diplomatic officials into matters of a clearly internal nature. This book, then, is as much a traditional diplomatic history of the relations between two governments as it is a political history of Chile in the period between 1964 and 1970. Unlike most accounts on the subject, however, this study develops a narrative of Chilean politics in the years of the Frei administration in which the United States, through the agency of the embassy in Santiago and the CIA, was not an external force but an actor deeply involved in affairs of a domestic character.[11] Until Allende's victory in 1970, U.S. officials sought inclusion in Chile's political system and political culture by exploiting the convergent interests between them and local actors, taking advantage of the leverage the United States could exert through its provision of economic aid and political support. The Johnson administration's policy toward Chile, executed with a great deal of independence by its diplomatic agents stationed in Santiago, pursued the construction of partnerships with local actors whose autonomy and preeminent position in the design and development of policy was never in question.

The United States asserted its undisputed continental hegemony in Chile between 1964 and 1970 in a moderate manner, more in the style of an "empire by invitation," as in the case of its relations with the countries of post-World War II Europe, than in the ruthless and oppressive form of capitalist imperialism so loudly denounced by Latin American Marxists and left-wing nationalists throughout the twentieth century.[12] What is more, much like in post-World War II Europe, U.S. foreign policy did not intend to set the boundaries for political action in Chile in the years of the Frei administration. To be sure, the asymmetry in power and resources between the countries was conspicuous in a few instances, such as the negotiations over copper prices in 1965 and 1966 (see chapter 4). Even then, however, the relationship was based on the shared assumption that Chile's institutions and legal framework were legitimate. Moreover, when U.S. involvement in Chilean politics did bend the legal norms, such as when the CIA provided funding for political parties and candidates, those actions did not depart from regular practice, as the Marxist Left—especially the Communist Party—also received money from foreign sources, albeit in much smaller amounts.[13] In any case, at no point did the Johnson administration adopt a threatening, much less a subversive, attitude toward Chile in the years of the Frei administration. As is well known, the attitude of the Nixon administration toward Chilean affairs was substantially different in light of Allende's election.[14]

The third argument of the book is that the intimate partnership developed by the Christian Democratic Party and the Johnson administration contributed significantly to further polarize Chilean politics during the years of the

Frei government and beyond. After Richard Nixon assumed the presidency of the United States in 1969, the Frei administration could no longer count on massive U.S. aid to buttress its political project—which by then had lost its original impetus anyway—but the close relationship between Frei, some of his closest aides, and Ambassador Korry remained strong and consequential for Chilean politics beyond Allende's accession to the presidency in 1970. The significant involvement of the United States in Chile since 1964 strengthened the anti-Marxist side of the political spectrum, especially Frei and his followers within the PDC, both materially and ideologically. Simultaneously, throughout the 1960s, the Marxist Left, especially Allende's own Socialist Party, assumed an ever more radical position and embraced ever more enthusiastically the spirit and political example of socialist countries, such as Cuba. Even more important, by the end of the 1960s Communists and Socialists had settled on the conviction that the goal of transforming Chile into a socialist country was achievable in the not so distant future. As a result, the gulf between the Marxist Left and their opponents widened and deepened.

Conservatives on the Right feared the imminent destruction of the political, cultural, and social order in which the interests of landed elites and the entrepreneurial class remained safe. Many among them preferred and even yearned for a strong, authoritarian government determined to stop the wave of radical change proposed by Christian Democrats and the Left and to impose order on what they perceived, not so mistakenly, as a volatile situation. On the other hand, many Christian Democrats and other middle-class groups had the certainty that the political project of the Marxist Left would eventually destroy the institutions of liberal democracy from the inside, as in Czechoslovakia in 1948, and establish a full-blown communist dictatorship, as Fidel Castro's revolutionaries had done in Cuba after 1959. Communists and Socialists, fully convinced of the righteousness and historical inevitability of their cause, did little to assuage the fears of their opponents, which could always be rationalized as desperate cries from reactionary forces watching their world fall apart or be exposed as imperialistic propaganda. Since these interpretations contained, in fact, a grain of truth, it was relatively easy for Communists, Socialists, and other left-wing groups to portray Chilean democracy as little more than a system of domination established by the national bourgeoisie in alliance with the forces of capitalist imperialism. Furthermore, imperialism in the Americas was represented by none other than the United States, enemy of all the countries and political forces admired by the Marxist Left and the main international sponsor of its strongest rival in the arena of Chilean politics, the PDC.[15]

By the presidential election of 1970, the common ideological ground underlying the country's political system and culture had shrunk significantly, not least because the language of the global Cold War had virtually taken over Chilean politics. By 1973, the common ground had all but disappeared. On 11 September 1973, the storm that began to gather in the years of the Frei administration unleashed all its fury over a society that too often and too conceitedly had prided itself in the sturdiness of its institutions and the uniqueness of its democracy. Thousands suffered directly the violence of a regime whose primary purpose was to root out once and for all the ideological project and the political culture of the Marxist Left; no one was left untouched by the radical program of neoliberal modernization ruthlessly implemented by the Pinochet dictatorship in the seventeen years that followed the brutal overthrow of Salvador Allende. This book tells the story of the first stage of the process that led to the destruction of what once was considered the finest democracy in Latin America.

Chilean Politics and U.S. Records

This book explores the involvement of the United States in Chilean politics between 1964 and 1970. It focuses on the political relationship between the Johnson and Frei governments and on the role in Chilean politics played by the U.S. embassy in Santiago from the presidential campaign of 1964 to Allende's victory in the presidential election of September 1970. The covert operations carried out by the CIA in Chile in the same period, thoroughly treated by authors such as Peter Kornbluh and Kristian Gustafson, are only marginally assessed here.[16] This thematic preference implies a broad thesis about the character and some specifics of the relationship between the United States and Chile in the crucial period between 1964 and 1970. Focus on CIA operations has overshadowed the more consistent and coherent involvement of the United States in Chilean politics during the Frei administration, which a number of books and essays have dealt with but no published work has comprehensively assessed.[17] This study provides an account of the relations between the United States and Chile in the years of the Revolution in Liberty, centering on subjects and instances of interaction so far ignored or only marginally considered in the existing scholarship.

The research for this book was conducted mostly with the records of the Department of State at the National Archives II and the John F. Kennedy, Lyndon B. Johnson, and Richard Nixon presidential libraries. Other published collections of U.S. documents, such as the *Foreign Relations of the United States (FRUS)* series and the online repositories of records declassified under the Freedom of Information Act, also have been of substantial value. In Chile, the records of the Frei Foundation, especially Frei's personal correspondence, expose his more intimate thoughts on the evolution of Chilean politics during his tenure. Finally, the records of the sessions of the Chilean Congress offer insight into the ways in which different political forces understood the relations between Chile and the United States throughout this period and contribute to the understanding of the debates on the propriety or convenience of some specific policies related to those relations.

The preponderance of U.S. archival material in this book requires an explanation. Even though Chilean sources were abundantly consulted, the information they offer is, in general, less substantial than the information provided by U.S. documents, in many cases even with respect to the inner workings of Chilean politics. In the case of U.S. and Chilean diplomatic correspondence, the differences in quantity, content, and character are enormous. While U.S. diplomatic documents cover an astonishingly wide range of subjects and are an excellent window into the more particular, and even intimate, aspects of the relations between U.S. diplomats and Chilean political actors, the records of the Chilean Ministry of Foreign Relations and its embassy in Washington are, in general, exceedingly formal and devoted mostly to state-to-state relations, with little to show for the more clearly ideological side of the relationship between the Johnson and Frei administrations.

In fact, one interesting finding of the research behind this book is that U.S. diplomatic records are indispensable for a thorough understanding of the political history of Cold War Chile. Besides the involvement of U.S. diplomatic officials in Chilean politics, these documents offer invaluable information about the ideas, opinions, intentions, and plans of important Chilean political actors in some specific instances in this period. Since many politicians, beginning with President Frei, viewed the United States as a redoubtable partner in meeting particular goals, they spoke quite freely about virtually all topics of relevance in Chilean domestic politics with their U.S. diplomatic interlocutors.

Consequently, the remarkably detailed reports sent by the U.S. embassy in Santiago to the State Department and the White House provide an extraordinary source for the study of Chilean politics in the 1960s and early 1970s. For instance, Frei's reaction to Allende's victory in 1970 and his intentions to provoke an institutional crisis in its wake—the subject of the last chapter of this book—cannot be properly assessed through Chilean sources, mostly because the main protagonists of those events, much like the Ventura family in José

Donoso's *A House in the Country*, have drawn a heavy veil of secrecy and denial over them.[18] Of course, these documents were developed from a distinctive and inevitably partial perspective. As a result, some views and facts are emphasized and others downplayed. In the same vein, some characters, such as Eduardo Frei, are shown in a better light than others, such as Radomiro Tomic and Foreign Minister Gabriel Valdés. Still, for all their biases and interests, the authors of these documents did not invent realities, mostly because it was not in their best interest to do so. Consequently, the records of the United States foreign policy apparatus, especially those of the Department of State, are an extraordinary source for the reconstruction of a story that few Chilean documents and testimonies address with the same degree of honesty and accuracy.

Chilean Politics and U.S. Hegemony

After serving as U.S. ambassador in Santiago for a year and a half, Ralph Dungan had acquired a keen understanding of the way in which his Chilean interlocutors, from President Frei down, saw him and the avenues these perceptions opened for him in the fulfillment of his duties. He was not just another diplomat residing in the capital city of a small yet influential South American country. He was the ambassador of the United States, one of the Cold War superpowers, and more important, the actual or potential partner of all the forces opposed to the revolutionary Left in the context of Chilean politics. President Frei could very well forget the name of the Soviet ambassador in Santiago and not incur any cost for that oversight; Dungan, on the contrary, was the representative in Chile of the main sponsor of his Revolution in Liberty and the leader of the ideological camp in which many Chilean politicians—Christian Democrats, Radicals, Conservatives, and Liberals—belonged in the context of the Cold War.[19] As a result, Dungan's name and his office carried a great deal of weight in the day-to-day functioning of Chilean politics. Without having to put too much effort into it, the ambassador was, as he described in a letter to a friend of his in 1966, a "big fish in a little pond."[20]

Dungan, his successor Edward Korry, and other U.S. diplomats stationed in Santiago took full advantage of the influence their formal positions granted them and, in some cases, of the pure awe with which many Chilean political actors held them. The deputy chief of the U.S. mission in Santiago, Joseph John Jova, was able to significantly influence the shape of the presidential race of 1964 because politicians in the Christian Democratic and Radical parties sought his advice regarding the election and, to a great extent, proceeded in accordance with the U.S. diplomat's counsel. Ralph Dungan, who also generated a great deal of goodwill among his Chilean interlocutors on account of his friendship with the late President John F. Kennedy, became a close friend of President Frei. Edward Korry became equally influential shortly after his arrival in Santiago in 1967. Both men supported the president in the implementation of his ambitious program of reform and, what is more, advised him on matters related to the divisions within his own party, not only because it was in the U.S. interest to do so but also because Frei himself saw the advantage of having the representatives of the United States on his side in these struggles.

The interest of Chilean politicians, starting with none other than the president of the Republic, in drawing U.S. diplomatic representatives into matters of domestic politics was a reflection of the hegemonic character of the foreign policy of the United States toward Latin America since the end of the nineteenth century and, especially, during the Cold War. Since the United States had become, in the first decades of the twentieth century, the main partner of Latin American countries in trade, investments, credits, military supplies, and aid, it was only logical that its diplomatic representatives enjoyed positions of privilege in their host countries in the region. After World War II, and with the onset of the Cold War, the strategic interest of the United States in Latin America deepened and took a more clearly delineated ideological character, so U.S. envoys also became representatives of the leading country of an ideological bloc and, as such, partners and adversaries of local political forces for which the Cold War had different implications but fundamentally the same meaning.[21]

The sheer material and military power of the United States, and its newly embraced ways to deploy that power after World War II, turned its diplomatic representatives, whose number grew steadily after 1945, into actors with whom politicians all across the world had to reckon—for better or worse.[22] To be sure, Central American and Caribbean countries had already experienced U.S. hegemony in a concrete and significant way during the first decades of the twentieth century.[23] On the other hand, South American countries, while accepting influence from the United States in economic and cultural terms, had been able to conduct their political affairs independently.[24] During World War II and in its immediate aftermath, the United States took a more assertive and, in some cases overbearing, attitude toward the politics of its South American neighbors, in much the same way it had done regarding the politics of Western European countries like France and Italy.[25]

Not all cases had the same character. In Argentina, the adversary was not a left-wing revolutionary but a populist leader, Juan Domingo Perón, perceived by many to be a fascist. In Bolivia, the United States supported a nationalistic government that, albeit quite radical in some of its measures, appeared to be the best way of containing revolutionary movements in the context of a perennially volatile political system and culture.[26] In Chile, the growing appeal and electoral success of Marxist parties, clearly identified with the socialist bloc and, after 1959, the Cuban Revolution, prompted the United States, under Democratic and Republican administrations, to become heavily involved in the domestic politics of the country between 1963 and 1973. Presidents Kennedy, Johnson, and Nixon approached the matter in different ways, both because the circumstances they had to face were dissimilar and because their strategic outlooks on foreign policy, especially toward Latin America, differed. At any rate, in all these cases what was at play was the full weight of U.S. diplomacy in the pursuit of a national interest that had acquired global dimensions in the post-World War II era; in other words, the clearly delineated hegemonic intent that underlay U.S. foreign policy during the Cold War.

This hegemonic intent of the United States, however, was not the result only of unilateral imposition and was not exclusively based on hard power. The case of Chile in the years of Eduardo Frei's Revolution in Liberty is an excellent representation of the interplay between unilateral intent and the interests of foreign actors in the creation and exercise of U.S. hegemony in the Cold War. The administrations of Lyndon B. Johnson and Richard Nixon, with different outlooks and by different means, sought to protect and promote what they perceived as the interests of the United States in the Cold War. In Chile, these interests were challenged—or threatened—by the growth of a revolutionary Left that looked admiringly toward the Soviet Union, Cuba, and other socialist countries. The national interests of the United States in this sense dovetailed with the views and interests of Chilean political forces that saw the ideological conflict of the Cold War in much the same way the agents of U.S. foreign policy did. For them all, the coalition of Communists and Socialists, no matter how democratic and institutional their means to achieve power, was a mortal threat to Chilean democracy and the permanence of the country in the international camp led by the United States.

A second aspect of this convergence between U.S. intent and the interests of Chilean political actors was the search for development and modernization. Ralph Dungan and Edward Korry became close friends with Frei and other Chilean politicians of similar ideological persuasions, but not only because they were all, as Frei once put it, philosophically anti-communists. The U.S. ambassadors and other U.S. diplomats shared with Frei and other Chilean politicians a set of ideas about the proper road toward development that put them all at odds with the traditional Right as well. Many Chilean politicians forged political partnerships and personal relationships with U.S. diplomats because they all spoke a similar ideological language, shared the broad lines of a diagnosis about the causes of Chilean underdevelopment, and had coincident ideas about the correct way to modernize the country. These Chilean politicians, especially but not exclusively Christian Democrats, felt comfortable around U.S. diplomats because of affinities that went far beyond their primordial opposition to communism.

The United States could not exercise its hegemonic intent on such an emblematic Cold War stage as Chile by associating with adversaries of the revolutionary Left exclusively on account of their common negative views of their rivals. Nixon attempted that approach after the victory of Salvador Allende in the presidential election of 1970, behind the back of his own ambassador in Santiago, and the results were tragic. What allowed U.S. diplomats to perform their duties in a comfortable environment and, to a large extent, successfully, was their image as representatives of a superpower that stood as a positive model and an engine for development and modernization. That image was built on the material prosperity and military power of the United States but also on the philosophically liberal character of its political system and its respect for the institutions of Chilean politics. To be sure, Chilean politicians who sympathized with the United States and recognized its leadership in the fight against communism did not approve blindly of every aspect of U.S. foreign policy. The more heavy-handed way in which the United States intervened in other places of Latin America and the rest of the world—the invasion of the Dominican Republic in 1965 is the most exemplary case—met the determined rejection of forces that otherwise were in agreement with the modernizing drive of U.S. foreign policy under the Democratic administrations of John F. Kennedy and Lyndon B. Johnson. Yet, for all the flaws in the exercise of U.S. hegemony, ambassadors Dungan and Korry, as genuine representatives of the benevolent side of U.S. foreign policy, enjoyed ample privileges of access to—and therefore could exert influence on—the higher echelons of Chilean politics.

Unfortunately, neither Frei's ambitious program of reform nor the constructive spirit of the policies toward Chile of the Kennedy and Johnson administrations survived the turbulence of the 1960s. By the end of the Frei administration, the Christian Democratic Party had endured a painful split, and its candidate for the 1970 presidential election did not embrace the ideological sensibility underlying Frei's project and his vision for the future of the country, of which philosophical anti-communism was a fundamental tenet. The Nixon administration, for its part, had no interest in supporting comprehensive projects of modernization and development in Latin America—and had little sympathy for Chilean Christian Democrats so clearly identified with the image and the program of John F. Kennedy. Ambassador Korry did not lose his friendship with Frei and some of his ministers because of this shift in U.S. policy; in fact, the Chilean president spent the night before the presidential election of 1970 discussing the likely results and their implications for the country with the U.S. diplomat. However, the sense of positive purpose that sustained the relationship until President Johnson announced his decision not to run for re-election in March 1968 was gone for good.

Along the road, the landscape of Chilean politics had changed in important ways, not least because of the influence exerted by U.S. diplomacy. By 1969, all major Chilean political parties, with the exception of the Communist Party, had experienced significant splits or reformulations; the United States had something to do with at least two of them. Furthermore, by supporting Frei's Revolution in Liberty politically and materially, the United States furthered the identification of Chilean politics with the ideological conflict of the Cold War in a way that mirrored processes occurring simultaneously across the world. If throughout the 1960s the Chilean Left embraced ever more decidedly the spirit and the language of the Cuban Revolution, the right wing of the Christian Democratic Party, led by Frei, grew ever more fearful of the possibility of the success of its revolutionary opponents. Certainly neither Frei nor his supporters within the party needed prodding from U.S. diplomats to convince themselves of the risks entailed by the prospect of a government of the Left. However, the determined support provided by the United States to the Christian Democratic government and to Frei himself in his battles against the left wing of his party certainly contributed to strengthening the anti-Marxist resolve of the president and his followers. Left-wing politicians, for their part, could not help but see the Christian Democratic Party, especially the wing identified with Frei, as an associate of the United States.

It is commonplace to assign a great deal of blame on U.S. hegemony for the polarization of Chilean politics and the subsequent destruction of Chilean democracy after 1973. Richard Nixon's decisions in 1970 and after certainly provide some substance to this argument. Nevertheless, a closer look at the relationship between U.S. diplomats and Chilean politicians in the years of the Frei administration show that the exercise of U.S. hegemony was only one factor, albeit important, in the erosion of Chilean democracy, and it was so because Chilean actors were as interested as their U.S. interlocutors in drawing the United States into matters of a domestic character. The hegemonic power of the United States, then, could influence Chilean politics not because of its unilateral intent but because the main actors of the institutional system of Chilean politics sought to take advantage of that hegemonic power and direct it toward their own purposes.

Those purposes, and here lies the crux of the matter, were not determined by the influence of the United States any more than the purposes of the Left were determined by the influence of foreign revolutionary models like the Soviet Union and Cuba. The polarization of Chilean politics, in which the United States played a significant supporting role, was the result of a complex process whose origins were both autochthonous and foreign, and in which a number of other international actors had some participation, too. Ultimately, in ways that were the consequence of the decisions of Chilean actors and, simultaneously, out of their full control, the polarization of Chilean politics in the years of Eduardo Frei's Revolution in Liberty was a faithful representation and a tragic subplot of the global Cold War, the story in which the United States played one of the leading roles.

Chapter 1

The U.S. Embassy in Santiago and the Presidential Election of 1964

In light of the competing political projects and candidates, the Chilean presidential election of 1964 took on the character of an emblematic event in the context of the Cold War. One of the leading candidates in the race, Salvador Allende, was an avowed Marxist and the standard-bearer of the Popular Action Front (FRAP), a coalition of Socialists and Communists formed in 1958. Allende, a longtime member of the Socialist Party (PS), and a senator since 1945, was committed to a program of economic, social, and political transformation that, if successful, in the long run could turn Chile, a democratic republic whose political stability and open society stood out among Latin American countries, into a socialist state. Allende's main contender was Eduardo Frei Montalva, the undisputed leader of the Christian Democratic Party.[1] Frei's political project also called for significant reforms in Chile but without a thorough reshuffle of political institutions. Encouraged by their strong showing in the presidential election of 1958, in which the Christian Democratic candidate obtained 20 percent of the vote, Frei and the PDC ran their 1964 campaign on the promise of a Revolution in Liberty. The slogan captured the minds of many Chileans who, while wishing for more equality and development, were reluctant to embrace socialism as this concept was understood by the Socialist and Communist Parties.

For the United States, an Allende victory in the presidential election would entail a huge setback in the Western Hemisphere.[2] The turn taken by the Cuban Revolution since 1960 had shaken up the politics of the entire continent. Cuba's close political approximation of the Soviet Union, moreover, had

Figure 1. Mapuche women marching through the streets of the southern town of Temuco in 1965 in support of Renán Fuentealba, candidate to the Senate. The banner in the back nicely captures the anti-communist aspect of the Christian Democratic project: "Switching overlords is not a revolution." *Courtesy of Archivo Fotográfico Casa Museo Eduardo Frei Montalva.*

posed a very real challenge to the United States and had brought the world to the brink of nuclear war in 1962.[3] The victory of a Marxist candidate who supported Castro and his regime in a democratic presidential election would deal another shocking blow to the hegemonic position of the United States in the Americas. Furthermore, it would disprove the idea that the imposition of socialism was inherently incompatible with the practice of democracy, one of the foundational assumptions of the Cold War divide, at least from the perspective of the United States and its liberal allies in Latin America and the rest of the world.

Consequently, since the last months of 1963 the Chilean presidential election, scheduled for 4 September 1964, became a matter of the utmost importance for the White House, the State Department, and the CIA. The primary objective of the United States was to prevent Allende's victory at the polls. Later on, as events in Chile unfolded in the first half of 1964, it became clear that the best way to bring about this result was for the United States to support the candidacy of Eduardo Frei, whose project seemed an excellent alternative to the revolutionary path proposed by the Marxist Left and a good representation of the goals and values of the Alliance for Progress, the policy of promotion of development and democracy in Latin America conceived and first implemented by the John F. Kennedy administration (1961–1963).

The United States provided generous funding for the Christian Democratic campaign through the CIA. These efforts were uncovered in significant detail in the reports issued by the Church Committee in the 1970s and have been treated in several scholarly works published in both the United States and Chile.[4] Covert operations carried out by the CIA, however, were not the only means through which the United States attempted to reach its objectives in the Chilean presidential election of 1964. The U.S. ambassador in Chile, Charles Cole, and more so the political staff of the embassy in Santiago, especially Deputy Chief of Mission John Joseph Jova, played an important role in shaping the race and advising the main chiefs of Eduardo Frei's political campaign, and even Frei himself, in the course of 1964.

While most scholarly works about the U.S. intervention in Chilean politics between 1964 and 1973 draw on the documents that were declassified after 1999 and the information provided by the reports and hearings of the Church Committee, few have explored thoroughly the unclassified records of the State Department. These documents offer an extraordinary window for the study of Chilean political history and reveal the ways in which U.S. diplomats involved themselves in Chilean politics, thus seeking to influence the course of events and direct it toward U.S. foreign policy goals. The mostly untold story of the U.S. embassy's involvement in the 1964 presidential race is an excellent example of the way in which U.S. foreign policy was carried out on the ground and, in many situations, in the open. Furthermore, it shows how U.S. intervention was as much in the interest of Chilean political actors who actively sought to engage U.S. diplomats to achieve their own objectives as it was in the interest of the United States. Indeed, U.S. intervention in Chile was not a unilateral display of power by a regional hegemon but a complex process of engagement and negotiation between the agents of U.S. foreign policy and Chilean actors with their own—and not always coincident—objectives.

The Naranjazo

On 15 March 1964, a by-election to replace a recently deceased deputy, Oscar Naranjo Jara of the Socialist Party, took place in the province of Curicó, about

120 miles south of Santiago. The region, agrarian and dominated by a few powerful landholders was widely supposed to be a stronghold of the traditional Right, represented by the Conservative and Liberal parties. At the time, the right-wing parties were allied with the Radical Party (PR) in a coalition called the Democratic Front (FD), and were formally aligned with and held cabinet positions in the government of Jorge Alessandri Rodríguez (1958–1964).[5] The FD had already nominated Julio Durán, of the PR, as its candidate for the presidential election of September 1964.

The candidate of the coalition for the Curicó seat in the Chamber of Deputies was Rodolfo Ramírez, a member of the Conservative Party. So much confidence did the FD have in its strength in Curicó that Durán himself bluntly expressed that, rather than only a competition for a single seat in Congress, the by-election of March was a plebiscite on the performance of the Alessandri administration and a forecast for the coming presidential election, despite the fact that the twenty-five thousand votes of the province amounted to less than 1 percent of the total national vote.[6] On the same day as the by-election, another member of the PR, Senator Ulises Correa, reiterated this idea.[7] The U.S. embassy in Santiago shared the optimism of the Radicals. A few days before the by-election, a report from the embassy asserted that "the Democratic Front candidate . . . should win . . . with a margin of between one and two thousand votes over FRAP candidate Oscar Naranjo."[8]

The PDC, then in the opposition to the Alessandri administration, presented Mario Fuenzalida as its candidate in Curicó, without much hope of his chances in the by-election. At the national level, on the other hand, the Christian Democrats were aiming high. Their candidate for the September presidential election, Eduardo Frei Montalva, had won 20 percent of the vote in the 1958 presidential election, had since strengthened his popular appeal, and had become a favorite of the Kennedy establishment in Washington. For the Christian Democrats, who had refused to enter any coalition with other major political parties, the presidential election of 1964 offered a great opportunity to reach the presidency and, thus, implement their ambitious program of reform.

The leftist coalition had also decided on its candidate for the presidential election: Salvador Allende of the Socialist Party. Allende had already run for president twice. In 1952, with the support of only a fraction of the PS and the then outlawed Communists, he won 5 percent of the vote. In 1958, backed by the coalition formed by the reunified PS and the now legal Communist Party (PC), the FRAP, Allende obtained near 28 percent of the vote against the 31 percent of the winner, Jorge Alessandri, who was eventually elected over Allende in the Congress runoff election. Allende's chances in 1964 were at least as high as those of Eduardo Frei in a three- or four-way race (Jorge Prat, a former minister of the second Carlos Ibáñez administration was at the time running on a self-styled nationalist platform).[9] Since Congress had elected as president the candidate with the largest vote count in the three elections in which the runoff had been necessary, the prospect of an Allende government seemed real.

In the Curicó by-election, the leftist coalition had reason to believe in the possibility of a victory even though the odds seemed to favor the traditional Right. Besides the sustained growth of the support for the Left in the agrarian regions in previous years, the candidate himself, Oscar Naranjo Arias, had an edge over his opponents that would prove decisive on the day of the vote: he was the son of Oscar Naranjo Jara, the late deputy whose vacant seat would be occupied by the winner of the by-election. At the end of the day, the FD bitterly lamented its ill-considered statements about the relevance of the by-election and its exaggerated optimism regarding its outcome. Naranjo obtained 39.2 percent of the vote, well ahead of his opponents. The results surprised most politicians and knowledgeable commentators, even within the ranks of the FRAP. To this day the event is known in Chile as Naranjazo, a name that represents its surprising and, to some, shocking character.[10] The traditional right-wing parties had misread the state of affairs in Chile, especially in the rural areas and, consequently, had held on to an electoral strategy that no longer worked. The report of the U.S. embassy on the election made this quite clear: "[Peasants] were much more influenced by the FRAP promises on land and power and the [Christian Democratic Party] concentration on their needs and interests than by the [Democratic Front] attempts to scare them with the communist threat and jolly them with free football games, wine and meat pies."[11] The Curicó by-election was a signal that the strategy, tactics, and even the ethos of the traditional Right were on the wane and that a new political landscape that neither Conservatives nor Liberals could fully comprehend was taking shape.[12]

The day after the Curicó by-election, Durán met with Senator Jacob Javits (R-NY), who was visiting Chile, and the deputy chief of mission of the U.S. embassy in Santiago, Joseph John Jova. Durán, who was in a depressed mood, acknowledged that the election "took [the] pulse of the country" and that his chances of winning the presidential election were almost nonexistent. He recognized that his campaign strategy had failed. The themes of "[the] Berlin Wall, anti-communism [and] save democracy had not impressed campesinos." He was angry at President Alessandri for his alleged "tolerance of communism and [the fact that] this had permitted hundreds of FRAP militants, many trained in

Cuba, to participate in the campaign in which FRAP promised everything to people without scruple."

Durán also assigned blame to the late President John Kennedy for the political situation in Chile. Besides "awakening people's aspirations and desires for change," some "Alliance [for Progress] statements over-critical of present Latin leadership groups had undermined their position without at [the] same time preparing [an] alternative system to take place of present one before this crumbled." Asked by Javits what the United States could do to help, Durán replied, somewhat melodramatically, "nothing, we must now fight the battle by ourselves." He added, in a critical and bitter tone, that the United States "should have tried harder under the Alliance for Progress to sell democracy as well as social and economic reform."[13] Undoubtedly, the FD defeat in the Curicó by-election had brought to the surface the deep resentments created by the process of social change sponsored by the Alliance for Progress in Chile, especially its push for agrarian reform, and the reconfiguration of the political map then taking place.

The outcome of the Curicó by-election wrought havoc in the center-right coalition. Durán's candidacy, an uneasy compromise between Conservatives, Liberals, and Radicals, did not raise massive enthusiasm. In fact, many within the FD considered Durán a poor choice and, even months before the Curicó by-election, recognized that his chances of winning the 1964 election were slim.[14] The victory of the FRAP candidate in what was supposed to be a right-wing stronghold dealt a tremendous blow to an already weak candidacy. A couple of days later, Durán announced his withdrawal from the race, with the purpose of facilitating "the search for solutions that contribute to the defense [of democracy]."[15] His party, however, did not accept Duran's withdrawal, and he duly stayed the course.[16] On 20 March, the PR decided to split from the FD and announced it would hold an extraordinary national assembly to reassess the position of the party regarding the September presidential election.[17] Everyone who knew Chilean politics, however, understood that the Naranjazo had killed any chance Durán may have had of winning before that fateful by-election.

Foreign Involvement in the 1964 Presidential Race

The FRAP victory in the Curicó by-election and the breakup of the FD prompted officials in the CIA, the State Department, and the White House to throw all the U.S. support behind Eduardo Frei, the PDC candidate. A few weeks after the Naranjazo the White House Special Group in charge of appropriations for covert operations abroad approved $750,000 for the Frei campaign with the provision, introduced to assuage the qualms of Ambassador Charles Cole that the PDC could lean too far to the left, that the money would also be used to gain some leverage within the party.[18] Cole, a non-career diplomat who had taught history at Columbia and Harvard, had a more conservative outlook on politics than the Democratic administration in Washington and many of the political officers who staffed the embassy in Santiago.[19] The amount granted by the Special Group ($1 million) was lower than what the Frei campaign had requested. However, more money was authorized by the Special Group in the following months. The total amount the CIA spent on the 1964 Frei campaign reached around $3 million.[20]

Whether Frei himself was aware of the extent of the U.S. involvement in his presidential campaign is not known for sure. According to the testimony of Robert A. Stevenson, one of the political officers in the U.S. embassy in Santiago in 1964, he and Rudy Fimbres, another member of the political staff of the embassy, met with two emissaries sent by Eduardo Frei on an unspecified date. The two Frei messengers told the U.S. diplomats that "[Senator Frei] really would like your help."[21]

If the PDC had found a formidable ally in the Democratic administration of Lyndon B. Johnson, the Left had international partners of its own. Unfortunately, because of the authoritarian and illiberal character of the regimes that supported the Chilean Communist and Socialist parties, little documentary evidence of the assistance provided to the Allende campaign by countries such as the Soviet Union and Cuba is available. Consequently, while the extent of the support provided by the CIA to the Frei campaign is well established, little was and is known of the foreign financial sources of the Allende campaign. Drawing on Soviet records, historians Olga Ulianova and Eugenia Fediakova have shown that Moscow provided the Chilean Communist Party with two hundred thousand dollars in 1963 and $275,000 in 1965. The records for 1964 could not be accessed by Ulianova and Fediakova, but it can be assumed that the amounts received by the Chilean PC were at least in the vicinity of the amounts given by the Soviet Union in 1963 and 1965.[22]

We also know that as early as 1962 the Czechoslovakian government responded favorably to a request of financial assistance from the famed Chilean poet and conspicuous member of the PC Pablo Neruda. According to historian Michael Zourek, Czechoslovakia gave the FRAP fifty thousand *korunas* and two movie projectors worth another ten thousand *korunas*.[23] Although such donations were no match for the massive involvement of the CIA in the

Frei campaign, their existence confirms that the Chilean Left sought and got financial assistance from countries on the other side of the Iron Curtain. However, no other known records from communist countries show information of this kind, so it is impossible to assess the relationship between the Chilean Left and its foreign sponsors with the same level of certainty and accuracy allowed by the records declassified and made available for researchers by the United States.

Nevertheless, a few U.S. documents from 1964 and 1970 offer a glimpse of the presumed relationship between the Allende campaign and foreign sponsors and, more important, the perceptions and convictions of U.S. diplomatic and intelligence officials regarding that relationship. On 5 May 1964, Deputy Chief of Mission in Santiago Joseph John Jova sent a cable to the State Department reporting that Frei had asked for information about funds coming to the Allende campaign from British and Canadian sources. Both the British and the Canadian ambassadors in Santiago had informed Frei that they had learned about an amount of around $1 million going from a Canadian bank account into the purse of the Allende campaign. Neither diplomat was able to provide more details about this presumptive foreign donation, but the British ambassador told Frei that he assumed Cuba was the original source of the money. This lack of absolute certainty notwithstanding, Frei told the U.S. diplomat he was convinced the FRAP was pouring much more money into Allende's campaign than the PDC was able to raise and spend on his own.[24]

Documents recently released by the CIA show that intelligence officials of the Johnson administration had the certainty that Cuba was providing generous financial aid to the Allende campaign. In a letter addressed to Henry Kissinger in the wake of Allende's victory in the 1970 election, John McCone, director of Central Intelligence between 1961 and 1965, informed the National Security Advisor that in June 1964 "Allende fielded 300 sound trucks and employed from 3,000 to 3,500 political workers." According to the former head of the CIA, this effort "was financed by $1,000,000 of United States currency which reportedly came from Communist sources outside of the country—presumably, Moscow." McCone offered this information as background for a concrete offer of money from the International Telephone & Telegraph company to help block Allende's road to power, so it must be taken with more than a grain of salt.[25] Nevertheless, considering the level at which the communication was held, the stature of both interlocutors, and the common assumptions on which they based their assessment of the Chilean situation in 1970, it seems highly unlikely that McCone was making it all up. After all, Kissinger could have easily checked the accuracy of McCone's statements by requesting information from the CIA if he had wished to do so.

Records from 1964 also show that the CIA had reached the conviction that the Allende campaign was receiving money from foreign sources, particularly Cuba. The President's Intelligence Checklist of 21 March 1964 reported that "Cuba has agreed to provide funds to Juan Lechín in Brazil [sic] and Salvador Allende in Chile for their presidential campaigns."[26] The intelligence briefing of 23 April 1964, for its part, informed President Johnson that Ernesto "Che" Guevara believed that "Allende, who has visited Cuba often and *is being bank-rolled in part by Havana*, will win the presidential election in the fall."[27] No further details about this presumptive Cuban funding for the Allende campaign are available. However, the very brevity of the information, presented as a solid fact to the president, suggests the CIA had gathered enough intelligence on the ground to reach the conclusion that the Castro regime was aiding the FRAP campaign. This is not necessarily contradictory with McCone's assertion in 1970 that Moscow was the foreign source of the funds received by Allende, as in 1964 Cuba did certainly not have on its own the capacity to dispose of large amounts of money. It is plausible, however, that Havana served as a channel for Soviet money flowing toward Chilean recipients. More important, it is undisputable that this was the conviction on which Frei, the CIA, and other U.S. foreign policy officials operated throughout the 1964 presidential race.

Shaping the Election

The defeat of the FD in the Curicó by-election opened the door for a realignment of the forces in competition in the arena of Chilean politics. The Conservative, Liberal, and Radical parties had their institutional and ideological roots in the nineteenth century and had become the parties of the establishment. Furthermore, while the PR promoted the interests and vision of the middle classes, and until the 1950s had been at the vanguard of reformist politics in Chile, Conservatives and Liberals represented mostly the interests and ideological outlook of socioeconomic elites and were, therefore, at odds with the evolution of the ever more inclusive and massive Chilean electoral body.[28]

At any rate, neither Conservatives nor Liberals had a political project in tune with the times, and their alliance with the Radicals in the FD was more the result of specific political circumstances than the crystallization of a common ideological vision. Consequently, when political circumstances turned adverse, as was the case after the Curicó by-election, the shaky coalition crumbled, and the other important political actors in the Chilean scene rapidly made their moves to take advantage of the new situation. The Christian Democrats, without much effort, obtained the unconditional support of the Conservative and Liberal parties and the undivided backing of the United States.

Allende and the FRAP, for their part, looked to the other party of the deceased Democratic Front. The PR had a flexible ideological identity, and many of its members were closer to the Marxist Left than to the traditional Right. After all, the Radicals had built a successful, if not enduring, political alliance with the parties of the Left in the 1930s and 1940s.[29] Consequently, the FRAP saw the outcome of the Curicó by-election as a chance to draw the support of some members of the PR, if not the formal endorsement of the entire organization, for the Allende candidacy. Four days after the Naranjazo, Allende himself called for the support of Radical voters in a mass rally, recalling the spirit of the Popular Front, the coalition of Radicals, Communists, and Socialists that supported Pedro Aguirre Cerda in the presidential election of 1938.[30] The next day, Raúl Ampuero, secretary general of the PS, confidently asserted in an interview with El Mercurio that the rank and file of the PR would vote for Allende.[31]

An electoral alliance between the FRAP and the PR—or at least a substantial number of its members—would significantly increase the chances of an Allende victory in the September election. Incorporating a traditional, bourgeois, middle-class party into the leftist coalition would help assuage the fears of those who favored reform and, in some cases, radical changes in Chilean society but were worried about the future of democracy under a Marxist government. In addition, the PR possessed an excellent electoral organization, a large roster of bureaucrats with vast experience in the functioning of government, and connections with powerful economic interests—the U.S. companies that owned the largest copper mines in Chile among them—that could be useful for campaigning and governing. In April, according to a report sent from Santiago to the State Department, Guillermo del Pedregal, an experienced and broadly respected politician who had held cabinet positions under three different administrations, approached Julio Durán on behalf of Allende to request the support of the PR for the Socialist candidate.

According to Durán's account, Del Pedregal told him that "Allende recognized [the] need for Radical support both to win and to govern." In exchange for their support, Allende would guarantee the "maintenance [of] democracy, constitutionality, continued non-political professional military and participation

[in] administration through certain ministries." Furthermore, Allende recognized that without the support of the PR, Chile would "lose foreign assistance, private investment [would] cease, pressures and troubles [would] immediately arise with Peru–Bolivia and Argentina."[32] Another testimony gathered by the embassy political staff said Allende went as far in his approach to Durán as to offer the key ministries of interior and defense to the PR in case he won the election with Radical support. The offer, however, was offset by Allende's affirmation that Communists would be appointed in other ministries and would continue to be fully entitled members of the coalition.[33]

According to an early assessment of the embassy, a good number of Radical deputies and senators were in favor of an alliance with the FRAP.[34] The U.S. embassy in Santiago and the State Department dreaded this prospect, as it would dramatically improve the position of the Socialist candidate in the presidential election. Political officers in Santiago and Washington agreed that such a situation had to be prevented. The State Department recommended that the embassy persuade members of the directorate of the PR of the need to postpone the assembly scheduled for 4 April so the anti-Allende forces could gain strength and, thus, confront more effectively those who favored an alliance with the Left.[35] Ambassador Charles Cole replied that seeking a postponement would be "futile and counterproductive." However, Cole added, the embassy had already been "involved in major effort to persuade Radicals not to endorse Allende and concurrently to persuade Christian Democrats to be more receptive and encouraging to Radicals."[36] Meanwhile, the CIA presented to the White House Special Group that decided on funding covert operations a plan that, besides supporting directly the PDC and the Frei campaign, included channeling money to the Radicals to dissuade them from switching their support to Allende.[37]

As a matter of fact, U.S. embassy officers began their efforts to influence the decisions of Durán and the PR shortly after the Curicó by-election. Eight days after the Naranjazo, political officer Joseph John Jova met with Radical senator Ángel Faivovich, who favored endorsing Allende. Jova tried to talk Faivovich out of such a preference by citing the examples of the communist takeovers in Cuba and Czechoslovakia and by pointing out the inevitable "difficulties envisaged in obtaining U.S. congressional support for loans or credits for a Chilean government which would contain Communists." Faivovich seemed somewhat persuaded by Jova's argument that once in power the Communists would "expand significantly," but he saw no way out. Jova made an emotional pitch, asking that "he and other leaders make [a] real attempt [to] find some better and less ignoble course for their historic party," offering in addition any help the embassy could provide. Faivovich, however, did not seem to change his mind.[38]

In a telling sign of the ideological contradictions and conflicts that beset the PR in the 1960s, by the end of the decade Faivovich would become the leader of the right wing of the party and would eventually leave it to become president of Radical Democracy, a party founded by disaffected Radicals who opposed an alliance with Communists and Socialists.[39] A week after his meeting with Faivovich, Jova met with another Radical congressman, Deputy Jacobo Schaulsohn, and made the same appeal. Schaulsohn's response differed little from Faivovich's. According to his view, "Radical participation with FRAP would really be an insurance policy against Communist domination of an Allende government . . . Allende was himself anti-communist [and had] a strong personality."[40] Jova's inquiries seemed to indicate that the PR would support Allende in the presidential election, thus posing a formidable challenge to the Frei campaign.

The CIA plan presented to the Special Group on 1 April also contemplated giving money to the Conservative and Liberal parties to persuade them to support Frei.[41] In fact, Conservatives and Liberals had drawn the same conclusions as everyone else from the results of the Curicó by-election: Durán had little chance of winning, and Frei seemed to offer the only real possibility of averting an Allende victory in September. No available document records any transaction between U.S. officials and members of the Conservative and Liberal parties, but it is likely that both parties or some of their members received funds from the CIA in the course of the 1964 campaign, probably in April. On 23 April, the Liberal Party (PL) decided to unilaterally support Frei in the September election; the Conservative Party followed suit a week later.[42] Frei and the PDC, however, refused to strike any kind of deal with the right-wing parties. Any formal accord, it was thought, would do more harm than good to the Christian Democratic candidate, since any link with the traditional Right would be widely considered an unacceptable compromise with forces that in reality opposed the reforms championed by the Christian Democrats.[43] So wide was the ideological gap separating the Christian Democratic Party from the traditional Right that Eduardo Frei publicly stated, in a sentence that has become the most famous and remembered symbol of the spirit of the 1964 campaign, that "he [would not] change his program even for a million votes."[44]

An alliance with the Radicals would not be well received either. Renán Fuentealba, president of the PDC, told embassy officers that "any formal [Radical Party] endorsement would cost his party more votes from working classes than [it] would gain."[45] Nevertheless, some Christian Democratic leaders, Senator Tomás Pablo and Deputy Carlos Sívori among them, approached members of the PR to dissuade them from throwing their support behind Allende. The Archbishop of Santiago, Cardinal Raúl Silva Henríquez, also tried to contact a few Radical leaders to assure them that a Christian Democratic government would bring about no changes in the relation between church and state, an issue of the utmost importance for the fiercely secular, anti-clerical Radicals. Knowing the PR had close links with the Masonry, Frei spoke with Grand Master of the Grand Lodge of Chile Aristóteles Berlendis to assuage fears harbored by the Masons about the relationship between the PDC and the Catholic Church.[46]

The efforts of the PDC to keep Durán in the race included channeling money from the Frei campaign to the PR. According to Germán Picó, a businessman of the right wing of the PR and a frequent interlocutor of embassy officials in 1964, in early May the manager of the Frei campaign, Álvaro Marfán, gave him sixty thousand *escudos* and would give him forty thousand more a few days later—a total that amounted to about $44,000.[47] Even Eduardo Frei met with Durán on 8 May to convince him not to quit the race. According to Juan de Dios Carmona, one of Frei's closest advisors, Frei promised Durán that he would consider appointing Radicals in ministries and other government positions after the congressional elections of March 1965 but did not give him specific assurances as to this possibility.[48] Frei's visit also had, according to Joseph John Jova, "a mollifying effect on Durán," as the Christian Democratic leader convinced the Radical candidate that there was "no danger in [a Christian Democratic] administration of change [in] present Church-state relationship and that Frei would not go directly to people with plebiscites but would work under [the] present constitutional system."[49]

While Durán and the Radicals brooded over the presidential election and Allende made serious efforts to draw the PR into the leftist coalition, another development favorable for U.S. interests took place in the last days of April. Jorge Prat, candidate of a couple of tiny nationalist parties, announced on 26 April that he would withdraw his candidacy. Jova had met with Prat on 20 March and heard the latter express his confidence that the Curicó by-election offered him a great opportunity to enlarge his following. In a sense, Prat's view of Chilean politics, characterized by a preference for a strong executive and a nationalist rhetoric, foretold the position that the majority in the military would adopt at the end of the 1960s and the beginning of the 1970s, especially regarding political parties and politics in general.[50] According to Prat, a former member of the Conservative Party and minister of the treasury in the second Ibáñez administration, the Curicó by-election represented "another failure of political parties and representative government."

In a three-way election without a Radical candidate, Prat went on, "with nationalistic appeal [he would] draw votes from FRAP and Radical rank and file as well as from right." In his view, "nationalism [was the] best weapon to defeat communism."[51] Whether Durán stayed in the race or not, Prat's nationalism could only draw votes from the anti-communist camp, thus hurting Frei. The U.S. embassy political staff were very much aware of this and, according to Jova, their efforts "aimed at discouraging Prat elements."[52] Neither State Department nor CIA records show how these efforts were carried out and whether they had an impact on Prat's decision to withdraw from the race. Since he did not have the support of any major party, his position was weak anyway, so his stepping down may well have been just the consummation of what was, indeed, inevitable. At any rate, Prat's renunciation left three candidates running, in accordance with what the Christian Democrats and the United States—the embassy in Santiago, the State Department, and the CIA—deemed best for their interests.

The embassy continued its efforts to dissuade the PR from aligning with the FRAP. Jova met again with Durán on 30 April. The latter bluntly told the U.S. diplomat that he was willing "to act as Frei's dupe so long as his candidacy helped keep the Radicals from going to Allende" and that he would campaign on the "theme of anti-communism but would withdraw if it seemed that his continuing in race would help Allende." This was in the best interest of the embassy, and Jova assured Durán that the U.S. government and the embassy political staff considered "his decision [to] continue anti-communist fight a noble one." For his part, knowing just too well what the main divide between the Radicals and the Christian Democrats was, Jova stated that he would try to "speak with Cardinal [Silva Henríquez] on [the] religious issue, agreeing that democratic forces need concentrate all [their] energy on [the] Communist enemy." Asked about what the U.S. government could do to help him and his position within the party, Durán replied, without any noticeable trace of embarrassment, that monthly installments of about $2,500 for each Radical deputy plus $3,500 to help prevent a national convention of the party, in all likelihood through bribes, "would do the trick."[53] In addition, Durán requested some financial aid for his own campaign, for what he was receiving from bankers friendly to the PR was not enough. In fact the CIA had begun providing funds for "moderate" members of the party in 1963, and it would continue to do so through the rest of the decade.[54]

Whether the money received by Radical members of Congress matched the request made by Durán is not known, and as CIA money continued to flow to members of the PR in later years, the question becomes for the most part irrelevant. Nevertheless, it is important to note that Durán, a presidential candidate and a politician of real national stature, seemed quite comfortable asking a U.S. embassy official for money, so much so that he even set a specific amount for his request.

Jova's conversation with Durán about the coming election covered more than just campaign strategies and tactics. Since both Jova and Durán understood the presidential election of 1964 in a similar key, as a momentous showdown between communism and democracy whose consequences would be felt throughout the world, they agreed that an Allende victory should be avoided at all costs. The election of Frei would be the best possible outcome. However, should Allende win, a military intervention to prevent him from becoming president could not be ruled out. Durán indicated that he would try to "feel out [the] military cautiously to see what possibilities may be generated for ultimate anti-Allende action." Durán would make these inquiries through fellow Radical and former vice president of the Republic Alfredo Duhalde, who had close ties with the military. For Durán, a military intervention to prevent an Allende government should the Socialist candidate win the September election was more than just a thought. In his view, Duhalde, a man with strong anti-communist leanings, should be appointed minister of defense in replacement of Carlos Vial, whom he considered "weak-kneed." In that position, presumably, Duhalde could manage to act in concert with the military to stage a coup in case of an Allende triumph in the presidential election. Jova did not explicitly express support for this move but was assured by Durán that the embassy would be kept informed about it.[55]

As it turned out, in another sign of the volatility of the Radicals' ideological convictions, Duhalde preferred an alliance between the PR and the FRAP and, in fact, attempted to facilitate this rapprochement by hosting a meeting between Durán and Allende in his own house in the first days of May. Apparently, Radical Senator Luis Bossay, the party's candidate in the 1958 presidential election, had been maneuvering behind the scenes to convince his fellow Radical congressmen to strike a deal with the FRAP regarding a possible runoff election in Congress, whether Durán continued in the race or not. Durán feared the scheme might carry the day within the party and openly expressed his concern about this possibility in a meeting with Jova on 11 May. He even gave Jova "names of 'weak' members with suggestions on how they might be kept firm."[56]

The negotiations between Durán and Allende did not lead to a deal be-tween the PR and the FRAP. On 10 May, the National Assembly of the PR decided by an overwhelming majority to uphold Duran's candidacy.[57] Al-though most Radicals knew Durán had little chance of winning the election or even finishing in second place, they were aware that throwing their support behind Allende or Frei—as some members of the party, such as Deputy Raúl Morales, quietly wished—the party would lose all the leverage it could have on a potential election in Congress, would be left in an uncomfortable posi-tion for the congressional elections scheduled for March 1965, and, in the worst scenario, would divide along ideological lines with some members aligning with the anti-communist camp and others joining the FRAP. The Radicals made their choice looking toward the elections of March 1965. Pragmatic political reasons played a larger role than ideological commitments in the decision to keep Durán in the race. Consequently, the extent to which U.S. diplomats influenced the Radicals' decision should not be overestimated. Nonetheless, the efforts of the political staff of the embassy, especially the well-connected Joseph John Jova, and the flow of money from the CIA to some members of the party undoubtedly contributed to shore up the attitude of the Radicals who did not want to join a coalition bent on thoroughly transforming a political environment they had helped shape and within which they felt exceedingly comfortable.[58]

The FRAP Case against Joseph John Jova

Jova's meddling in Chilean political affairs, though accepted with little hesita-tion and even welcomed by his interlocutors, became a matter of contention in the public debate after the tiny Democratic National Party (PADENA), then aligned with Communists and Socialists in the FRAP, announced that the U.S. diplomat had met with Julio Durán prior to the assembly in which the PR de-cided to turn down Allende's offer and keep Durán in the race. Senator Sa-lomón Corbalán, of the PS, spoke of this matter in the Senate without offering many details as to what specifically Jova had done.[59] The Communist newspa-per *El Siglo* kept the matter alive, devoting a few op-ed articles to Jova's deeds. In a piece published on 22 May, columnist Manuel Cabieses, who would later be one of the founders of the ultra-left weekly *Punto Final*, sarcastically pointed out that Jova's procedures "consisted of . . . lunching and dining several times a day," so as "to keep in touch with various politicians, members of parliament, journalists, businessmen, military officers, etc." For the columnist, these ways, although in line with the objectives of U.S. foreign policy, made Jova "the loudest secret agent in history" and "a shame for a policy tradition that finds its original sources in Fouche's inflexible coldness."[60]

Although little was said about what Jova had specifically done, Cabieses' depiction of Jova's actions was not far off the mark. Since the U.S. political officer had a broad range of contacts in Chilean political circles, it was almost impossible that his meddling in domestic political affairs went unnoticed. The character of his involvement in Chilean politics, moreover, could not help but reaffirm an image of the United States already prevalent in the Left, which exploited the episode to score points in the polarized campaign then underway.

Although the issue was potentially favorable for the Left—Jova had gone beyond what was acceptable for a foreign officer in his dealings with Chilean politicians—the fuzziness of the accusations vented in the Senate and the leftist press weakened the case against the U.S. diplomat before a public that was used to the frequent ramblings of the FRAP parties against the United States. For the FRAP, it was necessary to go beyond generalities and point out specific instances in which Jova had overstepped his legitimate functions as an officer of a foreign embassy in Chile. On 3 June, PADENA Deputy Luis Oyarzún announced in the Chamber of Deputies with great fanfare that he would "uncover before public opinion the frequent and reckless interventions in our internal political affairs of . . . Joseph John Jova, who, regarding the very recent acts of political parties and presidential candidates, made imprudent acts of meddling and pressure on politicians in order to favor a specific candidate." The situation, however, turned farcical when Oyarzún began to read his prepared statement. Instead of speaking about Jova's deeds, Oyarzún presented a long list of U.S. acts of intervention in Latin American countries, beginning with the issuance of the Monroe Doctrine in 1823 and ending with the U.S. involvement in the military coup that overthrew Brazilian president Joao Goulart a few months earlier.

The purpose of such a long introduction was to connect Jova's involvement in Chilean political affairs with the long history of U.S. interventions in Latin America, thus giving even more poignancy to the specific accusation against the U.S. political officer. However, just as he was about to enter the main matter of his speech—and right after he had lamented that "with the death of Franklin Delano Roosevelt died too the spirit of the Good Neighbor"—Oyarzún was interrupted by President of the Chamber Raúl Morales Adriasola and told that his time had run out and it was now the turn of the PS. Oyarzún replied that the PS had ceded him its time. Unfortunately for him, all the

Socialist deputies had left the room, so no one was able to formally give Oyarzún the time he needed to finish his speech. Morales Adriasola, following the procedural rules of the Chamber, denied Deputy Oyarzún the chance to keep speaking and moved on to another subject. The details of the accusation against Jova were not discussed at all in Congress.[61]

The full text of Oyarzún's speech was published a few days later in *El Siglo*. The text did not contain many specific details, so its effectiveness as an accusation was rather weak. However, Oyarzún rightly pointed out that "Jova, studiously, has managed to earn the trust, gratitude, and friendship of many key actors of our national life, especially in Chilean politics, [with whom] he meets in social engagements and other fora where matters that concern the whole country are discussed freely." Less accurate was Oyarzún's portrayal of the way in which Jova approached Durán. The implication in Oyarzún's account was that Durán had only reluctantly agreed to meet with the U.S. diplomat in the days before the convention in which the PR made its final decision regarding the presidential election. In Oyarzún's florid language, "Durán [suffered], as if in a vanguard writer's nightmare, the harassment of Mr. Jova. [Durán] tried to defend himself through the resourcefulness of his assistant, who replies evasively the repeated phone calls; but all is useless. Mr. Durán is beaten and has to accede to talk with the obsessing diplomat." Oyarzún's account mentioned, almost in passing, an actual meeting between Durán and Jova, purportedly recognized by the former, but did not offer any specifics as to the issues treated in the conversation. Nevertheless, the PADENA deputy finished his failed diatribe by demanding that Jova be ejected from the country.[62]

Even though Oyarzún did not get to read the full content of his speech in the Chamber of Deputies on 3 June, Raúl Yrarrázaval, a deputy from the Conservative Party, took some time to respond to his PADENA colleague and defend Jova from the accusations voiced in the leftist press. The content of Yrarrázaval's speech is worth noting because it highlights how the U.S. presence in Chile was perceived by politicians of conservative political persuasions. Whereas the FRAP accusations against Jova deliberately linked the actions of the U.S. officer with the long history of U.S. intervention in Latin America, thus reinforcing the Left's traditional ideological view of the United States, Yrarrázaval's defense of the U.S. diplomat extolled the positive aspects of Jova's actions as a U.S. embassy officer and of U.S. policies toward Chile in general. "We have seen U.S. ambassadors, and consequentially Mr. Jova, intervene on behalf of our country before the Agency for International Development, the Inter-American Development Bank, and many other important organizations that lend our country huge services," Yrarrázaval said. "We have seen them intervene before the Point Four Program and the Alliance for Progress to move forward with projects in housing, schools, sanitation works, potable water, sewerage, all with the purpose of improving the living conditions of our people," the Conservative deputy added. In addition, Yrarrázaval pointed out that of the aid received by Chile after the earthquake of 1960—the largest recorded in the twentieth century—the United States provided 85 percent, and to a great extent this was due to the efforts made by U.S. diplomats working in Santiago (Jova, however, did not arrive in Chile until 1961). Yrarrázaval concluded his speech by stating that "we want to make clear that it is not fair, gentlemanly nor correct to bring up . . . without any base, the name of a dignified foreign officer from a country that is an excellent friend of Chile, only because it is convenient for the interests of the Communist Party."[63]

Eventually the issue of Jova's improper meddling in Chilean political affairs died out without leaving much of an impact on the presidential race. Durán did ask Jova, however, to issue a public denial that the two had met, for the Radical candidate was afraid of the negative effects news of his conversations with the U.S. officer could have on his campaign.[64] Jova did not make any public statement regarding this matter and felt confident that nothing significant would come of the FRAP accusations against him. He did not meet with Durán in the week prior to the assembly of the PR that decided to reject the FRAP invitation, so the allegations of the FRAP were technically incorrect. Moreover, quickly after the first accusations against him were published in the leftist press, Jova received "many messages of friendship and support from government officials and from Liberal parliamentarians, President's aide, etc."[65]

Undoubtedly Jova's conversations with Durán and other politicians went far beyond matters with which a foreign officer could be legitimately concerned. Furthermore, Jova's main purpose was to shape the presidential election of 1964 in a way that would facilitate the achievement of the most important U.S. goal in the electoral contest, namely, that Salvador Allende be defeated. As the documentary record shows, the U.S. political officer played a significant role in the intense politicking that surrounded the issue of the Durán candidacy after the Curicó by-election and, although to an extent that cannot be thoroughly ascertained, Jova's involvement in discussions and negotiations certainly was a factor in the final decision of Durán and his party. Enough was known about Jova's actions that the FRAP could have built a strong case against the U.S. embassy and its involvement in Chilean politics. However, by attempting to directly link Jova's deeds with the broader ideological view of U.S. policies and attitudes toward Latin America held by the

Left, the FRAP weakened its case. Public opinion in Chile, and even some politicians of other persuasions, probably would have disapproved of Jova's actions if presented with a dispassionate account of them.

The sloppiness of the way in which the FRAP presented the accusations only reinforced the notion among its political opponents that the allegations against Jova were little more than another display of the traditional anti-Americanism of the Left. As such, it was countered by media and politicians of other sensibilities through the articulation of an opposite ideological view of the United States. For the Left, the United States had historically intervened in Latin American countries without any consideration of their interests and sovereignty, and Jova's meddling in Chilean politics was just another example of this pattern.[66] For the other political forces, the United States, the undisputed but not always righteous hegemon in the region, had been a supporter in times of need and a partner in the search for stability and development in Latin America, all the more so in the era of the Alliance for Progress. The issue of Jova's undue involvement in domestic political affairs, although important in its own merit, became eventually subsumed in the larger and ever more bitter ideological battle of worldviews that characterized Chilean politics in the 1960s.

Jova, for his part, continued his ascending career in the U.S. foreign service. His work in Chile eventually earned him recognition from the State Department, and a few months after Frei took office, Jova was appointed ambassador to Honduras, where he stayed for four years. In 1969 he was appointed ambassador to the Organization of American States by the Nixon administration. Finally, he served as ambassador to Mexico between 1973 and 1977.

Contingency Planning

In 1964 polls in Chile were scarce and largely unreliable. Politicians, commentators, and observers in general made their prognostications for elections relying mostly on the results of previous electoral contests—and there were plenty of these in Chile between 1932 and 1964.[67] In the Curicó by-election of March 1964, as has been pointed out, the U.S. embassy mistakenly predicted a victory of the Conservative candidate. The Naranjazo, moreover, came to complicate even further the matter of the 1964 presidential election. The uncertainty about the candidacies of Jorge Prat, who eventually quit the race in late April, and Julio Durán, who stayed in the race until the end but with the suspicion that he would withdraw always hovering, made forecasts even harder.

By the end of the campaign, it was widely acknowledged that Frei had a significant lead over Allende. However, whether Frei would be able to get a majority of the vote was still uncertain.

The issue, given the rules set out by the Chilean constitution for the election of the president, was an important one for all who had a stake in the 1964 race. If no candidate got a majority of the vote, Congress had to choose between the two larger pluralities. This situation had occurred three times since the constitution was drafted and promulgated, under strong military pressure, in 1925. Gabriel González Videla in 1946, Carlos Ibáñez del Campo in 1952, and Jorge Alessandri in 1958 were elected by the Congress after winning a plurality in the popular election. In all three instances, the candidates who finished second in the popular election received votes in the runoff in Congress, almost certainly from members of their own parties—Conservatives in 1946, Liberals in 1952, and Socialists in 1958. Nevertheless, the fact that Congress had elected as president the candidate with the highest popular vote consolidated the idea that this was the proper course to follow under any circumstances. Even though it had happened only three times, it had become the conventional wisdom that "tradition" obligated Congress to elect as president the candidate with the highest vote in the popular election.

In 1964, the momentous character of the electoral contest and the uncertainty about its likely results gave the issue of a potential election in Congress great significance. Frei, who had supported Alessandri in the election in Congress in 1958, found it hard to contradict that stance and act differently in 1964. In a television interview on 3 May, the Christian Democratic candidate stated that Congress should elect the candidate with the highest vote. Frei's assertion made U.S. embassy officers nervous. Allende and the FRAP knew very well they could not achieve a majority in the popular vote. The best Allende could do was to get a plurality, maybe top the unexpectedly high vote of Naranjo in the Curicó by-election (39.2 percent). If Frei, should he finish second in the popular election, was not willing to challenge the "tradition" of Congress electing the candidate with the highest vote, the FRAP strategy could confidently focus only on winning a plurality in the September presidential election. Should someone— Frei, Durán, parliamentarians of the right-wing parties, the military—question Allende's right to the presidency in the event of his winning the popular vote, the FRAP could agitate public opinion and garner widespread support beyond its ranks, claiming that political actors of other persuasions were not fulfilling their promises and were trying to overturn the people's decision.

Joseph John Jova spoke with Frei a few days after his remarks and questioned him about his stance on a possible election in Congress. Frei said that, though uncomfortable with the prospect of having to take a different position from the one he had taken in 1958, he had "very carefully chosen his words" and that "his view applied only in case of a clear triumph by one candidate over another." A clear triumph, in Frei's view, was "anything over a 150,000 vote lead." Furthermore, trying to assuage the fears of his interlocutor, Frei added that "he had left another loophole on television by saying that this [was] only his personal opinion and that Congress was sovereign in this matter." Jova, still uneasy about the situation, urged Frei not to be "over-pure" and expressed his hope the "he would not act impulsively and congratulate Allende too soon on Election Day if he seemed to be leading." Frei finally agreed that, if the future of Chilean democracy depended on it, Congress might have to choose the runner-up as president.[68]

Frei was more than a little uncomfortable with the general situation. The interlude between the popular election and a possible election in Congress, a period of fifty days, would likely see multiple and maybe violent displays of popular support for the candidates involved, thus creating an atmosphere of crisis that would put strong pressure on the deputies and senators in whose hands rested the decision about the political future of the country. Although Chile had seen political turmoil several times since its birth as a republic in the nineteenth century, its political system and society seemed to be much more stable and less prone to violence and disorder than those of other Latin American countries. More important, this idea was strongly ingrained in the minds of most Chileans. The prospect of a situation of popular violence, as opposed to a situation in which the state's monopoly of violence remained safe, scared Chilean political actors of non-revolutionary sensibilities almost as much as the possibility of a government headed by a Marxist coalition.

Frei's qualms about openly bidding for the presidency if he finished second in the popular election stemmed partly from his fear that such an attitude could trigger a political and social crisis of such proportions that it could, in turn, lead to a situation of violence and bloodshed theretofore unseen in Chile.[69] Nevertheless, for the most part he shared the U.S. assumption that the dilemma was not only between two candidates with different political platforms but also between two radically different worldviews. As a result, Frei seemed to recognize, however grudgingly, that every effort within the constitutional frame should be made to prevent Allende from becoming president.

Jova consulted with Frei on the latter's stance on a potential election in Congress because every possible scenario had to be seriously considered in order to avoid the loathed outcome of Allende taking office in November. Although their prognosis for the election had Frei as the frontrunner, even with a good chance of reaching a majority, the political staff of the embassy considered that the possibility of Allende winning the popular vote could not be ruled out, and they planned for that contingency. The candidate of the FRAP would not reach a majority of the vote, but he could reach a plurality if most of the new voters—a substantial number in 1964—and most of the traditional PR constituents decided to cast their ballots for Allende.[70] In this scenario, which was perfectly plausible, Congress would have to choose between Allende and the second highest vote, in all likelihood Eduardo Frei. Everyone with a stake in the election—Frei above all—had to be prepared for such eventuality.

The embassy plan for a scenario in which Allende won a plurality in the presidential election, as outlined in early June, contemplated various actions aimed at building up an environment favorable for a decision in Congress to choose the runner-up as president. Besides reaching out to influential parliamentarians, the political staff of the embassy considered it of critical importance to strengthen the links between the U.S. embassy staff and the U.S. military missions, on the one hand, and the Chilean armed forces, including the police, on the other. In the event of an election in Congress, it was indispensable that the Carabineros—the police—as well as the army were furnished with good and abundant anti-riot material so that any eruption of violence could be thoroughly repressed by the armed forces.[71] In addition, the chiefs of all the branches of the armed forces and the police had to be sounded out on their positions as to the possibility of Congress choosing the runner-up. Their resolution to back the constitutional process should the frontrunner in the popular election be denied the presidency had to be secured and stiffened. With the help of the U.S. Information Service (USIS), the embassy would try to "maintain a continued news media coverage of the constitutional provision permitting choice by Congress and, also, on the dangers of Communist 'participation' in government." Finally, some of the Military Assistance Pact items promised to the Chilean armed forces should be shipped as soon as possible.[72]

The efforts of the United States and the opponents of the Left concentrated on winning the election in September—or the election in Congress, in case no candidate obtained the majority of the popular vote. Unconstitutional means to impede an Allende government seemed more dubious, since the military were not well disposed to intervene in politics; the Chilean armed forces, in comparison with their Latin American peers, were reluctant to involve themselves institutionally in political matters. An intelligence report produced by the Department of State in May 1964 nicely captured the general attitude of Chilean society toward the relationship between the military and politics: "Chile leads all other Latin American countries in its record for maintaining constitutional government . . . Chileans cite their tradition with pride in contrast to the record of repeated military coups in neighboring Argentina and in some middle American countries, disparagingly called '*tropicales*' by the Chileans."[73]

To be sure, the military had played a significant role in the promulgation of the Constitution of 1925 and did not withdraw entirely from the political process until 1932. Nevertheless, the Chilean armed services were, indeed, less prone to intervention in politics than most of their Latin American counterparts. The Chilean military, especially the army and the navy, had developed a self-image as defenders of national security in a traditional geopolitical sense. The bordering countries, all of which had claims over Chilean territory, were naturally the biggest threat the country could face, and the first duty of the armed forces was to be prepared for the eventuality of a war against any of them (or any combination of them). Soldiers in Chile were trained fundamentally under these strategic assumptions.

As a result, most of them did not consider intervention in politics as part of their responsibilities. To the extent that the armed forces had a role to play in politics, it was to guarantee the normal constitutional process.[74] An intelligence report from 1963 described the Chilean military forces as "proud of their role as the ultimate guardians of constitutional order and their corollary tradition of non-intervention in politics in support of party interests." The report went on to say, presciently, that the Chilean armed forces "would almost certainly uphold the authority of any duly elected government, unless, in their judgment, the government itself had moved to subvert the established constitutional order."[75] Most U.S. officials, in both Santiago and Washington, considered that the armed forces would not intervene to prevent Allende from taking office if the Socialist leader were elected according to the rules of the constitution.

The professionalism and apoliticism of the Chilean military had been a cornerstone of the stability of the political system and, as such, drew praise from observers both in Chile and abroad. However, for those who considered communism the gravest threat for the Western Hemisphere, the attitude of the Chilean armed forces was rather troublesome, and something had to be done about it. According to General Andrew O'Meara, commander in chief of the United States Southern Command, the Chilean military had "held themselves aloof from politics for so long that their professionalism is quite narrow and unsophisticated in the light of today's threats." Therefore, it was necessary for the U.S. foreign policy machine to make them "more aware of the dangers which the Communists pose to their country today." Although the strategy of the Chilean PC by no means contemplated insurgency as a way toward power, O'Meara complained bitterly that Chilean high-ranking officers had consistently "resisted [U.S.] efforts to give them any type of counterinsurgency instruction on the basis that no insurgency threat exists in their country." O'Meara was so worried about the Chileans' apparent indifference toward the communist threat that he asked Attorney General Robert Kennedy to give a lecture at a seminar in the School of the Americas in Panama to draw "the right type of officers from the Latin American countries."[76]

The U.S. diplomats and military officers stationed in Chile found out that, indeed, there was little willingness among Chilean members of the armed forces to intervene in the political process if Allende were elected president in accordance with constitutional rules. Memoranda from the embassy reported that, although most officers did not want an Allende government, virtually none of them would be willing or able to do anything but continue business as usual if the Socialist candidate managed to win the presidential election. It is telling, however, that the possibility of intervention was considered and discussed among military officers. In fact, as an embassy report recorded, a navy officer complained a few months before the election that it was "becoming embarrassing to have so many people (Chileans) ask 'What will the military do if Allende . . . wins.'" The same officer, nevertheless, stated that "the navy would do nothing unless Allende strayed from the constitution."[77]

A few individuals did consider seriously the possibility of unconstitutional means to block Allende's taking office in case he won the presidential election. In February 1964, Carabineros Colonel Oscar Cristi, winner of a medal in the Olympic Games of 1952 in equestrianism, told a State Department officer in Washington that "so long as he [could] do anything about it, Allende [would] not take office as President." It is worth noting that Cristi's extreme views did not come from an identification with a specific political project but from a visceral hatred of communism. According to the U.S. officer, Cristi did not like "politics or politicians and [had] no political ambitions himself," but he "detested communism since it seeks to end democracy and liberty."[78]

Presidential candidate Julio Durán adopted a similar stance in the course of the 1964 campaign. He openly spoke about the possibility and desirability of a military move to prevent an Allende government in one of his conversations with Jova. Furthermore, by the end of the campaign Durán had become so concerned about the possibility of an Allende victory and what this would mean for Chile that, according to Radical businessman Germán Picó, he tried to raise money to buy arms and form a militia "to protect the country against a communist attempt to take over."[79] A CIA report stated that its agents in Chile had to dissuade Durán and some of his followers, assembled in a loose group called Legion of Liberty, from staging some sort of coup in case of an Allende victory in the election.[80] Durán had become one of the staunchest anticommunists in the Chilean political scene, and in 1969 his name would head a list of prominent Radicals ejected from the party when it joined the coalition of Socialists and Communists.

The strategy of the United States for the Chilean presidential election of 1964 did not contemplate explicitly the possibility of a military coup as a means to prevent the accession to power of the left-wing coalition. However, it was in the interest of the United States to instill in the military the idea that a left-wing government entailed grave dangers for Chilean political institutions and society. An embassy report from April expressed the political staff's hope "that open discussion in the military ranks [would] reveal to them that they [were] generally of the same mind and as the priority target that they [stood] to lose much if Allende [came] into the picture."[81] The contingency plan for the election devised by the embassy recognized that a military intervention in case of an Allende victory was unlikely. However, if Allende as president broke the constitutional framework, the armed forces might stage a coup and take over the administration of the country. In that case, the U.S. government should not appear in public as complicit with a military regime but it should still provide assistance to such a regime if significant popular resistance arose.[82]

The interest in the political stance and the politicization of the military showed by the U.S. foreign policy apparatus in the months before the 1964 election inexorably leads to the question of the attitude of the United States toward an eventual Allende government. Apparently, the military solution would not automatically become the prime objective of the United States if Allende was elected president. A State Department memorandum for McGeorge Bundy pointed out that the United States "should proceed on the assumption that Allende is bad medicine, but . . . should not slam the door because he might double-cross his communist friends."[83] In fact, none other than President Alessandri believed that Allende and the PS could be drawn away from their alliance with the Communists. For Alessandri, Allende was not a "true Marxist but merely an opportunist whose campaign was considerably less violent than that of González Videla [in 1946]." Should Allende win the election, the United States had to take a position "of reserved watchful waiting and readiness to move rapidly and with flexibility." In the scenario of an Allende government, the United States, according to Alessandri, had to avoid the hawkish attitudes taken toward the Cuban Revolution and choose, instead, the path taken regarding the Bolivian Revolution of 1952.[84]

Even though significant parts of the political program of Bolivia's National Revolutionary Movement (MNR), such as the nationalization of foreign mining companies, affected U.S. private interests, the United States provided considerable economic assistance to the MNR governments since 1952. This U.S. policy stemmed from the understanding that, for all its faults, the MNR and its left-wing nationalist program were the best means to provide a modicum of stability to Bolivian politics and prevent communist revolutionaries from gaining significant ground. What is more, supportive attitudes and policies gave the United States the ability to influence the course of the revolution, moderating the most radical intentions and views of its leaders.[85] In Alessandri's mind, the United States could conceivably influence an Allende government if its foreign policy apparatus adopted the pragmatic and understanding attitude it had displayed toward the Bolivian Revolution instead of implementing hawkish policies such as those that contributed to push Cuba toward communism in the aftermath of the 1959 revolution.

The situation, however, did not get to a point in which the United States had to choose between a Bolivian and a Cuban path. The resounding Frei victory in September (see Table 1) silenced the question as to what the United States should do if the Left came to power in Chile, though that issue would resurface in 1970. The response of the Nixon administration to Allende's victory at the polls was uncompromising. Would Lyndon B. Johnson and the foreign policy apparatus of the Kennedy era have reacted in a similar fashion had Allende won in 1964? As always, the counterfactual question is impossible to answer with certainty. According to the Church Committee report on U.S. covert operations in Chile published in 1975, in July of 1964 the CIA station and the embassy in Santiago received information from military officers about the intentions of men in the army and the air force to stage a coup in case of an Allende victory in the election. The report stated that the embassy's deputy chief of mission—Jova, although he is not identified by name in the report—and the CIA station staff rebutted such approaches.[86] However, it is clear that an important part of the U.S. strategy for Chile was to reinforce among Chilean military officers and non-revolutionary politicians the idea that a left-wing government headed by Salvador Allende would mean the end of Chilean democracy as it had functioned under the Constitution of 1925.

Table 1. Presidential Election of 1964

Candidate	Votes	%
Eduardo Frei (PDC)	1,409,012	55.6
Salvador Allende (FRAP)	977,902	38.8
Julio Durán (PR)	125,233	4.9
Invalid votes	18,550	0.7
Total	2,530,697	100

Source: Nohlen (editor), *Elections in the Americas. A Data Handbook*, p. 287.

The fundamental goal of this message was to avoid a cooptation of the armed forces by an Allende government, which would severely erode the military's capacity and will to oppose the transformation of Chile into a socialist country. Of course, if things came to a point in which the military had to assert their opposition to such a transformation, the natural way for them to do it would be some sort of coup d'état. In this sense, the tactics of cultivating the military, even while rejecting the most extreme plans of some officers, pointed inexorably to military intervention in political affairs. It did not happen in 1964 and it did not happen in 1970. It did happen in 1973, with a vengeance; the military who intervened to save Chilean democracy from the Marxist threat ended up suppressing democracy in the most brutal fashion for over sixteen years.

An Informal Actor in Chilean Politics

An embassy report from 5 May characterized a formal Radical endorsement of Allende as "the biggest danger for the democratic forces after Curicó."[87] A week later, the danger had been averted, to a large extent because the political staff of the U.S. embassy in Santiago were able to talk to and negotiate with Chilean politicians and, thus, influence their decisions. Members of the PR, especially the presidential candidate Julio Durán, considered U.S. diplomats to be perfectly legitimate interlocutors in conversations about electoral politics, party tactics, and even the personal affairs of some of their colleagues.[88] Moreover, Durán and other Radicals were not shy about asking for U.S. help, be it money or the leverage the embassy could exert on some Chilean politicians, to advance their positions in intra-party fights, as the story of the Durán candidacy shows.

The embassy, it can well be argued, played an equally significant part in the presidential election of 1964 as the role played by the CIA through its covert operations. The embassy staff—especially the political officer Joseph John Jova—became informal political actors who could talk frankly and negotiate with Chilean politicians of various persuasions, thus gaining the ability to influence some important decisions. This capacity did not stem exclusively from U.S. material power, nor was it purely the result of the hegemonic position of the United States in the region. For practical, ideological, and even sentimental reasons, Chilean politicians wanted to have close contact with the political staff of the U.S. embassy in Santiago almost as much as the U.S. diplomats needed to develop ties with political circles in Chile. The convergence of interests between the United States foreign policy apparatus and Chilean politicians opposed to communism and the revolutionary Left allowed U.S. diplomats to participate in discussions and influence decisions on what were, indeed, internal Chilean political affairs.

Frei won the presidential election by an ample margin, so all the fears about a government of the left-wing parties were put to rest after 4 September. However, just the possibility of an electoral victory of the Left awoke concerns among all who adhered to the institutional principles of Chilean democracy as it had functioned under the Constitution of 1925. Politicians of diverse persuasions and men in uniform, who could count on the sympathy of many U.S. diplomatic and military officers, assumed a government of the FRAP would sooner rather than later spell the end of Chilean democracy. Consequently, they were willing to consider, however tepidly, the possibility of unconstitutional actions to protect the constitutional order from what they saw as an imminent threat posed by Marxist parties bent on imposing a system modeled on the socialist regimes of Cuba and Eastern Europe. Chilean politicians and military officers had a genuine attachment to the way Chilean democracy had worked since the 1930s and did not need the prodding of U.S. diplomats and military officers to reach the conviction that a political project underscored by a Marxist ideology would mean the end of the political world they had helped build and consolidate. Nevertheless, this conviction was undoubtedly reinforced by the advice given to them by U.S diplomatic and military officers who wanted, above all, to talk their Chilean interlocutors out of, as it was put in an embassy report, "the common delusion that the Communists would not dominate an Allende government."[89] Ideological and personal affinities, U.S. leadership of the capitalist camp, the dependence of the Chilean armed forces on U.S. supplies, and the money generously disbursed by the CIA, among other factors, gave U.S. officials and their ideas a special status before their

Chilean counterparts, which in turn allowed them to exert influence on views and decisions made by Chilean actors. Although the extent of such influence is hard to ascertain precisely, it is safe to assume that Chileans who spoke openly about internal matters with U.S. officials considered seriously in their decisions what their interlocutors told them, as the examples described in this chapter have shown.

Chapter 2

Time of Hope, 1964–1967

Because its political alignments closely replicated the larger divide of the global Cold War, Chile was an important target for the Johnson administration's foreign policy toward Latin America. To be sure, the Americas, in general, were far less important to the United States than other areas of the Cold War (for example, Southeast Asia, Europe), so President Johnson and his foreign policy advisors spent comparatively little time on discussions and design of policies related to the rest of the continent.[1] Within Latin America, however, Chile had become a top priority, and it required and received a level of attention qualitatively different from other countries in the region—a prominence that was also reflected in the U.S. press, which, in general, covered Frei's victory and his tenure as president very positively.[2] The position of ambassador in Santiago, consequently, acquired an operational and symbolic importance above the level suggested by Chile's actual material capabilities and geopolitical weight. So much relevance did officials of the Johnson administration assign to the matter of the ambassadorship in Chile that even David Rockefeller and Milton Eisenhower were suggested for the post in White House discussions in the wake of Frei's victory in September 1964.[3]

Eventually Lyndon B. Johnson appointed Ralph Dungan ambassador to Chile. Dungan was a close friend of John F. Kennedy and had been one of his aides since before the 1960 election—a member of the "Irish mafia from the White House," as a foreign service officer who worked with Dungan in Chile described him.[4] In addition, he had met Frei and other Chilean Christian Democrats when they visited the United States in 1963.[5] Dungan did not speak Spanish, but he was a Catholic with a progressive outlook on political, social, and economic matters, which made him especially well-suited for the position of ambassador in a Latin American country with a government led by a progressive Catholic party. Moreover, Dungan adhered, broadly speaking, to the ideas encompassed in modernization theory that served as the intellectual basis for U.S. foreign policy in the Kennedy-Johnson era, so his personal convictions converged nicely with the political project of the Chilean Christian Democratic Party. The situation in Chile, in sum, offered him an opportunity for direct involvement in a political project for which the Johnson administration had high hopes and with which he felt ideologically identified.

Dungan, moreover, would have to take responsibility for a large part of the substance of U.S. policy toward Chile in his years as ambassador in Santiago. For all the importance attributed to Frei's Revolution in Liberty in the context of Latin American politics and the Alliance for Progress, the highest echelons of authority in Washington did not participate much in the making of policy toward Chile between 1964 and 1969. Other countries and regions of the world, particularly Vietnam, had much more relevance in the big picture of U.S. foreign policy under Johnson than Chile and Latin America. To be sure, President Johnson had to sign off on some particular policies toward Chile, such as the CIA undercover operations that had been carried out since 1964 and the program loans for the Chilean government presented for his review and approval almost every year, and did so well informed by his White House foreign policy aides.

The details of those operations and loans, however, were left, for the most part, to the concerned agencies. Particular negotiations with the Chilean government were conducted mostly by the embassy and the AID office in Santiago and the staff of the Department of State in Washington, all of which had a great deal of leeway in their dealings with their Chilean counterparts. As the political and economic objectives of the Frei administration coincided with those of the Alliance for Progress, there was little room for strategic differences between the two governments. In addition, PDC politicians and Frei administration officials were very much in tune with U.S. ideas about modernization, development, and fiscal policy—although naturally, both parties always wanted to get the most and cede the least in their negotiations. Only on a few occasions did Johnson and his foreign policy advisors judge it necessary to involve themselves directly in matters regarding Chile, most conspicuously after the Frei administration rejected the U.S. invasion of the Dominican Republic in 1965 and, later in the same year, when the Chilean government sought to increase the price of copper. As a result, between 1964 and 1969, relations between the two governments were conducted mostly through the channels established by the work of U.S. ambassadors and political officers assigned to Chile. This mode of operation was an underlying condition for the U.S. embassy's deep level of involvement in Chilean politics in the years of the Frei administration.

Dungan arrived in Chile in December 1964. He had become acquainted with Frei and other Chilean Christian Democrats in 1963, so he had an easy job developing a close relationship with members of the PDC, especially with Frei himself. These relationships, often established on a personal as well as a political level, became an important asset for the overall U.S. strategy toward Chile at the time; namely, to contribute as much as possible to the success of the Christian Democratic project. Dungan became personally identified with the Frei government and, unlike his predecessors and successors in the post, he did not reach out to actors of other political sensibilities. On the contrary, as a matter of strategy, the political staff of the embassy ceased almost entirely their contacts with Radicals and right-wing politicians while Dungan was the chief of the mission, a decision resented by some of the embassy officers who had been in Santiago at the time of the 1964 election, when those relationships had come in extremely handy.[6]

Conversely, Dungan's decision to reduce contacts with politicians outside the government and the PDC was seen by some prominent Chileans as the reflection of an ill-conceived U.S. policy toward Chile. Former presidential candidate Julio Durán, for instance, thought U.S. support for policies such as agrarian reform and the "Chileanization" of copper was a mistake, and let Ambassador Dungan know it in a conversation they had in June 1966. In his view, representative of what he called "the Center-Right" of Chilean politics, the Christian Democratic government, supported by the United States, favored U.S. corporations, whose ownership of copper mines would be partially bought under the "Chileanization" scheme, and discriminated against landholders, whose properties would be expropriated in exchange for long-term bonds. The Johnson administration's commitment to the Christian Democratic project, diligently implemented by Ambassador Dungan, was for Durán a big strategic mistake. In Durán's frank and somewhat prescient words, "the United States has put all [its] eggs in one basket and will be unprepared for the consequences in 1970 when that basket is dropped."[7]

Ambassador Dungan zealously played the role of partner of the Frei administration that he understood President Johnson had assigned to him. In general, his correspondence with the State Department and the White House shows his enthusiasm for the Christian Democratic project and, on occasion, his impatience with the sometimes bureaucratic nature of a diplomat's job.[8] As a well-connected Beltway insider, Dungan devoted a good deal of effort to spread and promote the spirit of Frei's Revolution in Liberty among congressmen—Democratic and Republican—journalists, businessmen, and his friends still working in Washington.[9] When difficult or uncomfortable situations arose in the otherwise good relationship between the Chilean and U.S. governments, Dungan generally chose to take the middle path, and in a few cases he even sided with the Frei administration outright. Such was the case, for example, of the Camelot Project, an academic project financed by the U.S. Army that sought to explore the potentiality of insurgency in the country. When the plan was outed by the left-wing press, Dungan reacted with great alarm and anger and emphatically informed the State Department that he considered that kind of project "seriously detrimental to U.S. interests in Chile."[10] The Camelot Project, at least as it pertained to Chile, never really materialized in concrete actions. In fact, the protests of the Chilean government led to a substantial review of the approach to government-funded social science experiments abroad by the Johnson administration.[11]

Dungan developed a close personal friendship with Frei, which naturally served the convergent purposes of the Chilean and U.S. governments very well. Frei and his closest circle felt comfortable around Dungan, for they all spoke an ideological language that, although coming from different sources, aimed at the same programmatic horizon. Modernization theory was related to the liberal intellectual tradition on economics and politics, while the ideology of the PDC was based on the social doctrine of the Catholic Church and the writings of Catholic philosophers such as Jacques Maritain, with whom Frei corresponded frequently; both schools of social thought, however, sought full inclusion of the masses in the formal mechanisms of a mostly open economy and the promotion and strengthening of liberal democracy as the legitimate model for the acquisition and exertion of state power.[12]

Intellectually and socially, Dungan was a perfect representative of the spirit of the Alliance for Progress and its underlying model of modernization, much like Frei and a good part of his following within the PDC. This ideological affinity made for smooth functioning of the relations between Chile and the United States while Dungan served as ambassador in Santiago even when the positions of both parties were at odds, as in the case of the U.S. intervention in the Dominican Republic in 1965. His stay in Chile, however, did not see as much trouble and certainly not the level of effervescence and polarization that increasingly characterized the landscape of Chilean politics in the last years of the 1960s.

Figure 2. Foreign Minister Gabriel Valdés greets Ambassador Ralph Dungan. The U.S. envoy developed good personal relationships with most of his Christian Democratic interlocutors while he stayed in Chile, but did not reach out to politicians of other sensibilities, as his predecessors and successors in the post did. *Courtesy of Archivo Histórico Gabriel Valdés—D&D Consultores, http://www.ahgv.cl.*

In 1967, Dungan was offered the position of chancellor of higher education of the state of New Jersey. He left Chile in August 1967 just as the fortunes of the Frei administration were starting to turn for the worse, but he continued to correspond with Frei and other Chilean politicians in the following years. Dungan, an archetypical liberal Democrat, opposed from the very beginning the military dictatorship that toppled Salvador Allende in 1973. He tried to mediate in favor of a few prisoners and exiles with both the U.S. and Chilean governments and even paid a visit to Socialist leader Clodomiro Almeyda, foreign minister of the Allende government, as he was held prisoner by the military dictatorship in 1974. The authorization slip for the visit remains in the collection of Dungan's personal papers as a chilling reminder of the methodical and bureaucratic character of the repression unleashed against the Chilean Left by the military dictatorship that took over power in Chile in 1973.[13] After stepping down from his position in New Jersey's system of higher education, Dungan served as an executive director in the Inter-American Development Bank. He died in Barbados in 2013 at the age of ninety.[14]

The Stabilization Program of the Frei Administration

The political project of the PDC was attractive to the Johnson administration—as it had been for John F. Kennedy and his entourage—because it offered a viable alternative to communism and other revolutionary sensibilities in Latin America. On the surface, the philosophical opposition to Marxism at the core of the Christian Democratic ideology and the PDC's commitment to the principles and practice of liberal democracy made for much of the sympathy earned by the party among many U.S. liberals. However, the ideological affinity between Chilean Christian Democracy and U.S. Cold War liberalism went well beyond their common philosophical and political rejection of Marxism. The Christian Democratic program offered a path toward development that embraced many of the propositions of modernization theory, the intellectual framework on which much of the foreign policy of the Kennedy and the Johnson administrations was founded.[15] Whereas the Marxist parties proposed to bring about equality and social justice through the establishment of an economy largely controlled by the state, the PDC sought to fully incorporate the majority of the population into the functioning of the formal economy, both in the city and the countryside, and to redistribute income in favor of workers and peasants. The Christian Democratic project did call for a larger presence of the state in some areas of the economy, such as the copper business, but it did not challenge the basic premise of capitalism: the regulated right to and the prevalence of private entrepreneurship in the context of a relatively free market.

Christian Democrats did feel uneasy about the concept of capitalism and presented their vision for the future—communitarianism—as different from both capitalism and socialism. What a communitarian order would look like the Christian Democratic ideologues never explained very well, but its characterization was always underscored by the conviction that private property, important as it was, should always be subjected to the common good; should play a role in the welfare of society as a whole and not only of the possessing individual; and should never overwhelm the deeper and richer spiritual dimension of an individual's life. For the moderate wing of the PDC, communitarianism was a true middle path between capitalism and socialism, although with much more in common with capitalism; for the left wing of the party, communitarianism belonged in the spectrum of socialism.[16] Nevertheless, for the majority of the PDC, and especially for Frei and the followers of his line, the means to achieve that end were very much in line with the main tenets of modernization theory and their concrete representation in the goals of the Alliance for Progress: expansion of formal education; a non-statist agrarian reform; a more progressive and efficient tax system; and the stabilization of the chronic issue of inflation.[17] In any event, the general economic policy of the Frei administration was not a sharp departure from the way capitalism was understood in several other countries of the world at the time, including the United States. At the most, it was a Chilean shade of the developmental type of capitalism promoted by institutions such as the United Nations Economic Commission for Latin America (CEPAL, by its Spanish acronym).[18]

While the Christian Democratic project, albeit rhetorically critical of capitalism, was, in general, acceptable for the then predominant sensibility of U.S. Cold War liberalism, Chile's economy and institutions seemed to provide a perfect context for the achievement of the goals of the Alliance for Progress.[19] Unlike many other Latin American countries, especially in Central America and the Caribbean, Chile had a relatively complex economy, still dependent on the export of raw materials—especially copper—but with considerable industrial activity and a stable political system. According to most assessments, Chile was not a typical Third World country but was still far from an optimal level of development. In his seminal work *The Future of Underdeveloped Countries* economist Eugene Staley, one of the founding fathers of modernization theory, placed Chile among the countries that had reached an intermediate stage of economic development, still far below the United States and Western Europe but on a par with countries such as South Africa, Argentina, pre-revolutionary Cuba, Italy, and even the Soviet Union.[20] According to the perceptions of U.S. policymakers, most of them imbued with the spirit of modernization theory, a consistent and generous flow of aid toward the Frei administration could conceivably help put Chile on a sure path toward development, thus making it a showcase for the Alliance for Progress. Certainly the flow of U.S. aid was contingent on the willingness of the Frei administration to pursue some specific policies consistent with the goals of the Alliance for Progress and largely in line with the programmatic prescriptions of modernization theory.

One of the cornerstones of modernization theory is the idea that the economic performance of a country is directly linked to political stability and the ability of the state to adequately perform its basic duties. Where the political situation is stable and the state is strong, the economy functions well, as the cases of the United States and the countries of Western Europe demonstrated; where instability reigns and the state is weak, the economy cannot conceivably reach its full potential, as was the case with most of the countries of the Third World. The key difference lay in the ability of the healthier states to sustain a formal economy encompassing the entire population through the effective enforcement of universally known laws and norms.

A thoroughly institutionalized state, able to reach the whole national territory and exercise its monopoly of violence over the entire population, moreover, could consistently obtain revenues through taxation, so it could further improve the economic performance of a country by spending on education and infrastructure and even redistributing income through the provision of specific benefits such as pensions or housing subsidies. In this scheme of things, Chile was, indeed, closer to the developed countries than to the typical underdeveloped Third World countries where state institutions were still exceedingly weak and most of the population lived outside the formal economy. As an AID report put it in 1964, "With its relatively advanced economy and society, and a political climate whose stability is unusual for the area, Chile has a potential for economic and social advancement that is among the highest in Latin America." Consequently, the report went on, "the long-range U.S. assistance objective for Chile is to help it become an early example of the success of the Alliance for Progress in action."[21]

Still, Chile's economy had not yet fully taken off, to use the term coined by the dean of modernization theory, Walt Whitman Rostow.[22] Full participation of the entire population of the country in the benefits of a modern economy and society was hindered by, among other things, an outdated social and economic order in the countryside, where peasants had little access to property and education and fundamentally depended on the decisions and fate of the landholders on whose land they lived and toiled. Furthermore, agricultural production was inefficient and insufficient for the needs of the ever-larger urban population of the country. A complicated structure of price controls for agricultural products, moreover, only compounded the situation.[23] In this context, a swift and significant agrarian reform, entailing the transfer of ownership of large portions of land to peasants, was necessary for both social and economic

reasons. The Chilean state, in addition, had expanded its obligations throughout the twentieth century without correspondingly expanding its revenues.
Consequently, the state's continuous need to resort to borrowing had contributed to consistently high levels of inflation, which had badly hampered the
performance of the Chilean economy. As the interests of urban labor were
represented by big and strong organizations and workers constituted the single
largest segment of voters, governments of different stripes were compelled to
grant wage increases at least as high as the inflation rate and usually above it.
Wage increases, in turn, pressed inflation further upward, in a vicious cycle that
no administration had yet been able or willing to tackle. For U.S. policymakers,
monetary and price stability were among the fundamental goals of the Alliance
for Progress, as they were critical to the consolidation of modern economies
and, therefore, indispensable for development and the universal inclusion of
national populations in the workings of a unified society. If the Frei administration wanted to make the Chilean economy take off for good, according to
the U.S. view, it had to take tough decisions regarding taxes, wages, price
controls, and monetary policy.[24]

Most U.S. aid toward Chile during the Frei years, about $420 million be-
tween 1964 and 1970 (see Table 2), was granted in the form of program loans,
which went directly to the Chilean state's coffers and had the purpose of cover-
ing expenses considered in the annual government budget—whose elaboration
was often discussed with U.S. officials. Along with the Johnson administration's
relative largesse, the Frei government could also count on the good disposition
of other creditor countries gathered in the Paris Club, which allowed for a favorable restructuring of Chile's external debt in early 1965, and the International Monetary Fund (IMF), with which the Frei administration signed a
standby agreement in 1966.[25] By and large, the Frei administration complied
with the requirements of the U.S. government and the IMF, at least until 1967.
A tax reform signed into law by President Jorge Alessandri in February 1964
helped increase state revenues from 14 percent to 16 percent of the country's
GDP in the first two years of the Frei administration.[26] The currency, the *es-
cudo*, was slowly but progressively devaluated to curb imports and stimulate
exports, and Central Bank borrowing by the government decreased significantly.[27] Inflation was brought down from 38 percent in 1964 to 17 percent two
years later. In 1966, moreover, the economy grew an impressive 11 percent.[28]
Finally, according to one quantitative analysis, real wages rose by over 10 percent
annually between 1964 and 1967.[29] In the first two years of his administration,
Frei seemed to be presiding over the sort of transformation, predicted and ac-

Table 2. U.S. Aid to Selected Latin American Countries, 1964–1970 (in thousands of current dollars)

Country	1964	1965	1966	1967	1968	1969	1970	Total 1964–1970
Argentina	9,600	5,300	6,700	1,600	2,800	1,900	1,000	19,300
Bolivia	77,200	18,800	37,301	19,200	18,600	21,501	8,000	123,402
Brazil	336,900	270,800	329,000	240,000	280,700	29,201	154,000	1,303,701
Chile	111,800	125,400	111,300	25,800	82,901	51,501	26,300	423,202
Colombia	105,700	27,200	101,600	117,300	100,000	110,901	131,100	588,101
Costa Rica	16,400	14,700	4,700	15,000	11,500	18,500	20,700	85,100
Dominican R.	14,500	66,200	100,600	58,800	58,700	26,300	19,800	330,400
Guatemala	9,300	13,200	9,000	14,101	16,500	8,600	32,200	93,601
Guyana	300.	12,300	7,500	9,700	8,601	17,600	1,601	57,302
Haiti	3,700	2,500	3,300	2,700	3,400	3,300	3,701	18,901
Mexico	52,500	36,400	300	300	200	200	1,000	38,400
Nicaragua	5,800	23,700	17,500	12,200	25,700	2,400	3,100	84,600
Panama	17,600	20,700	14,401	36,501	20,801	17,400	13,500	123,303
Paraguay	8,101	8,802	14,800	5,000	6,300	13,500	8,100	56,502
Peru	54,700	23,100	39,500	27,300	13,800	13,100	16,900	133,700
Uruguay	7,500	2,100	6,800	3,500	36,000	2,000	19,400	69,800
Venezuela	14,000	28,400	9,200	6,100	5,000	3,200	2,700	54,600

Source: U.S. Agency for International Development (USAID), and The Official Record of U.S. Foreign Aid, *Foreign Aid Explorer*, accessed 29 April 2019. https://explorer.usaid.gov/index.html.

tively promoted by modernization theory pundits, that had proved so elusive for less-developed countries: a seamless combination of economic growth, redistribution of income in favor of the poorest, and effective inclusion of the majority of the population in the institutions of a truly national society; all this against the backdrop of political and economic stability brought about by a responsible fiscal policy.

The stabilization features of the Christian Democratic project resembled some of the economic policies attempted by the populistic Carlos Ibáñez del Campo administration between 1952 and 1958 and the right-wing Jorge Alessandri administration between 1958 and 1964, which also had the blessing of the IMF and, with less enthusiasm, the United States.[30] In fact, they had an understanding of the relationship between the state and the economy that was very much in line with the way capitalism was practiced in the developed world. Nevertheless, the Frei administration's pursuit of stabilization policies ran parallel to the implementation of an ambitious program of wealth redistribution. Frei and his closest advisers understood that true modernization and development could only be the result of radical and rapid changes in some areas. In this sense, the Christian Democratic project was a novelty for Latin American politics. Historically, swift and radical social reform, in Latin America and elsewhere, had been associated with expansionary and frequently irresponsible fiscal policies—the populist road—or, in revolutionary contexts, with a thorough seizure of the state and the economy by those in power—the communist model. On the other hand, stabilization measures were usually advocated by those who either feared social change or did not prioritize the pressing needs of the working and middle classes. The Frei administration sought to bring about the social change so badly needed in the country without philosophically or practically challenging the standard liberal and capitalist understanding of the relationship between the state and the economy most widely held at the time.[31]

Riding the Crest of the Wave

The general alignment between the Chilean and U.S. governments notwithstanding, their emphases and short-term concerns were different. Policymakers in Washington followed a blueprint that, although generally in accordance with the stated purposes of the PDC, gave only secondary importance to the realities of day-to-day politics in Chile. This is not to say that officials in the State Department and the White House had a poor understanding of what was going on in Chile; on the contrary, they followed Chilean politics with great interest and understood it quite accurately. However, U.S. policymakers in Washington could think of and stick to a long-term strategy in a way that Chilean officials could not. The concerned officials in the State Department and the White House did not have to deal with the fierce opposition coming from five major parties—Conservatives, Liberals, Radicals, Socialists, and Communists— and were not under the scrutiny of a Chilean electorate that had the chance to go to the polls every other year. Frei and his closest economic advisers understood very well that the PDC's project could not be realized on the weak economic and fiscal foundations they had inherited from previous governments. They also understood that stabilization policies, though sound in the long term, could bring about social consequences in the short term and, as a result, could affect the political standing of those who promoted them. In some cases, politics would necessarily have to trump economic orthodoxy.

The negotiations between Chilean and U.S. officials for the 1966 program loan highlighted the inherent tension between the pressing needs of fiscal health and social reform in the context of an open society. By and large, U.S. officials had been pleased with the way the Frei administration had handled economic matters in 1965. Their expectation was that the PDC government could continue implementing its program of social reform without resorting to inflationary policies such as government borrowing from the Central Bank. The U.S. requirement on this matter was quite demanding, given the recent history of Chile's fiscal policy: in 1966, the Frei administration should not only reduce but actually eliminate borrowing from the Central Bank. The chief Chilean negotiator, Minister of Finance Sergio Molina, agreed on the technical soundness of the U.S. requirement yet could not fully concede on the matter. The budget for 1966 had to consider wage raises and spending on government-run social services such as social security and the National Health System that, although not necessarily in line with the long-term goals of the Alliance for Progress, were inevitable, for both legal and political reasons. Though Molina committed his best efforts to meet the U.S. requirements to the largest possible extent, he could not grant his interlocutors the assurance they wanted.[32]

Even President Frei weighed in on the negotiation at one point, making a rather melodramatic pitch for the Chilean case. Speaking with Ambassador Dungan, Frei complained about the inflexibility of the U.S. position. He, as did his finance minister, recognized the "technical soundness of [the U.S.] approach," but could not "in good faith" accede to the U.S. officials' conditions. Frei spoke of "the complexity of his political position," quoting the anti-U.S. vitriol of Socialist Senator Carlos Altamirano as proof of how difficult it was to tie his hands regarding monetary policy because of the conditions of an agreement between his administration and the U.S. government. Frei told Dungan, in a remarkably frank manner, that the image he had to sell to the Chilean public was practically a sham: "I speak to my country about our dignified position although small and weak, but in my heart I know this is not true. I have no dignity. I am a mendicant."[33]

An agreement between the U.S. and the Chilean government was, at last, reached in January 1966. Higher copper prices would bring more revenue than originally expected into the Chilean state's treasury, so public spending would not necessarily require expansionary monetary policies. Central Bank borrowing would not be definitely forsaken, but it could be lowered to a level that U.S. officials finally found acceptable.[34] The U.S. government would grant Chile a program loan of about $90 million, of which ten million had been added to the originally negotiated sum in compensation for the Frei administration's willingness to keep the price of copper at thirty-six cents per pound in the United States.[35] The Frei administration, in turn, would be able to keep inflation more or less at bay without hindering the implementation of its program, at least for the time being.

The increase in copper prices in 1966 allowed the Frei administration to maintain a relatively healthy fiscal situation while implementing far-reaching social reforms—a rare occurrence in Latin American history. By the end of the year, the situation looked so good that Frei and his economic team decided that a U.S. program loan for fiscal year 1967 would not be necessary for the Chilean budget. So exceptional was the decision of the Chilean government that National Security Advisor Walt W. Rostow introduced his memorandum to President Johnson informing him about this development as "a man bites dog item." The reasoning behind the Chilean government's decision to forgo a program loan for 1967 was, according to the reports coming from the embassy in Santiago, Frei's conviction that "[the] nation must understand its need to live within limits permitted by its resources and that Chile could not allow itself [the] luxury of external borrowing for normal budget levels at [a] time when copper prices [are] high." In addition, Frei thought the measure could help him contain demands for higher wages and public spending, which would, in turn, further his goal of keeping the fiscal situation in a relatively sound state.[36] In his presentation of the decision to the nation, which was broadcast by radio and television, Frei did not convey this line of thinking as explicitly—his preferences in this regard were well known—and, instead, emphasized the significance of the initiative for Chile's independent standing in the international scene.

The decision of the Frei administration to forego a program loan for 1967 did not, however, entail a complete renunciation of U.S. aid. Previously negotiated sector loans, which unlike program loans were granted for specific purposes, would be completed as planned. The AID had already negotiated with the Chilean government a $20 million loan for the agricultural sector and a $10 million loan for the education sector. According to the AID report to the president on these loans, the funds provided to the Chilean government by this means would make a significant contribution to a couple of well-established Alliance for Progress goals. The agricultural sector loan would contribute to boost food production by financing "technical assistance, fertilizer, pesticides, machinery and equipment for use in the private sector." The education sector loan, for its part, would provide funds for the continuing expansion of infrastructure necessary for the long-term goal of universal access to primary and secondary education. The way the money from these loans was supposed to be administered neatly illustrates the U.S. understanding of the role of the state in the process of capitalist modernization, which was also the most widespread ideological vision about capitalism held at the time in the Western world, still a decade before radical monetarist thought began to influence policymaking—ironically enough, in Chile. Agriculture was, in essence, a business whose ideal functioning, both from an economic and a social perspective, was better achieved by private actors; building infrastructure for a significant expansion in access to formal education, on the other hand, was a task to be carried out by the state.[37]

The sector loans negotiated for 1967, though small in quantitative terms, symbolized the ideological and technical affinity between a U.S. foreign policy fed by modernization theory and a Chilean government bent on a process of reform buttressed by a well-established and functioning bureaucratic state. Sector loans, unlike the program loans that went directly into the general budget, were provided for particular purposes and, more important, to specific agencies. In the case of the sector loans for 1967, the recipients and administrators of the funds would be the agriculture and education ministries. What made the 1967 sector loans so symbolically relevant was the fact that their concession and administration were negotiated directly between the AID and the concerned Chilean ministries. This was the first time the AID had proceeded in this way, and the records show there was a moderate expectation that this could be replicated in other cases. This methodological choice stemmed from the assumption, widely shared among U.S. policymakers, that Chilean institutions functioned reasonably well, as a result of a century and a half of steady state-building, and that officers of the Frei administration had a vision of development akin to the broad ideological and intellectual basis—modernization theory—on which the foreign policy of the Johnson administration stood. Unlike many other interlocutors in the Third World, Chilean policymakers, especially those of the Christian Democratic sensibility, were well trained in the complexities of a functioning bureaucratic system and, in broad terms, spoke the same ideological and technical language as their U.S. counterparts. Therefore, negotiating the concession and monitoring the administration of agricultural and education loans directly with the concerned ministries was a logical choice, even if it was an unprecedented one, for AID officers both in Washington and Santiago.[38]

A Bump in the Road

Needless to say, the Johnson administration's support for Frei's Revolution in Liberty was not unconditional. The most basic U.S. expectation was that Frei and the PDC would continue to oppose the parties of the Left, the main threat to U.S. interests in Chilean politics. Furthermore, the Frei administration had to meet a few important requirements regarding its macroeconomic and monetary policies to be eligible for U.S. aid. Frei made his best efforts to comply with such expectations and requirements, both because of the economic convenience of the partnership with the United States and because of his personal ideological convictions. The Johnson and the Frei administrations could maintain the most cordial relations above all because their officials and diplomatic representatives, not to mention Johnson and Frei themselves, by and large shared an ideological outlook on modernization, development, democracy, and the ideological confrontation of the Cold War.

The coincidence, however, was not absolute. As a middle-class and progressive party, the PDC had a vision of continental relations inherently critical of the imperialistic side of U.S. foreign policy toward Latin America. As a senator, Frei himself had expressed his condemnation of U.S. maneuvers to overthrow the government of Jacobo Arbenz in Guatemala in 1954. Frei and the PDC could and did recognize the leadership of the United States in the continental efforts toward modernization and development, especially through the Alliance for Progress. Besides, there was no point in denying the role of the United States as the economic and political hegemon in the Americas. As Frei put it in the same speech in which he condemned the intervention in Guatemala in 1954, "no judicious man in Latin America can deny that in this continent cooperation with the United States is fundamental for its economic development, its future prosperity and the well-being of its peasant, industrial and mining masses."[39] Nevertheless, accepting that such leadership and hegemony entitled the United States to unilaterally intervene in another sovereign country of the region, as the Johnson administration did in the Dominican Republic in 1965, was an entirely different matter.

On 28 April 1965, five hundred marines landed in the Dominican Republic to help the *de facto* ruling junta put down an insurrection of adherents of Juan Bosch, who had served as the constitutional president until he was overthrown in 1963.[40] The cables sent from Santo Domingo to Washington by U.S. diplomats and intelligence agents reported that the situation was becoming increasingly dangerous for U.S. citizens and, even worse, that Cuban-backed communists had a significant presence in the anti-government forces. The fear of losing the Dominican Republic to the communists, for the most part groundless, prompted Johnson to take the hawkish road and send the Marines, just as another progressive U.S. president, Woodrow Wilson, had done, for different reasons and in a different context, forty-nine years earlier.[41] The Johnson administration attempted to legitimize its intervention, which was reinforced with

more troops in the following days and weeks, by requesting that the Organization of American States (OAS) sanction it as legal and that other American
countries join the United States in the military occupation of the Dominican
Republic. A good number of Latin American countries, however, reacted
negatively to the intervention and to the U.S. request for troops.

The Chilean government did not approve of the intervention in the Dominican Republic, and its diplomatic representatives publicly expressed their
rejection of the decision made by President Johnson. Foreign Minister Gabriel
Valdés denounced the intervention as a breach of the OAS charter and demanded that the organization condemn the U.S. invasion.[42] Alejandro Magnet, the Chilean ambassador to the OAS, submitted a proposal that called for
an immediate end to the U.S. presence in the Dominican Republic and for the
formation, if requested by the Dominican government, of an inter-American
military force that would preserve order until the political process became
normalized.[43]

In directly calling for an end to the unilateral U.S. intervention, Chile took
a position of full disagreement with the United States in even more forceful
terms than other countries that also rejected the U.S. invasion of the Dominican Republic. Colombia, for instance, also called for an intervention sanctioned
by the OAS but avoided placing blame explicitly on the United States. Furthermore, Chile was the only country that refused to vote for the establishment of
a committee that would propose specific courses of multilateral action after
visiting the Dominican Republic. The idea of an *ad hoc* committee had even
been proposed by the Chilean representation, but the final resolution was
stripped of an explicit rejection of the unilateral U.S. intervention. Magnet
explained that there was no explicit guarantee that the start of multilateral action would entail the end of unilateral intervention in the Dominican Republic. Thus, the establishment of such a committee would only mean a legitimi-
zation of the U.S. actions. Chile would not lend itself to such approach.

The Johnson administration decided to send Averell Harriman on a quick
tour of Latin American capitals to present the position of the United States
and request the support of the governments of the region for its actions in the
Dominican Republic. On 7 May, Harriman had a long conversation with President Frei about the Dominican Republic affair—almost entirely in English. Frei
replied to Harriman's request for support by explaining that he understood the
position of President Johnson regarding the situation of the Dominican Republic; he asked, however, that his position be understood by the United States, too.
Frei stated that his policies were pro-American and referred specifically to the
agreements with the U.S. copper companies as a sign of his goodwill toward the

United States. He personally admired Johnson's domestic program and recognized that "American liberalism had given inspiration and courage to the [PDC]" in its years of growth and consolidation.[44] Ideological affinity did not mean, however, that Chile would follow blindly the United States in the international context. Just as Johnson had acted on the assumption that the interests of the United States required an intervention in the Dominican Republic, Frei thought that the interests of Chile were best served by opposing the U.S. unilateral action on this specific case.

Frei knew very well that the success of his project required the political and material support of the United States, so antagonizing the Johnson administration was not in the best interest of the Chilean government. On the other hand, Chile's longstanding diplomatic tradition, the particular features of the Chilean political culture, and even Frei's personal convictions as a progressive politician made it impossible for him to side with the United States on the Dominican issue. As he told Ambassador Dungan a few days after the invasion, he was much aware that the interests of Chile lay with the United States, but "we cannot be in the position of 'yes-men.»'"[45] Besides the fact that the intervention in the Dominican Republic was hard to swallow for almost everyone outside the United States, something U.S. foreign policymakers did not seem to understand or even care about, Chile had interests of its own in the international system. The advancement of those interests demanded strong opposition to foreign intervention in the domestic affairs of other countries, especially in Latin America. Ambassador Dungan explained to the State Department that the position taken by Chile on the Dominican crisis followed the traditional pattern of the country's foreign policy, which was "based very strongly on [an] extremely juridical interpretation of treaties." Chile had acquired large parts of its territory through war in the nineteenth century, and its annexations had been formalized through treaties. As a result, "a cornerstone of [Chile's] foreign policy, regardless of which party in power, has always been strict (often infuriatingly so) adherence to [the] letter of treaties and agreements."[46] From the Chilean foreign policy perspective, the U.S. intervention in the Dominican Republic was, above all, a breach of the legal commitments subscribed to by the countries of the Americas and sanctioned in the OAS charter. Any specific political analysis of the necessity or legitimacy of the intervention according to the particular circumstances in which it was carried out had to be subordinated to the fact that it was a unilateral intervention in the domestic affairs of a sovereign country and, as such, it was a violation of the legal framework for inter-American relations enshrined in the OAS charter.

Domestic politics also influenced Frei's decision to take a principled stance on the Dominican crisis. The Chilean Left voiced its strong rejection of the U.S. intervention in Congress, in the press, and on the streets. Communists and Socialists rallied against the U.S. intervention, finding once more an opportunity to voice their ideological anti-imperialist tropes. The official Socialist Party's statement on the Dominican crisis was quite extreme, going as far as to assert that "any Yankee on our soil, as peaceful as they may seem, is a danger for our fatherland, for behind every American citizen looms large, under any pretext, the shadow of an invasion."[47] In a more sober fashion, Socialist Deputy Clodomiro Almeyda aimed his darts at the OAS and, more broadly speaking, the inter-American system. Almeyda, who would later serve as minister of foreign relations in the Allende government, pointed out that the OAS had met in the wake of the U.S. intervention not to condemn it as a violation of the OAS charter but to find ways to channel the unilateral U.S. actions into a Pan-American operation.[48] The reaction of the OAS to the Dominican crisis was especially irksome for the Chilean Left, as a few years earlier Cuba had been ejected from the inter-American organization for its support of Venezuelan revolutionaries.[49] The double standard of the United States and the OAS was so apparent to the Left—and it was, indeed, very hard to see it in a different way—that Communist Senator Carlos Contreras referred to the OAS as the "U.S. Department of Colonial Affairs."[50]

In an exchange of letters published in the Chilean press, Senator Salvador Allende and Ambassador Ralph Dungan engaged in an argument that nicely highlighted the positions of the Left, as articulated by one of its senior leaders, and the United States on the Dominican crisis. Allende signaled his condemnation of the U.S. intervention in the Dominican Republic by refusing to attend a social gathering organized by the U.S. embassy in Santiago. Allende argued that "the United States [was] violating . . . the most essential principles of international coexistence, taking in bloody fashion a road which wipes out at its very roots the right of free determination of peoples." The U.S. intervention in the Dominican Republic signified, in Allende's words, "the predominance of force over all the moral, cultural and spiritual values which, after an arduous struggle, have come to be considered part of civilization."[51] Ambassador Dungan responded that the United States also "[believed] deeply in the principles of non-intervention and self-determination." Nevertheless, pointing to the case of Cuba without identifying it explicitly, Dungan asserted that "failure to interest ourselves collectively in the interests of our fellow citizens has resulted in the citizens of at least one country losing their free press, their right to vote, a rule of law, freedom of conscience, and all the other essential rights of free men in democratic societies." (An argument like this would make no impression on Senator Allende, who in his Senate speech against the U.S. intervention in the Dominican Republic had referred to Cuba, echoing the official line of Castro's regime, as "the first free territory in Latin America").[52] The United States, according to Dungan, would not accept the sacrifice of the liberty of the Dominican people to the principle of self-determination.[53]

Other political forces also expressed their condemnation of the U.S. intervention in the Dominican Republic. The Radical Party issued a formal declaration condemning U.S. unilateral action and stated their support for the position taken by the Frei government on the matter. According to the Radicals, not only did the U.S. intervention violate the OAS charter, it also entailed a breach of the Inter-American Treaty of Reciprocal Assistance—a more poignant indictment, as the treaty, even more than the establishment of the OAS, had been a cornerstone of the Cold War U.S. foreign policy toward the Americas.[54] The Radicals' condemnation of U.S. intervention in the Dominican Republic stemmed from a deeply held ideological conviction as to the way in which the international system should work. In his speech in the Senate regarding the Dominican crisis, Senator Ulises Correa emphasized that his party held a principled stance—a rather counterintuitive position, as the PR was in many ways the least ideological of all the major forces then competing in Chilean politics. In fact, on this matter the Radicals, along with the Christian Democrats, were more consistent than all the other political parties. The Radicals were on the record rejecting the overthrow of Guatemalan president Jacobo Arbenz in 1954, the Soviet invasion of Hungary in 1956, and the joint French and British war on Egypt over the nationalization of the Suez Canal by Gamal Abdel Nasser that same year.[55] The Radicals would also condemn the Soviet invasion of Czechoslovakia in 1968, which was vindicated by the Communists and criticized only softly and unconvincingly by then Senator Salvador Allende.[56]

More important for the position of the Frei government, the PDC unanimously rejected the U.S. intervention in the Dominican Republic. In some specific cases, the language and tone of that condemnation matched the invectives of left-wing politicians. Deputy Patricio Hurtado, who would leave the party years later to join the more left-leaning Unitarian Popular Action Movement (MAPU), expressed his repudiation of the U.S. intervention in the Dominican Republic and asked rhetorically what the attitude of the United States would have been had Salvador Allende been elected president in 1964. Under the newfangled doctrine that bore his name, President Johnson may have "felt authorized to send the marines to Arica, Valparaiso or Punta Arenas," Deputy

Hurtado pointed out.[57] Hurtado went even further in his general assessment of the situation, showing that the left wing of the PDC—the so-called *rebeldes* in the lingo of Chilean politics of the late 1960s—did not feel comfortable with the ideological affinity and the political closeness between the party and the United States. Hurtado asserted, "Latin America [is] in the middle of the evolution of its revolutionary process and [understands] that its destiny is not linked to—in fact it is incompatible with—the destiny of the North American nation."[58]

The U.S. actions in the Dominican Republic ran so clearly against the principles of non-intervention and national sovereignty so cherished to the PDC that even its more conservative members, including Frei, had little choice but to condemn the decision of the Johnson administration. Moreover, the independent position taken by the Frei government on the matter had given a boost to "the mystique of the 'Revolution in Liberty,'" as Otto Boye, a prominent member of the PDC intelligentsia, told a U.S. embassy officer. In the specific case of the Dominican crisis, the principled stance of the Christian Democrats squared nicely with the sensibility of the majority of Chilean public opinion and allowed the Frei government to score valuable points in the internal political arena. According to Boye's cold assessment of the situation, it was politically useful in Chile "to give the impression of lofty independence and martyrdom in the defense of sacred principles and the rights of the people in the face of U.S. pressures." Furthermore, the evidence of significant Castroite infiltration of the constitutionalist forces in the Dominican Republic was at best flimsy, so U.S. intervention was all the more indefensible in this case.[59]

Only the traditional Right, which had suffered a crushing defeat in the congressional elections a few months earlier, expressed some support for the U.S. actions in the Dominican Republic. The Conservative daily *El Diario Ilustrado* justified the U.S. intervention on the grounds that the Dominican rebel movement had been infiltrated by "Castro-Communists." In remarkable coincidence with the position expressed by Dungan in his letter to Allende, the *El Diario Ilustrado* editorial that justified the U.S. intervention maintained that the principle of non-intervention "becomes the right and the moral and legal duty of intervention in defense of life and the essential rights and liberties of man."[60] In Congress, Conservative Deputy Manuel Tagle stated: "At this tragic crossroads, the U.S. government chose to risk even its prestige and to take a rapid and virile decision, imposed by the urgency of events."[61] In a very odd speech, Liberal Deputy Jaime Bulnes said that he and his party did not favor a unilateral intervention in the sovereign affairs of other countries such as the U.S. invasion of the Dominican Republic. However, such interventions were common occurrences in the international context of the times, so everyone "should have become used to them."[62]

The position of the right-wing parties on the Dominican crisis reflected their dogmatic anti-communist conviction and, worse, it highlighted their inability to show themselves as a positive, creative alternative to the project of radical change proposed by the Left and the path of reform promoted by the PDC. Communist Deputy Volodia Teitelboim said it caustically: "These salt statues, which can only look to the past, have been whipped out by the people, because they understand nothing about the twentieth century."[63] Indeed, the stance of the right-wing parties seemed radically at odds with the atmosphere of Chilean politics and society at the time, and naturally the Frei government did not want to have anything to do with that kind of posture. If anything, the right-wing support for the U.S. intervention in the Dominican Republic gave the Frei administration another reason to oppose U.S. actions.

Notwithstanding the opposing views on the matter of the Dominican crisis, the Johnson administration did not try to strong-arm the Frei government into supporting or even accepting the U.S. position. Secretary of State Dean Rusk and another high State Department officer, William Dentzer, hinted that future aid could be hard to get in Congress as a result of the Chilean position in the Dominican crisis, but these passing comments did not strike Radomiro Tomic, Chilean ambassador in Washington, as a significant warning.[64] Rusk did tell Tomic, in a somewhat more bullish tone, that "the Caribbean was not Chile's responsibility and that [Chile] should let the directly affected countries ascertain the level of the Communist threat in the region and take timely measures."[65] In any case, should the United States change its friendly attitude toward Chile because of the disagreement over the Dominican crisis, Tomic thought the Frei administration could and should shift "toward Europe the center of gravity of its scheme of international solidarity," an assertion that attests to the deeply ingrained habit of Chilean politicians at the time to think of development and modernization as ends to be achieved only if richer countries were willing and able to provide economic assistance.[66] In the end, these tepid attempts of the United States to bend the position of the Frei administration on the Dominican crisis did not succeed. Toward the end of May, Chile voted against the U.S.-sponsored resolution to provide the inter-American force with a specific OAS mandate. The resolution was, in any case, approved by the majority of the OAS members.[67]

The Chilean position toward the Dominican crisis generated some resentment among some U.S. diplomats and strained the relations between the two countries a little. Finance Minister Sergio Molina, for instance, thought that

U.S. aid to the Frei administration decreased and came with more strings attached after 1965.[68] The documentary record, however, shows that the impasse over the Dominican crisis did not leave a lasting mark on the friendly relationship between the Chilean and the U.S. governments. Ultimately, the Johnson administration did not really need the support of the OAS to do in the Dominican Republic what it thought best for U.S. interests. Much less indispensable was the support of one specific country. Furthermore, the international political campaign to garner support among Latin American countries launched in the wake of the Marines' landing in the Dominican Republic was reasonably successful, and the Johnson administration did not have to change the course it had originally taken. Troops and police forces from other Latin American countries (Brazil and Argentina among them) joined the United States in its occupation of the Dominican Republic. The inter-American force led by the United States stayed in the Dominican Republic until new elections were held in 1966. By that time, the original opposition of the Chilean government to the unilateral U.S. intervention in the Dominican Republic had become an innocuous and remote thing of the past.

The Massacre in El Salvador

For all his progressive convictions, Frei responded much in the same way as his predecessors to episodes of social mobilization that he perceived as unacceptable challenges to the rule of law and public order. Since the end of the nineteenth century, many strikes and protests of the working class, and a couple of attempts of political insurrection, had met the implacable response of the state, leaving hundreds dead as a result.[69] For the Left, the consistent attitude of presidents of virtually all political sensibilities regarding social mobilization and its repression bespoke an inherent quality of the Chilean state, which, according to this critical view, was designed to keep the social and economic status quo intact. Along with the inequality inherent in the practice of capitalism in an underdeveloped country, the state's frequent choice of violent repression of the manifestations of the working class constituted one of the key points in the Left's structural critique of the Chilean institutional order. The Frei administration's response to episodes of social mobilization was very much in line with the ways in which other governments had dealt with similar situations. This decision certainly did not help endear Frei to the traditional constituencies of the Left and the left wing of his own party, but, in a telling sign of societal attitudes toward forms of social mobilization perceived as challenges to law and order, it did not significantly hurt the president's standing in public opinion either.

The first episode of deadly repression for which Frei had to take responsibility occurred in March 1966 in the mining town of El Salvador, in northern Chile. The El Salvador miners had been on strike for a few weeks, in solidarity with workers of the El Teniente copper mine, then conducting their own legal strike following the failure of the process of collective bargaining with their employer, Braden Copper. The strike of the El Salvador miners, employees of Andes Copper, a subsidiary of Anaconda, was illegal and, in response to it, the Frei government declared a state of emergency in the area. As a result, a military squadron took over the town and, as the workers stationed in the union headquarters refused to leave the building and resisted an attempt of the military to seize it, the commanding officer gave soldiers the order to open fire against the crowd. Six men and two women died, and three dozen other people were wounded.

Frei had assumed from the beginning that the strike was a political maneuver from the parties of the Left, bent on opposing his government by any means at their disposal. The declaration of a state of emergency had already sent the message that the government would not tolerate forms of mobilization outside the letter of the law and that, in addition, were economically costly for the country. Furthermore, the fact that the military had a great deal of autonomy in their administration of the area under the state of exception meant that a violent resolution of the conflict was more than likely. The apparent ineptitude of the military officer in charge of the operation, Lieutenant Colonel Manuel Pinochet, who was shot during the failed attempt to seize the union building, added another explosive element to an inherently volatile situation.

Even though the government strategy to deal with the strike was deadly, Frei did not consider that the blame for the events in El Salvador lay with him or his administration. In a televised speech on the night of the massacre, Frei stated that, as regrettable as the outcome had been, the armed forces "were fulfilling their duties." In addition, the president presented the country with his own view of the illegal strike in El Salvador and the legal strike in El Teniente. According to his interpretation, copper union leaders across the country, following the strategy of the parties of the FRAP, were trying to "make the government fail," with an attitude of "determined and premeditated subversion."

Moreover, Frei linked the mobilization of copper miners to assertions made by Chilean and foreign revolutionary leaders in the meeting of the Tri-Continental Conference held in Havana in January 1966. Salvador Allende had, in fact, stated in the conference that his and other revolutionaries' obligation was "to link anti-imperialist action with the daily struggles of the people: strikes, seizures of land, collective mobilization."[70] The enthusiastic presence of elected parliamentarians in an international conference whose official declaration vindicated violence as a means to attain political goals was certainly problematic for Chilean democracy. However, it was highly unlikely that the actions of Chilean copper workers, who had a robust history of autonomous mobilization, were related to the conference in Havana. In fact, even the staff of the U.S. embassy in Santiago thought that, while Frei had a point in his interpretation of the strike as part of a political strategy of the FRAP aimed at destabilizing his government, there was no evidence of any link between the mobilization of copper workers in El Salvador and other mines and the Tri-Continental meeting held in Havana a couple of months earlier.[71]

The killings in El Salvador put Frei in a most uncomfortable position with respect to the left-wing opposition and his own past attitudes toward similar instances of state repression of working-class protests. Frei had resigned from his post of minister of public works in 1946 in protest of the bloody quashing of a demonstration in downtown Santiago that had resulted in the death of eight people.[72] Twenty years later, as head of the government, his perspective was different. Frei's response to the strike in El Salvador, and his attitude after the incident, for the most part coincided with the actions of many of his predecessors, including Alfredo Duhalde, the vice president to whom he tendered his resignation in 1946.[73] The biggest political problem, however, lay in the fact that the government's reaction to the strike and Frei's justification of the actions of the army seemed to substantiate one of the fundamental claims of the Left and the source of much of its popular appeal: namely, that the Chilean state, regardless of the party or coalition in government, had historically resorted to violence when challenged by the mobilization of workers and other social movements. Indeed, military and police repression of strikes and other forms of social mobilization had resulted in the deaths of scores of workers many times since the end of the nineteenth century. In this sense, from the point of view of the Left, Frei's handling of the situation in El Salvador offered more proof that the path of reform proposed by the PDC was, at best, insufficient; at worst, it was a sham meant to preserve the fundamental structures of an inherently unjust capitalist society.

Frei's reference to the Tri-Continental Conference in his speech of 11 March gave the incident in El Salvador an international character marked by Cold War alignments that, in the end, favored the position of the government. A few days after the incident, in a speech given at the University of Havana, Fidel Castro took up the gauntlet thrown by Frei and denied the existence of any relationship between the Tri-Continental Conference held in the Cuban capital a few months earlier and the strikes of copper miners in Chile. Not one to mince words, Castro went on in his diatribe against Frei and called him "a liar" and "a reactionary." Moreover, he accused the sitting president and the Alliance for Progress of doing the exact opposite of what the PDC had promised in the 1964 campaign: "[Frei's government] is not a bloodless revolution, but a policy of blood without revolution." Finally, Castro asserted with great conviction and eloquence that what Chile needed was "a socialist revolution."[74]

Castro's reaction, much in line with his view of the dichotomy between reform and revolution in Latin America, gave Frei and his administration some ammunition in the public debate on the massacre. Just as the deaths of the miners could be interpreted by the Left as one more occasion in which the Chilean state had crushed a workers' movement, Castro's words, along with the fact that Allende himself had to explain his participation in the Tri-Continental Conference in the wake of the massacre, seemed to give some plausibility to Frei's argument that the illegal strike in El Salvador was, in fact, part of a broader strategy of destabilization of his government carried out or at least condoned by the parties of the FRAP. To be sure, there was no evidence whatsoever of any link between the Tri-Continental Conference and the mobilization of workers in El Salvador and other copper mines, as Frei asserted in no uncertain terms in his speech of 11 March 1966. Nevertheless, as with many other domestic situations in Chilean politics during the Cold War, and particularly in the years of the Frei administration, international alignments and ideological affinities, to a large extent, shaped the image projected by political parties and leaders, and the perceptions of their rivals. For Frei and many of his party comrades, the enthusiastic participation of Chilean politicians, including Allende, in the Tri-Continental Conference was sufficient proof of the subversive intent of the parties of the Left.

In the end, the El Salvador incident did not cause major problems for the Frei administration. The parties of the FRAP maintained their position regarding the government and their historic interpretation of the relation between a bourgeois state and the working class, which only reinforced their conviction regarding the necessity of a revolutionary transformation of the economic and political structures of the country. Nevertheless, the line of argument offered by Frei and the PDC regarding the incident sounded convincing for a large part of the population, too. Illegal strikes were, indeed, a part of the mobilization repertoire of the Left and certainly had political intentions that went beyond the corporate interests of organized labor. Frei's strong response to the strike in El Salvador, in this sense, drew on a conception of the role of the government and a view of the legitimacy of his authority as president that had a good deal of support among the population. What is more, Castro's intemperate utterances reinforced Frei's position about the incident and, more important, his conviction that the parties of the Left, in his mind directly linked with a strategy of international revolution promoted by Cuba, bore the greatest responsibility for the tragic events in El Salvador.[75]

Chapter 3

Time of Trouble, 1967–1969

The first two years of the Frei administration were, for the most part, quite successful. The "Chileanization" of copper of 1965 and the agrarian reform law passed in July 1967 were the most emblematic achievements of a government deeply engaged in a program of substantial social and economic reform.[1] In addition, the expansion of public education and a visible redistribution of income in favor of the poor, all against the backdrop of a decreasing level of inflation and a healthy fiscal situation, seemed to reaffirm the feasibility of the Christian Democratic project. President Frei had built a highly positive international reputation, underscored by a lengthy and triumphant trip to several European countries in 1965.[2] It seemed, then, that the promise of a Revolution in Liberty could be fulfilled and that the Christian Democratic Party could build a base of popular support large enough to afford it another go at the presidency after Frei had to step down in 1970.

Despite the seemingly favorable situation for the government, in 1967 things would begin to go in a very different direction. After the first two successful years of the Frei administration, the attitude of the opposition stiffened noticeably, and even within the PDC some leaders began to voice their disagreement with the character and the pace of some of the reforms implemented by the government. Frei himself was still a popular figure, a condition he would continue to enjoy for most of his tenure and beyond. In addition, his positive international standing reinforced his image in Chile. However, his own personal popularity would not translate into a continuation of the success of the first two years of his administration. The changing winds of Chilean politics and the declining fortunes of the Lyndon B. Johnson administration would get in the way, and it was, in fact, a situation connected to the close relationship between the Frei administration and the United States that marked the beginning of the end of the Revolution in Liberty.

The Tide Begins to Recede

In late 1966 Frei received a formal invitation to visit the United States and personally meet with President Johnson. The encounter would be a crowning moment of sorts. For Johnson and the U.S. foreign policy apparatus, the visit could help attract attention, at least for a brief moment, to a successful case of the Johnson administration's foreign policy, beyond the nightmare of the Vietnam War.[3] For Frei, it would be an excellent opportunity to personally meet with President Johnson and further the reach of his international image. The domestic political convenience of such a trip was an important factor in the consideration, as the generous praise Frei was bound to receive would boost his image as a statesman in Chile, as well. The tour, with its accompanying publicity and fanfare, would perfectly symbolize the excellent relationship between two governments and presidents that shared a vocation for progressive reform and an ideological outlook on the means to achieve economic, social, and political goals.

The State Department and the embassy in Santiago put a great deal of effort into the planning of the trip. Biographical sketches were produced, topics of conversation were thought of, and even ideas about gifts for Frei and his wife were suggested; a good history book for him and a silverware set for her seemed appropriate.[4] From President Frei's dislike of instant coffee to Mrs. María Ruiz-Tagle de Frei's self-consciousness about her looks to the negative views of the Soviet Union held by Foreign Minister Gabriel Valdés' wife Sylvia Soublette, the biographic briefs prepared by the staff at the State Department covered the lives and characters of the Chilean visitors thoroughly.[5] Speaking to Chileans about *terremotos* (earthquakes), both in the actual and figurative sense, would probably lead to a jolly conversation; bringing up the issue of Bolivia's breaking of diplomatic relations with Chile a couple of years earlier, not so much.[6] The State Department drafted a welcome speech to be presented by President Johnson and another for the introduction of Frei's address to a joint session of Congress.[7]

Even the character and idiosyncrasies of Chileans were a matter of interest. One document described Chileans as appreciative of "evidence that they are not considered to be, like other Latins, impetuous, volatile, pursuing fancy with vain ambition" and "imitators of everything French, [but admirers of the U.S.] drive and material progress."[8] Everything was carefully considered and planned so the visit of President Frei to the United States would be a complete success.

The story, however, would not end as planned, and its actual denouement was among the first of several hard blows the Frei administration would receive. According to the Chilean constitution, the president required authorization from the Senate to travel abroad. Frei had already visited Europe and other South American countries, and the upper house had granted its authorization on those occasions almost as a matter of course. This instance, however, was different. Frei's visit to Europe in 1965 had received a good deal of international attention and had, arguably, contributed to boost his standing both in Chile and abroad. Moreover, it did not sit well with the Left that Frei publicly criticized the Berlin Wall and let himself be photographed next to it along with West German politicians.[9]

From the point of view of Frei's opponents, the U.S invitation very clearly underscored the political and ideological affinity between the Johnson administration and Frei's Revolution in Liberty. Frei's visit to the United States would probably become another moment of triumph for the already popular president and would contribute to further identify Chile with the Christian Democratic project in the international scene. Consequently, for the opposition—a composite of parties on the Right (the recently founded National Party, or PN), the Center (the ineffable Radicals), and the Left (the uncompromisingly anti-U.S. Communists and Socialists)—the prospect of a state visit by Frei to the United States was undesirable. Unfortunately for the president and his party, the motley crew of the opposition held a majority in the Senate and, therefore, could deny Frei the constitutionally required permission to travel to the United States.

The debate in the Senate and the final vote on the issue must rank among the lowest points in the long history of the Chilean legislature. Senators of the PN—members until only a few months earlier of the Liberal and Conservative parties—joined their mortal ideological enemies, Socialists and Communists, and the opportunistic Radicals in voting against granting permission to the president to leave the country and visit the United States for three days. All but three opposition senators voted against Frei's trip. Not surprising, every party chose its own reason, different from the reasons of the rest, to justify its course of action. The PN argued that the invitation was not meant for Frei as head of the Chilean state but as the political leader of a particular ideological program—one the Liberals and Conservatives had supported in 1964 as a lesser

Figure 3. The Chilean Left did not like Eduardo Frei's public visit to the Berlin Wall in the company of then mayor of the city Willy Brandt in 1965, and one senator brought it up as an argument to deny the Chilean president permission to visit the United States in 1967. *Courtesy of Archivo Fotográfico Casa Museo Eduardo Frei Montalva.*

evil in the fight against communism but which the PN now fiercely opposed. The Radical Party, whose National Executive Committee backtracked in its original recommendation of approval of the constitutional permission for Frei's trip, scrambled to find a reason to justify its negative vote and, not surprising, did manage to find a few. Frei's visit to the United States, although it would last only three days, would have the president out of the country when important constitutional matters were being discussed (the Law of the Agrarian Reform), was meant mostly to extoll the achievements of the Revolution in Liberty, and would, thus, have an unidentified impact on the municipal elections of April 1967.[10]

For the Left, the Johnson administration's invitation to Frei offered an excellent opportunity to make an ideological stand by showing once more on the parliamentarian stage its intellectual and political opposition to the foreign policy of the United States and strike an actual blow to the Christian Democratic government. The senators of the left-wing parties joined their National and Radical counterparts in denouncing the political intent of the invitation but put much more emphasis on the reasons for which they were ideologically opposed to the United States and its foreign policy, at the time identified almost exclusively with the Vietnam War. The Communist and Socialist senators voted against granting Frei permission to visit the United States because manifesting their genuine ideological view of the relationship between the Frei and Johnson administrations was strategically convenient, considering that this time the stand of the left-wing parties coupled with the actions of the other opposition parties would hurt the government in both actual and symbolic terms. As was the case with so many other issues of Chilean politics at the time, the language of the Cold War took center stage in the debate about one particular and, in the grand scheme of things, largely innocuous event.

The effort of Communist Senator Volodia Teitelboim to explain the position of his party is extraordinarily telling of the ideological forces and political convictions at play in the uniquely open and diverse stage of the Cold War that was Chile until 1973. In drawing the line between the position of the left-wing parliamentarians and that of their National and Radical bedfellows, Senator Teitelboim made clear that the Communists had always been anti-imperialists, unlike all the other parties in Chilean politics. The Communists represented "an anti-imperialism of all seasons, objective, scientific, founded on the fact that Latin America's biggest tragedy is to be not fully independent . . . [for] its riches do not belong to the countries that comprise it, but to big U.S. consortia." Senator Francisco Bulnes (PN) interrupted Teitelboim's speech to accuse the Communists of supporting Soviet imperialism, "the most brutal there is." Teitelboim's response provides a nice illustration of the Communists' vision of history and the unbendable ideological convictions derived from it. For the Communist senator, imperialism was "represented by any capitalist country that, having reached the stage of financial capitalism, exports capitals and takes over the basic sources of raw materials of the economically weaker countries." Evidently, this textbook Leninist interpretation of imperialism excluded the Soviet Union, as there was no case in which the communist superpower took possession of the economic resources of other countries—never mind, of course, the hijacking of the political systems of the countries of Eastern Europe or the actual annexation of independent nations by the Soviet Union in the wake of World War II. When Christian Democratic Senator Tomás Pablo brought up the crushing of the Imre Nagy government in Hungary by Soviet troops in 1956, Teitelboim responded, without much arguing, that the Hungarian Revolution of 1956 was, in fact, a counterrevolutionary situation. The Soviet Union, therefore, had dealt with it as the leading country in the world revolutionary process must.[11]

The Communists' understanding of imperialism, at least as it was presented publicly, allowed them to side unconditionally with the Soviet Union in the international context, including particular situations, such as that of Hungary in 1956 and later Czechoslovakia in 1968, and also criticize the actions of the United States as imperialist without necessarily projecting an image of inconsistency. In comparison with the most immediately pressing domestic economic and political matters, these largely philosophical discussions, including the debate about Frei's possible trip to the United States, certainly had little importance. Nevertheless, they illustrate with great accuracy the wide gulf that separated the world visions, conceptions of history, and even the language on which the positions of the competing forces in Chilean politics stood.

Ambassador Edward Korry

A few months after the U.S trip debacle, Ambassador Dungan presented his resignation to take the position of chancellor of higher education of the state of New Jersey. In his replacement, President Johnson appointed Edward Korry, another man without formal diplomatic training. Korry had become familiar with international affairs, especially in Europe, as a journalist working for the United Press and *Look* magazine in the 1940s and 1950s. In 1963, President Kennedy, on Dungan's recommendation, appointed him ambassador in Ethiopia, another country in whose development the United States had invested a good deal of money and effort through the 1960s.[12] In his capacity as ambassador in Addis Ababa, Korry led a task force, appointed by President Johnson, that assessed U.S. policies toward development in Africa.[13] After four years in Ethiopia, Korry indicated to National Security Advisor Walt W. Rostow that he wanted a change, preferably the ambassadorship in Belgrade, where he had spent some time and made acquaintances as a journalist in the 1950s. According to his own unpublished memoirs, he was also vetted to replace Bill Moyers as White House press secretary, but he refused to take the position.[14] Korry had also been offered a vice presidency at the World Bank in early 1967, an offer he seemed willing to take if no change of position within the U.S. foreign policy apparatus was forthcoming.[15] That change, neither a promotion nor a demotion, became possible in mid-1967, when Dungan presented his resignation to the ambassadorship in Chile.

If Dungan was a strong-willed and temperamental man, Korry performed his tasks as a diplomat with as much dedication and passion. Moreover, Korry assumed the political responsibility of his position as chief U.S. diplomatic representative in Chile with a personal zeal that surpassed that of his predecessor and sometimes had a negative impact on the image he projected. Joseph John Jova, for instance, considered both Dungan and Korry egomaniacs and persons with whom it was very difficult to work.[16] According to Domingo Santa María, Chilean ambassador in Washington from 1968 into 1971, Korry had an "excessively vehement and somewhat imbalanced personality" and was full of "personal ambitions [and] enmities."[17] As a result of his rather idiosyncratic character, Korry developed a singular type of relationship with several important Chilean political actors. The most important cases in point were Foreign Minister Gabriel Valdés and Radomiro Tomic, who became one of Korry's biggest nemeses in the Chilean political scene, for both political and personal reasons.[18] Nevertheless, and even though both men were well aware of their mutual dislike, they maintained an outwardly friendly relationship until the end of Korry's presence in Chile.

On the other hand, Korry's strategic approach as ambassador to Chile differed dramatically from his predecessor's. Dungan had prioritized the relationship of the embassy with the Frei administration and the PDC to the point of cutting off almost all contact between U.S. diplomatic officers and political actors of other persuasions. In later testimonies, Korry dubbed this closeness between Dungan's embassy and the Frei administration an "incestuous relationship."[19] The new ambassador set out from the very beginning to change this situation and reached out to politicians of other parties and sensibilities.[20] Korry's new strategy was reasonably successful. Establishing working, let alone close, ties with the parties of the Left was all but impossible, so other than some feelers sent out to Allende and other left-wing politicians, Korry did not devote much effort to this endeavor. On the contrary, the new ambassador successfully managed to rebuild some of the bridges burned by Dungan, especially those that linked the U.S. embassy with the Right and the more conservative wing of the PR.

As a direct consequence of his strategy, Korry was able to have a lengthy and frank conversation with Jorge Alessandri, former president and likely candidate of the Right in the 1970 election only a couple of months after his arrival in Chile. Alessandri very liberally spoke his mind to Korry, who was rapidly learning about the intimate polarization of the spirits that underlay the more structural polarization of the Chilean political system then underway. Besides telling the ambassador of his bitterness about the way the United States had handled its relations with Chile since the late 1950s, Alessandri candidly exposed his views on the current state of political affairs. Frei's predecessor had no hope in the future of Chilean democracy, especially if the candidate of the Left won the presidential election of 1970, which he thought was the most likely scenario. As terrible as the prospect was, however, Alessandri bluntly expressed his preference for a victory of the Left in 1970, for such an event would prompt a military intervention that would "save the country."[21] In all likelihood, at that time this kind of talk was little more than the thoughtless expression of a deep frustration, recognizable among those who loathed the rapid undermining of the political, social, and cultural status quo to which they were accustomed. Nevertheless, it was also a sign that the consensus around the worth and the strength of Chilean democracy was eroding, slowly but noticeably. Korry would have to perform his diplomatic duties in an atmosphere much more heated and much less favorable for the Frei administration than that in which Dungan served his stint.

Even though Korry's strategy sought primarily to establish or reestablish ties between the embassy and parties other than the PDC, the close relationship developed between Dungan and some officials of the Frei administration, including the president himself, continued; in fact, it became even closer. Korry and Frei became personal friends, and the ambassador established good relationships with some of the most important names in the economic team of the administration: Carlos Massad, Sergio Molina, and Andrés Zaldívar, among others. As early as December 1967, only three months after Korry's arrival in Chile, the ambassador was speaking with Frei about matters of national political importance and, more significant, about the affairs that troubled the PDC.[22] And only one month later, Korry was already giving advice to the president on intra-party issues, as one lengthy report of the ambassador presumptuously—and characteristically—titled "Fitting the President for Pants" describes.[23] While Frei stayed in power, Korry always enjoyed preferential access to the president and some of his ministers and participated actively in some important policy discussions, such as the design of the national budgets of 1968 and 1969 and the negotiations between the Chilean government and the Anaconda corporation for the nationalization of the latter's assets in Chile in 1969.

Ironically, Korry's most visible mark in history came about mostly on account of an operation in which he did not participate directly and whose particulars he largely ignored. During the 1970 presidential campaign, Korry recommended that the United States not support any specific candidate and limit its undercover efforts to fund an anti-Allende campaign. After the candidate of the Left won the presidential election on 4 September 1970, Korry did what he could to support the stillborn attempts by Frei, some of his ministers, and other PDC politicians to prevent Allende's accession to the presidency. Even though he was as convinced as his Chilean counterparts that a

Figure 4. Before arriving in Chile in 1967, Edward Korry served as U.S. ambassador in Ethiopia, appointed by President John F. Kennedy in 1963. *Courtesy of the John F. Kennedy Presidential Library.*

government of the Left would spell the end of Chilean democracy, which he genuinely cherished, Korry understood that the success of any attempt to block Allende's definitive election as president depended on Frei's initiative and on the United States and himself staying on the sidelines.

As a result of Nixon's explicit orders, Korry did not know of the foolish attempts of the CIA to provoke a coup by supporting the actions of two paramilitary groups comprised of mostly inexperienced young men who lacked any other meaningful support. The ambassador, albeit ignorant of the details of the operations, could not be thoroughly fooled. And although he wrote a memo to the White House comparing any CIA attempt to provoke a coup through these groups to the Bay of Pigs fiasco, he could do nothing to avoid the events that led to the murder of General René Schneider.[24]

As the chief diplomatic representative of the United States in Chile at the time, however, Korry was almost automatically identified with the worst part of Nixon's anti-Allende efforts. Korry served in Chile until 1971, when he was replaced by foreign service diplomat Nathaniel Davis. In later years, Korry grew bitter about his experience in Chile, especially because he felt he was unjustly treated by the Church Committee, which in the mid-1970s assessed the involvement of the United States in Chilean politics between 1964 and 1973, among other intelligence operations conducted through the period.

In later testimonies, Korry complained that the congressional investigations on U.S. intervention in Chile were no more than a political maneuver to tarnish even further the image of the Nixon administration and to disentangle the Democratic Party from a foreign policy in which it had been deeply involved all along, deliberately ignoring the real political situation at stake in Chile.[25] He never abandoned the conviction that Allende and his coalition sought to destroy Chile's democracy in the pursuit of the construction of socialism. In one of his latest interviews, he even referred to the Popular Unity political project as "Fidelismo sin Fidel," (Fidelism without Fidel).[26] Consequently, he did not regret having participated in overt and covert operations aimed at opposing Allende and the Chilean Left; on the contrary, as a convinced liberal cold warrior, he, to the end, owned his actions as U.S. ambassador in Chile, including all the anti-Allende efforts in which he did participate.[27]

Korry began writing a book on the U.S. involvement in Chile and even sent a draft of the introduction and first chapters to the McGraw-Hill publishing house. A copy of that draft can be found, oddly enough, in the personal papers of another man for whom Korry harbored ill feelings, his predecessor in the embassy in Santiago, Ralph Dungan. Not much that is unknown can be found in those pages, and we do not know whether he kept writing what would have likely been a very successful book. The fact that he did try to write his memoirs but did not publish them is intriguing. After all, thousands of pages about the U.S. involvement in Chilean politics in the 1960s and 1970s have been published in the United States, many of them unworthy of any reader's time; even the memoirs of his successor in the U.S. embassy in Santiago, Nathaniel Davis, a man who did not engage in the kind of political activity in which Korry thrived, were published in 1985.[28] At any rate, Korry did not serve as a diplomat again after his stint in Chile nor in any other position of high visibility. Any chance he may have had of a successful and prominent career in international politics, whether as a U.S. diplomat or in some other capacity, died because of his presence in Chile at the time Salvador Allende won the presidential election of 1970. After leaving Chile, he taught at a couple of universities and briefly headed the Association of American Publishers. Korry died in Charlotte, North Carolina, in 2003.[29]

The 1968 Wage Readjustment Bill

The Senate's denial of permission for Frei's trip to the United States in early 1967 was a sign of much worse things to come. With the conspicuous exception of the killing of eight striking workers in the mining town of El Salvador in March 1966, which put the Frei administration on par with almost all its twentieth-century predecessors in bloodily crushing workers' protests or strikes, the first two years of the Christian Democratic government had been largely successful.[30] However, starting with Frei's stillborn trip to the United States, in 1967 the triumphant tide began to retreat. In July, the left wing of the PDC won the internal elections, and one of its leaders, Rafael Agustín Gumucio, assumed the presidency of the party. The national assembly of the PDC, moreover, approved a programmatic document that questioned the pace of the process of reforms implemented by the Frei administration and proposed a much more radical plank for the party, calling for the pursuit of a "noncapitalist path toward development."[31] Frei himself had to intervene in a national assembly of the PDC in January 1968 to help the more moderate wing regain control. To make matters worse, the gulf separating Frei from Radomiro Tomic, the most likely candidate of the party for the 1970 presidential election, was becoming ever wider and deeper.

The real turning point for the Frei administration, however, came in early 1968, and it was, to a large extent, a consequence of the inherent tension between the reformist vocation and the stabilizing intent of the Christian Democratic government. The monetary and fiscal measures taken by the Frei administration in its first years had been successful in lowering the rate of inflation. In 1967, however, it became clear that the combination of economic policies geared toward redistribution of income and long-term growth were pressuring prices up again.[32] Consequently, Frei's economic team decided to check the resurgence of inflation by attempting to implement a more restrictive wage policy and simultaneously increase national savings. In November 1967, Finance Minister Sergio Molina proposed a plan under which a 20 percent wage increase, an amount already below the inflation rate for 1967, would be granted, partly in cash and partly in bonds of what would be a national savings fund. The savings fund, according to Molina's conception, would eventually become a state investment fund, managed by representatives of organized labor and the government.

If successful, the scheme would go a long way toward socializing investment, for the fund would be allowed to both capitalize and create enterprises. The latter, according to the original idea, would not be the property of the state under the existing statute of public corporations but of the fund itself, therefore giving its stakeholders direct participation in the ownership of the means of production. For its designers, this plan was a perfect representation of the doctrine of Christian Democracy. On the one hand, the creation of an investment fund in which workers were the main stakeholders would do much for the redistribution of wealth in the long term. On the other hand, the forced savings scheme on which the creation of the fund was based would help increase national savings and reduce inflation in the short term. The obvious problem of such vision, however, lay on its very forward-looking nature. Giving up part of their wage raises in exchange for savings bonds that they could not freely dispose of and whose value could be negatively affected by inflation was not a likeable prospect for workers and certainly not for the parties most closely associated with organized labor, the Socialist and Communist parties. The political battle about the plan was bound to be fierce and decisive.[33]

If Molina's plan could not be materialized, the government would have to return full swing to the practice of borrowing from the Central Bank to meet its obligations. The social and political costs of the plan were not lost to Frei and his economic team, but their convictions about the proper way to manage the economy led them to go forward with the proposed scheme. However, Frei and his advisers probably did not foresee the extent to which the plan would be opposed by their political adversaries. The CUT (*Central Única de Trabajadores*) called for a national strike against the forced savings plan, cleverly dubbed "*chiribonos*"—a combination of the words *chirimoyo*, which in Chilean parlance refers to bounced checks, and *bono* (bond)—by the left-wing press. The repression of the strike resulted in the death of four people.[34] Once again the Frei administration took the traditional position of the Chilean state against strikers and working-class protesters, thus giving substance to the Marxist Left's ideological claim that Chile's democracy had an unmistakable class bias. Furthermore, the left wing of the PDC also opposed the scheme and let it be known to the president and the concerned ministers. Consequently, considering that the project seemed doomed to fail, Frei decided to withdraw the proposal, which resulted in Molina's resignation in February 1968—only one month after the more moderate wing had regained control of the PDC, largely thanks to Frei's personal intervention in the party assembly.

Molina's replacement, Raúl Sáez, was as committed as his predecessor and the president to the stabilizing features of the Christian Democratic project. In fact, Sáez had been one of the nine members of the Inter-American Committee on the Alliance for Progress constituted at the inception of the policy to monitor its functioning and make recommendations for the optimal appropriation of the funds.[35] Sáez did not belong to the PDC, and, like Molina, he had also served in other administrations. The plan advanced by Sáez did not differ significantly from Molina's. The wage increase for public employees would contemplate a forced savings component, in the form of shares of the government housing corporation (CORVI) fund, and would not be equally granted across the board. In addition to the provisions related to wages, the proposed bill contained a few clauses that would have effectively suspended the right to strike. These clauses were, in the end, struck out after negotiations with the Communist Party. The politicking behind the changes to the original bill was more than Sáez was willing to take, especially as the stabilizing features of his plan had to give in before political considerations. Sáez tendered his resignation only a month after he had taken up the job. His replacement, the young lawyer Andrés Zaldívar, had basically the same outlook on economic matters as his predecessors, but he was a member of the PDC. Still, ideological and technical continuities notwithstanding, Sáez's resignation was another hard blow to the stabilizing intent of the economic program of the Frei administration.[36]

Frei and his entourage took the widespread opposition to the wage readjustment bill as a manifestation of the intransigence of their political adversaries. Not surprising, Ambassador Korry, who had arrived in Chile only a few months earlier, shared this view. For him, the opposition parties simply "[refused] to deal with the economic problems Chile [confronted]" and were "dedicated to [the] proposition that [the] failure of Frei [was of] overriding importance."[37] As in any democratic and competitive political system, this was partly true. However, the battle over the wage readjustment bill was also a contest between political forces with different ideological views regarding the role of the state on the road toward development. Those views, in confluence with long- and short-term strategic considerations inherent to a competitive political system, determined the positions of the major Chilean parties regarding particular policies and decisions. In some instances, the parties of the opposition, for different reasons, reached the conclusion that they could not afford to block initiatives critical to the success of the program of the PDC. The hallmark policies of "Chileanization" and agrarian reform, for instance, could be enacted because the parties on the Right and the Left, respectively, gave their votes for them. In the case of the 1968 wage readjustment bill, the opposition parties considered that the Frei administration's proposed schemes were too far from what was acceptable for them and, in the case of the Marxist parties, their base constituencies.

The debate over the matter on the Senate's Joint Committee on Government and Finance highlighted the deep ideological divides that separated the major Chilean political forces from each other and how they played out in the complex and often cumbersome process of policymaking. The PR, represented by senator and former presidential candidate Luis Bossay, rejected the proposal of the Frei administration mostly because of the relative prejudice its passage would entail for public employees, who under the terms of the government bill would receive part of their wage readjustment in bonds instead of cash.[38] This position was a logical one to take for the PR, for public employees constituted a significant, if not the largest, part of its constituency. For the PN, on the other hand, the bill was little more than a ploy to increase the funds allocated for the 1968 budget and, therefore, it was an inflationary policy. For the Right, the Christian Democratic government had gone well beyond the limits of the spending capacities of the Chilean state, taking advantage of the circumstantial high prices of copper as a consequence of the Vietnam War. More important, the Christian Democratic project ran against the most basic tenets of the political ideology of the PN. According to Senator Francisco Bulnes, the Frei administration, by undermining the right to private property through policies such as the agrarian reform, had struck a hard blow at the main asset of Chile's economy, which, according to the PN, was not copper but private entrepreneurship.[39]

On the other side of the aisle, the Communist Party opposed the original Molina plan fiercely. The attitude of the PC toward a wage readjustment bill, nevertheless, could not be totally uncompromising, as an exceedingly lengthy legislative process would probably end up hurting in very practical terms the immediate interests of the working class, the party's natural constituency. After negotiations between the government and the opposition, represented by Senator Rafael Tarud of the Alianza Popular Independiente party, the Sáez bill was stripped of its harshest anti-strike measures.[40] Consequently, the PC could commit its approval of the bill, which was modified through the legislative process anyway.

For the Socialist Party, on the other hand, the Frei administration's bill was utterly unacceptable. Senator Aniceto Rodríguez pointed out, as did the other opposition parties, the economic inconvenience of the proposed plan for many workers, both in the public and the private sector. More significant, however, was Rodríguez's questioning of the structural character of the proposed wage readjustment plan and its deep ideological roots. For the Socialist senator, "the rejection of the bill was a rejection of the entire government policy, which has been characterized by a thorough submission to the norms imposed by the International Monetary Fund." The economic policy of the Frei administration, according to Rodríguez, aimed at "the maintenance of the old 'status', the strengthening of the monopolies, the same old submission to foreign voracity and, ultimately, every attempt at economic development is still based on the participation of U.S. investors."[41] Rodríguez's evaluation of the economic policies of the Frei administration may have been exaggeratedly harsh; his reading of the character of those policies, however, was essentially correct. In the implementation of its development plan, the Christian Democratic government followed (or tried to follow) the basic rules of macroeconomic and monetary policy advised by the United States and international institutions of capitalism, such as the IMF. Furthermore, the Frei administration did not attempt to thoroughly transform the structure of property in Chile, even though some of its policies (the agrarian reform, the "Chileanization" of copper, the nationalization of some utilities companies, and, theoretically, the creation of the savings fund) certainly had an impact in that regard. In sum, the Frei administration's project of development, much attuned with the core ideas and practices of developmental capitalism, was, at its roots, contrary to the model promoted by the Marxist Left.

The Frei administration's stabilization effort suffered a hard defeat in the political confrontation over the 1968 wage readjustment bill. Inflation rose again, and the parties of the opposition could legitimately claim a victory over a government that had lost the initiative and could not even count on the unanimous support of the party of the president. Ambassador Korry's assessment of the episode as it was still unfolding was extraordinarily sharp and prescient: "However the current maneuverings among the Chilean parties may end, the inescapable fact is that we are witnessing the end of the noble and necessary Frei experiment in 'Revolution in Liberty' . . . because . . . the government of President Frei has reached the limit in its ability to carry forward its program of economic and social reform within a democratic framework."[42]

To make matters worse, a severe drought hit the country in the winter of 1968, forcing the government to spend even more on food imports. The bountiful fiscal times of 1966, when the Frei administration had proudly declined to ask for a U.S. program loan for the following year, were gone for good. In July 1968, the Frei administration obtained a program loan in the amount of $20 million from the Johnson administration for the remainder of the year. Unlike the program loans of previous years, not much thought was given either in Chile or the United States to the developmental impact of this batch of U.S. aid. National Security Adviser Walt W. Rostow was brutally blunt in his request for President Johnson's approval of the loan: "[It] is primarily a political bailing out operation to help President Frei and the moderate Christian Democrats make the best possible showing in the Congressional elections in March 1969."[43]

The Denouement

By the time Lyndon B. Johnson authorized the $20 million program loan for the Frei administration in July 1968, he was already a lame-duck president. The widespread support received by Johnson's liberal platform in 1964 had receded substantially. Lyndon B. Johnson had assumed the presidency riding on the popularity of John Kennedy, and his administration got off to a great start with the passing of the Civil Rights Act and his landslide victory in the 1964 presidential election. When Frei assumed the presidency in Chile in November 1964, the spirit of the Alliance for Progress was still very much alive; if not in its democratic intent, at least in terms of its development goals.[44] The early success of the Frei administration showcased for a brief moment the bright possibilities offered by the combination of generous U.S. developmental aid and a government committed to the modernization goals of the Alliance for Progress. That success roughly coincided with the highest point of the Johnson administration, marked by landmark legislation on civil and voting rights for African Americans and the project of broad social reform promoted under the banner of the Great Society. This moment of intense and high hopes, however, would not last long. The escalation of the war in Vietnam rapidly superseded every other issue in the political and societal debate in the United States. As a result, Johnson's ambitious domestic program fell victim to the needs imposed by the war.

The Alliance for Progress, for its part, quietly faded away, too, as a consequence of the changed U.S. political environment. Still, the inconspicuous and rather painless death of the Alliance for Progress owed much to the fact that the Latin American countries that had signed on to the policy in the early 1960s did not embrace it as decidedly as the endeavor required. In many of the Latin American countries, in fact, the era of the Alliance for Progress saw the rise of military dictatorships instead of the promised democratic consolidation apparent in the intent of the late President Kennedy. Frei, a man of high intellectual capacity and a statesman of recognized international stature, published a bitter complaint about the state of the Alliance for Progress in 1967 in the magazine *Foreign Affairs*. The title of the piece penned by Frei, "The Alliance that Lost Its Way," illustrates precisely the fate of the policy on which so much hope had been placed in the beginnings of the turbulent 1960s.[45]

By mid-1968, it was clear to everyone that the relation between the Johnson and Frei administrations had suffered greatly as a consequence of the changes in the political winds in the United States and Chile. The partnership for modernization and democracy forged between the two governments in 1964 had more than a few accomplishments in Chile, much in the same way that Lyndon B. Johnson's ambitious domestic program did in the United States. However, after Johnson announced he would not run for reelection on 31 March 1968 and the Frei administration lost the battle over the wage readjustment bill a few weeks later, in both countries a widespread sensation of failure took over large sections of the parties in power and public opinion in general. Neither Frei's Revolution in Liberty nor Johnson's Great Society bore in 1968 the sense of optimism and hope they had offered to the Chilean and American peoples four years earlier.

Nevertheless, the appearance of failure that somewhat unfairly accompanied Frei's and Johnson's programs of reform since 1968 did not affect the images of the two leaders in the same way. While in 1968 Lyndon B. Johnson was a highly unpopular man, reviled by a great part of U.S. and world public opinion because of his responsibility in the escalation and continuance of the Vietnam War, Frei was still widely respected and admired in Chile and abroad. This apparent contradiction lay, in part, in the fact that a large part of Chilean public opinion attributed the supposed failures of the Frei administration to the political opposition and, more important, to infighting within the PDC. There were no equivalent attenuating factors for the decisions made by Johnson regarding the Vietnam War.

Eduardo Frei read with great sharpness the situation in the United States and his own in the context of Chilean politics. The close relationship with the Johnson administration that had been so instrumental in his accession to the presidency and the implementation of a large part of his program was no longer a high-quality asset. Consequently, when a new opportunity for a trip to the United States arose in 1968, Frei preferred not to take it. The prospect of a meeting with a lame-duck and highly unpopular U.S. president was certainly not attractive for the Chilean head of state. In his personal letter to President Johnson explaining his decision to visit Brazil but not the United States, the Chilean president manifested very warmly his deep and genuine appreciation for his embattled U.S. counterpart, praising Johnson's statesmanship and his intentions toward peace in the Vietnam War.[46]

Still, Frei's decision not to travel to the United States was correctly seen and resented as a rebuff by the State Department. In a tragic paradox of history, the figure of Lyndon B. Johnson had become almost exclusively identified with the war. Next to the decisions he made, sometimes against his own instincts, regarding the conflict in Southeast Asia, the monumental domestic achievements of his presidency—civil and voting rights legislation, a significant expansion of the welfare state, deep changes in discriminatory immigration rules, to

Figure 5. Eduardo Frei could not make a presidential visit to the United States as was his desire. The only time he met President Lyndon B. Johnson was at the meeting of American presidents in the Uruguayan beach town of Punta del Este in April 1967. The image suggests that Johnson did not miss the chance to give Frei his famous "treatment." *Courtesy of Archivo Fotográfico Casa Museo Eduardo Frei Montalva.*

name only a few—ended up mattering little in most contemporary assessments of his administration.[47] As one of the most reputable scholars of the Vietnam wars has put it, Johnson's story in the presidency "bears all the markings of a tragedy."[48] So much so that even the president of a less-developed country, and one especially favored by the foreign policy of the United States at that, felt it would be inopportune to visit Lyndon B. Johnson in his moment of defeat.[49]

A Different Paradigm

The winner of the 1968 presidential election, Republican candidate Richard Nixon, had a much different outlook on domestic and foreign affairs from that of his Democratic predecessors. If by 1969 the spirit of the Alliance for Progress was all but dead, Nixon's arrival to the White House hammered the last nail in its coffin. The commitment to a particular path to modernization in underdeveloped countries that had characterized the foreign policies of the

Kennedy and the Johnson administrations gave way to a much more tepid attitude toward development.[50] In the grand scheme of Nixon's foreign policy, Latin America mattered little and the United States had no obligation to underwrite long-term, state-directed plans for development. Moreover, partly because he had to face different challenges, Nixon took a much tougher position regarding the nationalization of assets of U.S. corporations in Third World countries. In the case of Latin America, during his first year in office Nixon confronted the nationalization of oil fields by the Peruvian military government from an initially unforgiving position. Even though he did not apply the Hickenlooper amendment, which mandated the automatic suspension of U.S. aid to countries that expropriated properties of U.S. corporations without proper compensation, Nixon wanted to send a strong message to Third World governments with similar intentions toward U.S. corporations established in their national territories.[51]

Frei and some of his ministers understood well that Richard Nixon would take a different approach to Latin America and Chile. In a conversation with Korry in March 1969, a frustrated Frei informed the ambassador that the denial of a new program loan by the United States would force his government to recalculate its entire economic policy for the remainder of his term. He understood the intellectual roots of the shift in U.S. foreign policy under Nixon and was aware that "the days when Chile counted for something in Washington were gone." Still, he needed to know with more certainty what the United States would decide regarding aid for Chile. In making his case, somewhat theatrically, the president asked Ambassador Korry to take into consideration the fact that "he had been the most loyal friend of the [United States] in these past four years in South America" and had paid a high political price for this, especially with the left wing of his own party.[52]

Eventually, Nixon chose to deny a program loan to the Chilean government in 1969, ostensibly for technical reasons. In actuality, Nixon and his foreign policy advisors did not see much success in the type of foreign aid their Democratic predecessors had provided Latin American countries during most of the 1960s, so separating U.S. policy toward the region from that foundation was a priority for the Republican president. Denying the loan to the Frei administration was consistent with and a powerful signal of the new attitude. In addition, Nixon may have had more emotional reasons to proceed this way. Ambassador Korry stated in his unpublished memoirs that Nixon refused to sign off on the loan because the Frei administration and the ambassador himself were too closely identified with President Kennedy.[53] Although there is no other evidence that supports Korry's testimony, it is not unconceivable that considerations of this sort played a part in Nixon's decision.

Attitudes had changed in Latin America and Chile, too. While Frei and his economic team adhered to the spirit of U.S.-Latin American cooperation underlying the Alliance for Progress, other Christian Democrats had a more overtly critical position toward the United States and its hegemonic position in the inter-American system. Foreign Minister Gabriel Valdés, for instance, had been a vocal advocate for reform of the OAS, an effort in which he enjoyed a mild success with the modifications introduced to the charter of the organization through the Protocol of Buenos Aires of 1967. In addition, Valdés was critical of the purposes and mechanisms of U.S. provision of foreign aid to Latin America, which, in his view, had no real impact in the development of the region.

In a most frank and tense conversation with Ambassador Korry in October 1968, Valdés told the U.S. envoy, for whom he felt no sympathy at all, that the Alliance for Progress did not amount to even 5 percent of the "internal effort of Latin America" toward development and that the "United States had to revise its entire policy toward the region, help ten times more, or not do it at all, but accepting the consequences." Korry's argument that the United States had given Chile five times more than President Kennedy had promised at the inception of the Alliance for Progress in 1961 did not make much of an impression on Valdés, a man who clearly did not share Frei's general outlook on the relations between Chile, Latin America, and the United States.[54]

For Valdés and other Christian Democrats, such as Foreign Undersecretary Patricio Silva, Nixon's arrival in the White House was the conclusion of a process of deterioration in relations between the United States and Latin America that had begun with the death of President Kennedy in 1963. As attested by his conversation with Korry in October 1968 and by the interpretation offered in his memoirs, Valdés considered that the Johnson administration did not do for Latin America as much as its predecessor, regardless of the amounts of aid provided by the United States to the Frei administration and the support given to the Christian Democratic Party.[55] Valdés' views were representative of the sensibilities of a group within the PDC, the *rebeldes*, that, at the time, was moving ever further from Frei and his program, even though the minister himself did not belong to that faction of the party. In any case, as a consequence of the changes in U.S. foreign policy brought about by Nixon's assumption of the presidency and the situation of Chilean politics and his own party, by mid-1969 it was clear there were no compelling reasons for Frei to keep the same friendly attitude toward the United States that he had shown in the past five years. This is not to say the Chilean president changed his own personal views of the United States and its foreign policy or that his personal relationship with Ambassador Korry soured significantly. However, both the domestic and international situations had objectively changed, and he could not ignore the shift. As a result, Frei and his foreign ministry made some decisions involving Chile's relations with the United States that reflected a new, more distant attitude. In June 1969, for instance, Nelson Rockefeller, touring Latin American countries in an official mission for President Nixon, had to cancel his stop in Chile after the Frei administration informed him of the political inconvenience and risks his visit could entail.[56]

The most visible manifestation of the new attitude of the Frei administration toward the United States was the solemn deliverance of a document titled "Latin American Consensus of Viña del Mar" to President Richard Nixon. The document, the result of the deliberations of the Special Committee of Latin American Coordination (CECLA) at a meeting held in Viña del Mar in May 1969, consisted of a set of proposals aimed at the development of Latin America and calling for a more proactive U.S. participation in the effort through initiatives regarding trade, aid, and technical cooperation. While the content of the document was neither radical nor confrontational, its explicit recognition of the dependent character of Latin American economies with respect to the developed countries of the northern hemisphere and the fact that it was elaborated without U.S. participation did mark a departure from the way relations with the United States had been handled throughout the era of the Alliance for Progress.[57] Gabriel Valdés, accompanied by the Latin American ambassadors in Washington, presented President Nixon with the document on 11 June 1969. Somewhat oddly, Eduardo Frei's doubts about the convenience of having his foreign minister personally deliver the Viña del Mar Consensus in Washington were resolved by the foreign minister of Brazil, José de Magalhaes Pinto, who thought it would be a good idea to have Valdés represent the coordinated voice of the Latin American countries in front of President Nixon, despite the obvious ideological and political differences between the Brazilian military dictatorship and the Chilean Christian Democratic government.[58]

According to Valdes' memoirs, neither Nixon, whom he characterized as probably "one of the worst—maybe the worst—president of the United States," nor Henry Kissinger cared much for the Viña del Mar Consensus. In fact, as per Valdés' recollection, Kissinger was blunt in his response to the Chilean minister's speech, pointing out that Latin America did not matter much in the big scheme of world power, whose axis went "from Moscow to

Washington to Japan."[59] The message was clear: Nixon's foreign policy would deal with Latin America only as a secondary stage of world politics and certainly without the emphasis on modernization and development that had characterized the approaches of the Kennedy and Johnson administrations—which had not pursued those goals very consistently anyway. In this vein, the Nixon administration did not want to forge the same close links with Frei and the PDC as the Johnson administration had done. Ironically, but not illogically, after Allende won the presidential election in 1970, Nixon became involved in Chilean affairs to an extent and in a way that went far beyond what any of his predecessors had done during the 1960s.

1969, *Annus Horribilis*

Two other heavy blows, one of them of its own doing, hit the Frei administration in 1969. On 9 March, only a few days after the congressional elections, the police opened fire against a group of squatters occupying a plot of land in the southern city of Puerto Montt. Nine people, including one toddler, died as a consequence of the actions of the police.[60] Once again, the Frei administration had chosen to deal with a localized social protest in the hardest possible way, leaving a number of poor and innocent people dead as a result and giving substance to the Left's claims about the historic position taken by the state against protests and other social manifestations.[61]

Speaking in the Senate, Salvador Allende chastised the Frei administration for its responsibility in the deaths of the Puerto Montt squatters, going as far as to accuse the government of premeditated murder. In the first of his interventions on the matter, Allende gave a detailed and poignant account of the events leading up to the incidents of 9 March, countering the government's official line that the situation had been the result of a deliberate provocation, led with political intent by Socialist councilman Luis Espinoza. Allende denied with great ardor that either Espinoza or the PS had any malicious intention in their presumptive involvement in the events of Puerto Montt. Yet, in a rather extemporaneous twist toward the end of his speech, Allende uttered a stern warning: "To reactionary and murderous violence, we will respond with revolutionary violence."[62] A few days later, again speaking in the Senate, Allende doubled down on his words about the massacre of Puerto Montt, this time quoting what President Frei had said in 1946 when he tendered his resignation to the cabinet of Vice President Alfredo Duhalde in protest of the killing of nine people in a workers' rally in downtown Santiago.[63]

But once again, Allende went beyond the particular issue in discussion to locate his and his party's position on the matter of the Puerto Montt killings within the larger landscape of contemporary revolutionary politics. Addressing the justification provided by Minister of the Interior Edmundo Pérez Zujovic for the actions of the police in Puerto Montt, which blamed the incidents on the supposedly subversive intent of the Left, Allende once again referred to the concept of revolutionary violence as a legitimate response to reactionary violence. Moreover, the Socialist senator cited Lenin's *The State and Revolution* as the source for "the interpretation of us Marxists of what bourgeois society is, and what the government and the state of that bourgeois society are," adding that the Socialists wanted the "transformation of the bourgeois state into a socialist republic."[64] To finish his intervention, Allende quoted Fidel Castro's harsh words against the Frei administration: "Christian Democracy offered Chile a revolution without bloodshed and has given it bloodshed without revolution."[65]

Frei and the right-wing of the Christian Democratic Party, known as *oficialistas*, blamed the incidents of Puerto Montt on the PS and backed the decisions of Pérez Zujovic and the police. For Frei and the *oficialista* wing of the PDC, the events of Puerto Montt, just as the massacre of El Salvador three years earlier, were a tragic consequence of a confrontation deliberately sought by the Left as a matter of political strategy. The leading presence among the squatters of Socialist councilman Luis Espinoza, who had just been elected deputy in the election of 2 March, was for the government sufficient proof that the *pobladores* of Puerto Montt were acting in connivance with the parties of the Left, a view that the U.S. embassy in Santiago, for the most part, shared.[66] Certainly the relationship between party and social mobilization, especially among people looking for a place to live in cities throughout the country, was much more complex and nuanced than Frei and the most conservative wing of the PDC believed.[67] Nevertheless, Frei, Pérez Zujovic, and the *oficialistas* were genuinely convinced that the parties of the Left, as instigators of illegal forms of social mobilization such as the seizure of land in cities and the countryside, bore responsibility for the events of Puerto Montt.

Senator Patricio Aylwin, one of the most prominent representatives of the conservative wing of the PDC, responded to the speeches of Allende and other senators of the opposition by pointing out that many politicians of the Left, particularly in the PS, adhered to "the *fidelista* thesis of violence." For Aylwin, the link between some Socialist politicians' adherence to revolutionary violence and situations such as the one in Puerto Montt a few days earlier was unmistakable. The last words of his speech nicely sum up the way in which the conservative wing of the PDC, led by Frei, understood the contemporary reality of Chilean politics: "those who support violence as a system cannot elude the responsibility they bear in episodes like this. To discharge that responsibility on a democratic government, which respects the law and is habitually trying to solve the problems of the people, reveals a frustration that is typical of the Latin American Left."[68] Even though in his speech Aylwin allowed for the possibility that the actions of the police may have been circumstantially wrong, he made very clear that, in trying to remove the squatters from the land they had occupied, the government was only fulfilling its duties as enforcer of the law, which, according to their point of view, was being breached deliberately and with clear political intent by a Socialist politician.

Besides the left-wing opposition, more than a few Christian Democrats of the *rebelde* line blamed the Puerto Montt massacre on Pérez Zujovic, thus furthering the ideological divide that afflicted the PDC. Only a few months later, a sizeable number of members of the party, particularly from its youth branch, would split and form their own movement, which would later join the coalition of the Left shaped by Communists and Socialists. Pérez Zujovic's image before public opinion suffered greatly as a result of the events of Puerto Montt.[69] Famous folksinger Victor Jara publicly singled out Pérez Zujovic as the main culprit of these sad events in a famous song, *Preguntas por Puerto Montt*. In July 1971, a band of far-left revolutionaries, some of whom had been pardoned by President Allende early in his tenure, killed Pérez Zujovic. The murder, perpetrated by fanatics with no formal party affiliations widened the gap that separated the Left from the PDC, many of whose members blamed the assassination of their comrade on the public campaign against him run by the left-wing parties since the events of March 1969.[70]

The second heavy blow to the Frei administration, and a chilling warning of the military's potential for intervention, occurred on 21 October 1969. In the previous weeks, army general Roberto Viaux had been trying to meet with President Frei to inform him of some grievances widely held among commissioned and noncommissioned officers. Viaux made his moves from his base in the northern town of Antofagasta without authorization from the head of the army; partly as a result of this, the army's promotion board recommended his dismissal. Other officers then made public a letter in which they demanded that Viaux keep his position. On 20 October, Viaux arrived in Santiago, called by the army's high command. Instead of meeting with them, Viaux went to the Tacna regiment and, from there, directed a mutiny with the purpose of extracting concessions from the government. Even though it was not a political military coup, the attitude of some high-rank army officers was alarming and threatening. One CIA cable from a few weeks before the mutiny identified then largely unknown General Augusto Pinochet as one of the high-rank officers supporting Viaux's plan.[71] All political parties, with the notable exception of the PS, rallied behind the constitutional government and condemned the putsch. The rebellion, which quickly became known as the Tacnazo, was put down by loyal forces. An unknown number of soldiers were killed and a few civilians were wounded by fire opened from the regiment.

In the days and weeks after the Tacnazo, a presumptive involvement of the CIA in the mutiny became a matter of high contention between Ambassador Korry and Foreign Undersecretary Patricio Silva, who saw the hand of the United States in the military attempt. A CIA spokesperson said in the days after the Tacnazo that the agency knew something was going on within the Chilean army and, coincidentally, Ambassador Korry was in Washington at the time of Viaux's putsch. For Silva, these facts suggested U.S. intervention in the military movement. No such intervention existed, but the fact that a high official of the Frei administration thought that way and so informed the U.S. embassy in Santiago is very telling of the shift in the character of the relations between the Chilean government and the United States since Nixon's assumption of the presidency and of the relevance acquired by the left wing of the PDC, to which both Minister Valdés and Under Secretary Silva belonged, in the management of the country's foreign relations.[72]

Viaux's mutiny succeeded partially. The general himself had to retire, as had been decided before the putsch, but the Frei administration had to concede on some important matters: Sergio Castillo, commander in chief of the army, was replaced by General René Schneider, and Minister of Defense Tulio Marambio stepped down and his post was assumed by Sergio Ossa. Viaux, Schneider, and Ossa, albeit on different sides of the divide and suffering different consequences, would play significant roles in the events surrounding the election of Salvador Allende in 1970.[73] Although the Tacnazo did not provoke—because it did not seek—substantial political changes in Chile, it was a sign that many in the military, widely believed to be doctrinally opposed to and incapable of political intervention, had crossed a threshold in their willingness to stand against the constitutional order if they believed that the general and their own situation warranted their intervention.

Chapter 4

Chilean Copper and U.S. Companies

After the world market for nitrates crashed during the Great Depression, copper took over as the main staple of the Chilean economy. From the 1930s to this day, copper has been Chile's signature export and one of the main sources of foreign currency and state revenues. In addition to its economic importance, copper has become, for better and worse, one of the most potent signs of Chile's national identity. Two of the largest copper mines in the world, Chuquicamata and El Teniente, are located in Chile. During the twentieth century, towns with distinctive characters—Chuquicamata, Sewell, El Salvador—grew around these and other mines, imbuing the individual and community lives of copper miners with a particular identity that became an important feature of Chile's cultural imagination. Those towns, built by U.S. companies that exploited the mines next to them, no longer exist or are now only a shadow of what they once were, serving mostly as silent testimonies of the way in which the production of copper created social and cultural landscapes around its sites of exploitation during the twentieth century.[1]

A few U.S. corporations, notably Kennecott and Anaconda, carried out the exploitation of the largest copper deposits. In the early twentieth century, Chile's economy, mostly reliant on the export of one product (nitrates), dependent on foreign investments, and lacking a significant industrial base, had been unable to generate the capital necessary to extract its awesome mineral resources, particularly copper. As was the case with so many other countries in the world in the nineteenth and twentieth centuries, the capital and know-how necessary to begin large-scale exploitation of Chile's mineral resources came from the industrialized powers, fundamentally the United States. In 1904, Braden Copper Company began exploiting El Teniente, the largest underground copper mine in the world, some fifty miles south of Santiago. Braden was later acquired by Kennecott. In 1912, the Chile Exploration Company, owned by the Guggenheim brothers, began exploiting Chuquicamata, now the largest open pit copper mine in the world, located in the mountains east of the Atacama Desert. Later, that company was acquired by the U.S. multinational giant Anaconda. Other copper mines, most notably Potrerillos, also came under ownership of Anaconda in the 1920s.[2]

Ownership of the large copper mines, the *Gran Minería del Cobre* in Chilean parlance, increasingly became an issue of contention in Chilean politics, much like the exploitation of natural resources by foreign companies in other parts of the world—bananas in Central America and oil in the Middle East, for instance. After World War II, the Chilean state tried several pricing and taxation frameworks to keep in Chile as much revenue from the export of copper as possible.[3] Still, the astounding profits made by the U.S. companies stood in stark contrast with the widespread poverty and sense of scarcity that constituted the experience of a majority of the Chilean population. If copper was a sign of cultural and social identity because of its importance for Chile, it was also a symbol of the position occupied by Chile in the large scheme of the world economy: a country dependent on the export of one raw material exploited by foreign companies and, thus, unable to reach a level of optimal economic development. Consequently, the idea of nationalizing the assets of the U.S. copper companies, with the purpose of keeping in Chile all the revenues generated by the export of the red metal, gained ever more weight in Chile's political debate, especially through the efforts of the parties of the Left.[4]

During the Frei administration, the political debate on copper policies reached a climax. Since U.S. capitals were among the most significant actors in the story, the discussions around the issue of copper converged with the ideological visions of the United States and the Cold War held by the different Chilean political parties. As the Frei administration tried to introduce the most comprehensive and consistent reform around the structure of the property of the *Gran Minería*, eventually leading to nationalization in the case of Chuquicamata, the forces in competition in the arena of Chilean politics stood by their ideological convictions, regarding both copper and the United States, in their opposition or grudging support for the policies proposed by the Christian Democratic government. Furthermore, the U.S. government became deeply involved in the matter of copper in Chile, first by pressuring the Chilean government into rolling back a price increase in 1965 and then, mostly through the personal efforts of Ambassador Korry, by mediating in the negotiation between the Frei administration and Anaconda on the nationalization of the U.S. company's largest mine, Chuquicamata, in 1969. The big picture of the relations between the United States and Chile during the Frei administration, especially as they relate to the developmental efforts of the Christian Democratic project, cannot be fully understood without exploring the role played by copper policies in those years.

The Policy of "Chileanization"

An important part of the long-term Christian Democratic project was the "Chileanization" of copper. When Eduardo Frei assumed the presidency in 1964, copper accounted for the largest share of Chile's revenues and had become an issue of sharp confrontation within the political debate. According to the State Department, by 1964 Anaconda and Kennecott produced over 60 percent of Chile's foreign exchange earnings.[5] Moreover, the companies projected an image of "tremendous foreign economic power within Chile," as they were entirely owned by U.S. parent firms. Only a few Chileans held top management positions, no shares were traded in the Santiago stock exchange and, last but not least, the companies operated in enclaves with an autonomy that, although inherent to the economic activity, caused resentment among Chileans.[6] In this context, calls for outright nationalization had become increasingly louder, especially as the left-wing parties gained followers in the 1950s.

In the 1964 campaign, Allende promised nationalization of the largest copper mines if elected, and the issue became a matter of contention between him and his Christian Democratic contender. Frei and the Christian Democratic Party in general shared the idea that Chile should get more revenue from the export of copper. However, they took a more gradual, conciliatory, and pragmatic approach. The key for Frei and the Christian Democrats rested as much on increased participation of the Chilean state in the decisions regarding the production and the sale of copper as it did on a significant expansion of production, for which large investments were needed. Even though some Christian Democrats favored nationalization—Radomiro Tomic among them—Frei and some of his closest advisers on economic matters, Javier Lagarrigue and Raúl Sáez, concluded that the Chilean state could not raise the capital to make the investments needed for the expansion of production nor could it pay compensation for the expropriation of the U.S. companies' assets. Throughout the presidential race, Frei's campaign explicitly ruled out nationalization, for it was "contrary to the interests of the People of Chile," as one pamphlet of massive distribution explained.[7]

Instead of nationalizing the assets of U.S. companies in Chile, the Chilean government, under the Christian Democratic plan, would buy the majority of the shares of Braden, the subsidiary of Kennecott that worked the El Teniente mine. The Chilean government also reached agreements with Cerro Corporation and Anaconda for the future development of two new mines, Río Blanco and Exótica. In these cases, the Chilean government's participation in the joint ventures reached only 30 percent and 25 percent, respectively. Anaconda, which had undertaken a program of investment and expansion of production under its own initiative in the years prior to Frei's presidency, refused to negotiate its ownership of the Chuquicamata and El Salvador mines, at least for the time being.[8] Under the new arrangement with Kennecott, undoubtedly the most significant breakthrough in copper policy until 1969, the Chilean government would be able to make the most important decisions regarding the production and sale of copper without losing the know-how provided by the U.S. company. In addition, with funding from the Export-Import Bank, the new partnership would invest heavily on expanding production, the most important goal of the reform. The negotiations were cordial, and the final terms satisfied both parties.[9]

Congress began discussing the bill sent by the Frei administration to legally enforce the copper agreements in September 1965. The Christian Democrats had won a majority of the seats of the Chamber of Deputies in the March 1965 elections but still were a minority in the Senate. The Christian Democratic senators did their best to defend a position that had become closely identified with their party and, as a result, was a major matter of confrontation with the other political groups represented in Congress. Since its founding as the PDC in 1957, the party had strived to develop a distinct identity, different from the identities of the other Chilean political parties, and had worked to build a following of its own. Throughout the 1964 campaign, moreover, Frei made it conspicuously clear that the party would not trade any part of its political platform for the support of other political parties. This attitude made both the Left and the Right angry at the Christian Democrats, who had a hard time getting the parliamentary support needed for some of its policies. The "Chileanization" of copper, a key project in the Frei program, was one of those issues in which Christian Democrats faced stiff opposition from the Left, and they received the parliamentary support needed for the passage of the bill only after some hard discussions and bargaining in the Senate.

The Christian Democratic senators closed ranks behind the government bill, even if their own personal preferences seemed closer to the position of the Left, as was the case, for instance, of Rafael Agustín Gumucio, one of the senior leaders of the party. In his speech in the Senate arguing in favor of the agreements, Gumucio asserted explicitly that "the attitude of the United States as an imperialist country [was] concrete and precise and [had] meant, for the underdeveloped countries, asphyxiation, misery and hunger."[10] The position represented by Gumucio did not differ significantly from what left-wing politicians said in the same forum and, indeed, a number of Christian Democrats held similar views, typical of Third World politics, regarding the asymmetries of the international order and, more specifically, the position of the United States as the hegemonic power in the Americas. Despite these ideas, Gumucio joined his Christian Democratic colleagues in supporting the government bill and the agreements with the U.S. companies because he agreed that Chile did not possess the capital necessary for nationalization and, for the time being, the main purpose of the Frei administration was to expand the production of copper. In fact, the copper agreements were as much a policy as they were a business transaction, and the Christian Democrats were not shy about acknowledging this. Senator Benjamín Prado recognized that "in the matter of investments made by foreign capitalists, [we] must still speak in business terms." Furthermore, he recognized that those terms were not necessarily favorable for a country like Chile, which, as any country looking for its way toward development, was "conditioned by some determinate elements that [could not be] dealt with by us."[11] The agreements were a pragmatic measure aimed at increasing the income perceived by the state by the export of copper, not an expression of ideological principles. Senator José Musalem summed up the Christian Democratic position nicely: "It is not the time for romantic, programmatic, idealistic or utopian testimonies; the people demand, in the short term, efficient solutions that provide them with more welfare."[12]

The Liberal and Conservatives senators eventually voted in favor of the bill, even though they did not agree with some of its specific terms. In fact, outright nationalization had its advocates even on the Right. Liberal Senator Julio von Mülhenbrock, for instance, stated his preference for nationalization during the discussion. Von Mühlenbrock argued in the Senate, reiterating a ubiquitous topic in Third World politics—usually identified with, but certainly not exclusive of the Left—that "the State which does not control its basic sources of wealth will be sovereign only in name, and not in fact; it will be at the mercy of those who really manage its economy, and its destiny will be compromised forever." Presciently, the Liberal senator asserted that national-ization, if not realized then, would be carried out by others in the near future. In a foretelling remark, von Mühlenbrock manifested his hope that such a step would not be taken "by force, violence or theft, but in democracy, in freedom, and under the protection granted by sound judgment . . . and Chilean legality."[13]

Von Mühlenbrock countered the reasoning of the PDC as to the financial feasibility of nationalization, although he conceded that the agreements, espe-cially the one reached with Kennecott regarding the El Teniente mine, were a step forward in Chile's copper policy. The Liberal senator also argued, showing his sympathy for the United States, that nationalization was politically plausible given the shift in U.S. foreign policy brought about by the "advent of the policy of the great President Kennedy and the Alliance for Progress." In 1965, unlike what could have been expected a few decades earlier, the U.S. government would not oppose the nationalization of Chilean copper, as the United States was at the time coming back "from the super capitalism of preying and utilitar-ian morals, which placed profit above everything else, even if that meant for ever sacrificing and alienating the loyalty of those being subject to its exploita-tion." Moreover, there were precedents; the United States had eventually ac-cepted without resorting to undue measures the nationalization of oil in Mex-ico by President Lázaro Cárdenas in the 1930s and, more recently, the more modest policies toward petroleum in Argentina of President Arturo Illia. In the latter case, the United States had reacted favorably, "vigorously supporting Ar-gentina in its struggle to stabilize its economy and triumph over the crisis." The United States in 1965 truly understood the problems besieging Latin America, "had nobly assumed the task of lifting Latin America from underde-velopment, poverty and misery and [was] making a huge effort to raise the conditions of living of [the Latin American] peoples."[14] Nationalization of U.S. assets, therefore, would not entail a furious and ruthless reaction from the U.S. government, as some feared.

Others on the Right did not favor nationalization but still criticized the agreements for other reasons. Senator Pedro Ibáñez, one of the heavyweights in the Liberal Party, chided the government for the deal struck with Kennecott over the property of the El Teniente mine. Ibáñez argued that, contrary to what the Christian Democrats believed, the agreement would not really mean the "Chileanization" of copper. According to the terms of the deal, the Chilean subsidiary of Kennecott, Braden Copper, would sell the majority of its shares to the Chilean government for $80 million, and then it would loan the amount to the new company to carry out the expansion of production that was at the core of the Christian Democratic project. Senator Ibáñez, as did the Popular Action

Front senators, considered that this clause meant that Kennecott would be able to profit from the expansion of production planned for the following years without having to make any real investment. According to Ibáñez, there was no "Chileanization," but "the escape of a foreign company that is given an award for leaving."[15] Liberals and Conservatives did not reject the rationale underlying the agreements. Ibáñez asserted that he "considered convenient that the country is associated with big international companies operating in Chile, for they guarantee stability and security for our very important copper activities."[16] In fact, Ibáñez criticized the Christian Democrats for not having supported the Alessandri government a few years earlier when it tried to offer better conditions to U.S. companies with the purpose of expanding production.[17] Nevertheless, the agreements established a particular system of taxation for the U.S. companies, so they entailed discrimination against Chilean capitalists. The Liberals, in more ways than one the party of the Chilean entrepreneurial class, were not opposed to the idea of establishing favorable conditions for foreign investment as long as those conditions favored Chilean capital, too. Ibáñez was blunt about this: "I have defended and will keep defending the foreign companies against any injustice, but at the same time, I defend with the same or higher passion Chilean capital and businesses."[18]

The Radicals, who had received hard blows in the 1964 presidential election and the 1965 congressional election, eventually voted in favor of the government bill, although some of them shared the concerns of the other opposition parties. The issue of discrimination against Chilean entrepreneurs was raised by Senator Jonás Gómez, who called it "racial discrimination."[19] The most pressing issue for the Radicals, however, was their demand that a percentage of the taxes paid by the U.S. companies be earmarked for spending in the area where the mines were, specifically for housing developments. The government agreed to meet this demand, or so the Radical senators understood, but the final version, passed after President Frei vetoed some articles, did not include a clause that would satisfy this particular Radical concern.[20] This specific issue, a minor matter in the grand scheme of things, contributed substantially to widen the gap between Radicals and Christian Democrats, as the former felt betrayed by the latter. In later testimony, Senator Jonás Gómez even suggested that, from that point onward, no compromise between the Radical and the Christian Democratic parties would be possible, a situation that further contributed to the progressive polarization of Chilean politics.[21]

As expected, the Socialist and Communist parties rejected the copper agreements and voiced their opposition to the policy of "Chileanization" in Congress. Coinciding with their Liberal, Conservative, and Radical colleagues, the

Communist and Socialist senators considered that the government bill went too far in granting powers to the president to enter into agreements with the U.S. companies and not far enough in establishing a state monopoly over the sale of copper abroad. The left-wing senators also questioned the convenience of the agreements on economic grounds, along the same lines as the right-wing parties had done.[22] Senator Raúl Ampuero, one of the leading figures of the Socialist Party at the time, also questioned the legality of establishing contractual terms as laws.[23] All the left-wing senators who took the floor to argue against the agreements reiterated, with more or less emphasis, the idea that Chile should nationalize the U.S. owned copper mines. Communist Senator Julieta Campusano even suggested that paying compensation to the U.S. companies was financially feasible at the time—a remarkable assertion given the way nationalization would be handled by the Allende government a few years later.[24]

The fundamental argument of the Left against the agreements, however, was neither economic nor procedural. An association between the Chilean state and the U.S. companies like the one proposed by the Frei administration ran against the core ideological principles embraced by both Communists and Socialists. The Chilean Left considered the copper agreements as an unmistakable representation of U.S. imperialism and a willing surrender to it on the part of the Christian Democratic government—a deal between "the horse and the jockey," in the expression of Communist Senator Volodia Teitelboim.[25] A negotiation of this sort—and the Christian Democrats' conciliatory attitude that underscored it—clashed violently with the revolutionary paradigm followed by the Chilean Left. Senator Salomón Corbalán, of the PS, asserted in his speech against the agreements that "to be revolutionary in an underdeveloped country, subjected to imperialism, one must be anti-imperialist." More specifically, Corbalán maintained that "the problem of underdevelopment cannot be confronted if the foreign companies that dominate and strangle the economies of the underdeveloped countries are not confronted."[26]

Communists and Socialists subscribed to a historical interpretation of the relations between the developed and the less developed countries quite common in the Third World. Since the nineteenth century, imperialist powers had injected capital into underdeveloped countries, by establishing colonial dominance if necessary, and had taken profits quite disproportionate to the original investment. Senator Salvador Allende pointed out that the original investments of both Kennecott and Anaconda in Chile had amounted to about $3.5 million and, in the course of fifty years, the companies "had taken $4.106 billion from Chile, an impoverished country, to the United States, a rich country." All the companies had left behind, as had the British companies that extracted and exported nitrates in the last decades of the nineteenth and the first decades of the twentieth century, were "exploited workers, sick with silicosis."[27] The only solution to this problem, as the Left understood it, was to nationalize the copper mines, imitating what other Third World countries—such as Mexico, Egypt, Indonesia, and Syria—had done. All of them, according to Senator Teitelboim, had progressed significantly after nationalizing their natural resources.[28] In the same vein, Socialist Senator Aniceto Rodríguez pointed to the examples of Cuba, Egypt, and Algeria, which had forcefully reacted against and eventually defeated imperialism.[29]

Other left-wing senators focused their criticisms of the agreements on the imperialist features of U.S. foreign policy. Socialist Senator Raúl Ampuero, for instance, wondered why anyone should doubt that the United States would use all the means at its disposal to force compliance with the agreements if it was widely known that there was "a battalion of marines behind every Mormon pastor, every [Peace Corps] volunteer, every Yankee journalist, every American consul."[30] In an intervention announced as a Marxist-Leninist analysis of the matter, Senator Jaime Barros rejoiced in speaking vitriol against the United States and its Christian Democratic friends. Americans were "war-mongers [whose] Peace Corps carry a milk can and a cross in one hand and, in the other, a machine gun to shoot the people with the pretext of anti-communism." The Christian Democrats, in Barros' view, meekly followed the spirit of the Alliance for Progress, "a sedative meant to stall the liberating and revolutionary movement of the Latin American peoples by granting small demagogic reforms and even reigning in to some degree on the most reactionary groups so that Yankee imperialism can, without risk, continue to grow rich and intensify its exploitation." Even the stupefying Alliance for Progress was in its death throes, according to Barros' invective, for its father had been killed, and the United States under President Johnson "[understood] ever less of reformism and [was marching] rapidly toward fascism."[31]

The PDC had enough votes in the Chamber of Deputies and was able to negotiate and obtain enough votes in the Senate, despite the opposition of the other parties, to pass the bill much in the way the government had drafted it. The copper agreements became formal associations between the Chilean state and the U.S. companies, most notably Kennecott, shortly after the bill was passed. As had happened before with other Chilean policies toward copper, the "Chileanization" law was supposed to set the rules of the game for at least a quarter of a century. For its sponsors, the new set of rules promised the expansion of production and the increase in fiscal revenues the country so badly needed. For its left-wing detractors, the association between the Chilean state and the U.S. companies produced benefits only for the latter and, even worse, legitimized and strengthened the imperialistic yoke the United States and its capital held over Chile.

Exercising Leverage: The 1965 Rollback in the Price of Copper

By the end of 1965, the U.S. economy was beginning to experience the effects of the ambitious domestic program of Lyndon B. Johnson and the parallel escalation of the Vietnam War. The expansion of government subsidies and social programs under Johnson's War on Poverty and the ever-larger military and political U.S. presence in Vietnam obviously required a significant increase in public spending. Higher spending was bound to lead to higher inflation, which, indeed, would occur consistently from 1966. In the last months of 1965, the conviction within the Johnson administration was that the price of copper could become a significant factor in the expected increase in inflation in the United States and, consequently, it was necessary to do something about it.

The U.S. copper market had a distinct oligopolistic character, and the few companies that dominated production and sales in the United States— Anaconda and Kennecott among them—set what was known as the "producers' price," much lower than the price of the mineral in the London Metals Exchange, an indicator for transactions made in other parts of the world. The U.S. government, for its part, held a large stockpile of copper, ostensibly for national security purposes, and could buy or sell depending on the specific circumstances of the market, so that the price would remain relatively stable. The copper market in the United States, at least during the first half of the Cold War, was largely shaped by the decisions of the directors of a few big companies and a handful of U.S. government officials, although by the 1960s this oligopolistic character was beginning to weaken with the incorporation of new companies and ores from all over the world into the large-scale production of copper.[32]

An important portion of the copper traded in the U.S. market, however, came from Chile's Anaconda mines. Consequently, the price of Chilean copper, which was largely set by the Chilean government, also had an effect on the price of copper in the United States. In October 1965, the Frei administration decided to raise the price of copper from 36 cents to 38 cents per pound. This decision pushed U.S producers, at least according to the view peddled by Anaconda and Phelps Dodge to U.S. officials, to raise the price to 38 cents as well.[33] As the Johnson administration feared that the increase in the price of copper could add a new factor in an already inflationary situation, it set out to convince the Frei administration to reverse its decision and return to the more convenient—for the United States—rate of 36 cents per pound.

As had been the case with the crisis in the Dominican Republic earlier in 1965, Averell Harriman, this time accompanied by Assistant Secretary of the Treasury Anthony Solomon, traveled to Santiago in mid-November to persuade President Frei to roll back the 2-cent price increase. Without referring explicitly to the Vietnam War, Harriman and Solomon described the presumed effects of the new price set by the Chilean government on inflation in the United States. A spiraling inflationary situation in the United States and an excessive increase in the price of copper in world markets were, according to the U.S. envoy's argument, inconvenient for Chile, as they could, respectively, lead to a reduction in U.S. foreign aid and risk the substitution of cheaper materials for the ever more expensive red metal.

Frei was in a tough spot. He felt obliged to evaluate in good faith and even make a serious effort to comply with the request of the U.S. government. The Johnson administration had generously supported him since the presidential campaign. Moreover, the rank of the emissaries sent to present the U.S. case meant that the issue was of the utmost importance to the Johnson administration. On the other hand, as the president of a country whose main source of income was copper, he could not put U.S. interests ahead of Chile's in any decision regarding the price of the mineral. Furthermore, in a political environment where all major political parties other than his own PDC opposed him, any policy regarding copper was bound to be controversial anyway, as the ongoing parliamentary discussion on the agreements between the Chilean government and the U.S. companies demonstrated.

In his conversation with Harriman and Solomon, Frei expressed that even Conservatives and Liberals had pushed for a copper pricing policy more aggressive than his administration's. Reversing a decision that had already been criticized as too tepid would certainly give ammunition to his adversaries. On the other hand, Frei agreed with the assumption that too high a price for copper would eventually lead to its replacement by cheaper materials, probably aluminum.[34] This fear, perpetually hovering over international copper markets, was reinforced in the Chilean case by the traumatic experience of the early twentieth century, when the development of synthetic nitrates in Germany during World War I set the production and export of saltpeter in Chile on its way toward collapse.

Negotiations between the Chilean government, represented by President Frei himself, and the representatives of the Johnson administration, assisted by Ambassador Dungan, were held in the most cordial terms. The U.S. officials, especially Dungan, familiar with the alignments and cleavages of Chilean politics, understood that their request was most delicate and put Frei on a difficult position. Consequently, the U.S. negotiating strategy privileged carrots over sticks. The U.S. government was at the time negotiating with the Chilean government a program loan in the vicinity of $80 million for 1966, but the U.S. officials who spoke with Frei and his economic advisers did not use it as a bargaining tool. On the contrary, they offered to increase the amount of the loan by about $10 million to compensate for the loss of revenue resulting from the rollback in the copper price. In the meantime, Secretary of Defense Robert McNamara announced that, as part of the plan for controlling the price of copper in the United States, the U.S. government would request Congress to temporarily suspend the 1.7-cent tax levied on imported copper, which at least momentarily satisfied a long-held aspiration of the Chilean state.[35] The particular offers of the U.S. government and the relative dependence of the Christian Democratic program on the continuous flow of U.S. aid and political support, which the U.S. negotiating team did not need to explicitly point out, eventually led Frei to accede to the Johnson administration's request. Chile committed the sale of ninety thousand tons of copper in the United States in 1966 at the agreed price of 36 cents a pound.

The story, however, did not end there. By the end of 1965, the growing imbalance between the demand and the production of copper, the reason the Johnson administration had sought the arrangement with the Chilean government in the first place, kept pressuring upward the price of the mineral in the world market. In early January 1966, the Frei administration, in agreement with the government of Zambia, decided to raise the price of Chilean copper exports again, this time to 42 cents a pound. Chile would still honor its recent agreement with the United States; however, the new pricing policy established by the Frei administration meant widening the spread between the price agreed upon with the United States for 1966 and the price at which Chilean copper was sold in the international market. As a result, the loss of revenue for the Chilean government would also increase. Representatives of the Frei administration traveled to Washington to request further compensation for the loss, but the Johnson administration refused to grant additional aid, among other reasons because the funds for foreign aid had already being appropriated. The Chilean government did get Anaconda, whose sales subsidiary handled almost all the Chilean copper sold in the United States, to partially make up for the loss of revenue resulting from the wider spread between the 36-cent price for the U.S. market and the 42-cent price for the rest of the world. Anaconda agreed to pay $3.5 million to the Chilean government in excess of its tax obligations for 1966.[36]

Figure 6. Since Chile and Zambia were among the largest producers of copper in the world, the two countries developed a warm relationship in the 1960s. The first president of Zambia, Kenneth Kaunda, in the photo having a laugh with Foreign Minister Gabriel Valdés, visited Chile in 1966, thus becoming the first African head of state to go to a Latin American country. *Courtesy of Archivo Histórico Gabriel Valdés—D&D Consultores, http://www.ahgv.cl.*

As everyone involved in the negotiation expected, the deal between the Chilean and the U.S. government drew much criticism from the opponents of the Frei administration. The terms of the agreement seemed highly unfavorable for Chile. Frei and his advisers made the decision to accede to the U.S. request mostly on political grounds, as maintaining good relations with a U.S. government that had been so generous to Chile and the PDC in the past few years was critical for the success of the Frei administration. However, this reasoning made good sense only for the Christian Democrats. For all the other political forces, especially those on the Left, no political reason could justify a decision that clearly ran counter to the short-term economic interests of the country.

The agreement, from the perspective of the Marxist parties, was a concrete example of what they had been denouncing ceaselessly since their founding: the United States was an imperial power bent on continental domination and willing to resort to all the economic, political, and military means at its disposal to secure its hegemony. Part of that strategy depended on the complicity of local actors willing to accept the U.S. imperialistic grand design in exchange for U.S. material support for their own projects. The PDC and the Frei administration, emblematic and proud representatives of the spirit of the Alliance for Progress and outspoken opponents of Marxism, fitted very well into the Left's narrative of U.S. imperialism and Third World subordination; the agreement on the price of copper between the Frei and the Johnson administrations was, for them, another example of the true character of the relations between the capitalist superpower and one of its Latin American subjects.

In February 1966, the Radical Party introduced a motion to impeach Minister of Mines Eduardo Simián in the Chamber of Deputies for his responsibility in the copper price agreement with the United States. According to the Radicals, the deal hurt Chile's finances, which meant that Simián had not performed dutifully his role as head of the Copper Department and, in fact, had imposed an injury to the honor of the country. The impeachment proceedings were held as the constitution mandated and highlighted once again the ideological divisions that characterized Chilean politics at the time and the concrete and symbolic importance of the United States in those cleavages.

The Radical deputies presented their arguments forcefully, chiefly pointing to the economic disadvantages of the deal. The Liberal and Conservative deputies agreed that the decision of the Frei administration had been unsound but refused to vote in favor of impeaching Simián. The Communist and Socialist deputies framed their criticism of the agreement in their core ideological narrative of international politics, portraying it as another example of the inexorably imperialistic character of U.S. foreign policy. In addition, the Communist and Socialist deputies pointed out that the decision of the Frei administration to roll back the price of copper to 36 cents a pound was a subsidy to the U.S. war effort in Vietnam. They were right.[37]

Yet for all the reasonableness of the arguments on the inconvenience of the copper price agreement, the impeachment proceedings were largely an exercise in futility. As minister of mines, Eduardo Simián was the head of the Copper Department. His role, however, was largely symbolic, since the main executive decisions, including those regarding the price of copper, were made by other officials, foremost among them the vice president of the department, Javier Lagarrigue. It was the latter, moreover, who conducted the technical negotiations with the U.S. government in November 1965, when Harriman and Solomon visited Chile, and January 1966, in Washington. Simián, a man with considerable technical expertise on mining and oil drilling, had little to do with the commercial aspects of the copper business and had not participated in the negotiations between the Frei and the Johnson administrations. Furthermore,

Simián was not a member of the PDC and had even worked for Radical governments in the past, so he was hardly a good political target.[38] The Radicals went after him because, besides President Frei himself, he was the only government official who could be impeached in regard to the copper price agreement. Since the Christian Democrats enjoyed a large majority in the Chamber of Deputies, the impeachment attempt was doomed to fail, as even the Radical deputies who introduced the motion acknowledged. In the end, the impeachment motion was rejected by the votes of the Christian Democratic, Liberal, and Conservative deputies, and the issue was laid to rest for a while. However, as the price of copper in world markets continued to rise consistently in the following months and years, the matter would arise again later, this time in a context of different political alignments both in Chile and the United States.

Negotiated Nationalization

The policy of "Chileanization" and the accords signed in 1965 by the Chilean government and the U.S. companies rested on the assumption that the price of copper would remain below or around 40 cents per pound. The Frei administration calculated the revenues the Chilean state would receive in profits and taxes and presented the project before the country with that figure in mind.

The price of copper in the world market, however, went upward rapidly after 1965, to a large extent because of the Vietnam War (see Table 3). As a result, both the Chilean government and the U.S. companies enjoyed a windfall of profits for a few years. This temporary bonanza allowed the Frei administration to implement some of its key reforms, without putting much pressure on inflation in 1965 and 1966, and to forgo a U.S. program loan for 1967. On the other hand, the favorable tax structures established for the U.S. companies under the "Chileanization" accords did not contemplate the eventuality of a substantial price increase in the following years. Consequently, the companies had benefited significantly from the higher prices of copper since 1965, enjoying enough profits to cover their share of the investments committed under the "Chileanization" agreements. On the contrary, the Chilean state had received a proportionally smaller amount of revenues through taxes than would have been the case under the previous tax structure.

By 1969, voices from all political quarters, including Frei's own PDC, were questioning the economic convenience of the "Chileanization" agreements and calling for a new copper policy. With the 1970 presidential election already in sight, the issue had the potential of becoming—as it eventually did—a political

Table 3. International Price of Copper, 1958–1973

Year	President	Dollars per pound. London	Dollars per pound. United States	2003 dollars per pound. London	2003 dollars per pound. United States
1958	Ibáñez-Alessandri	0.25	0.26	1.08	1.15
1959	Alessandri	0.30	0.31	1.30	1.35
1960	Alessandri	0.31	0.32	1.34	1.41
1961	Alessandri	0.29	0.30	1.26	1.33
1962	Alessandri	0.29	0.31	1.28	1.35
1963	Alessandri	0.29	0.31	1.28	1.36
1964	Alessandri-Frei	0.44	0.32	1.92	1.41
1965	Frei	0.58	0.35	2.50	1.51
1966	Frei	0.69	0.36	2.88	1.49
1967	Frei	0.51	0.38	2.11	1.58
1968	Frei	0.56	0.41	2.27	1.66
1969	Frei	0.67	0.47	2.58	1.84
1970	Frei-Allende	0.64	0.58	2.40	2.17
1971	Allende	0.49	0.52	1.79	1.89
1972	Allende	0.49	0.51	1.69	1.79
1973	Allende-Pinochet	0.81	0.59	2.48	1.82

Source: Díaz, Lüders, and Wagner, *La República en Cifras*, p. 399.

goldmine for the Left and a heavy liability for the PDC. Frei, who was also persuaded that the U.S. companies had gained much more than the Chilean state from the higher prices of copper, decided to take the bull by the horns and establish a new regime for the production of copper in Chile, thus simultaneously responding to the new realities of the world market and, at least from his perspective, settling the issue for the long term.

The matter of nationalization of U.S. assets had become highly relevant for the Nixon administration after the Peruvian military government decided to nationalize the International Petroleum Company in 1968.[39] Frei knew very well that he was treading on delicate ground, so he made a conscious effort to avoid alienating the Nixon administration. On 3 May 1969, Frei met with Ambassador Korry to inform him about his decision to alter the tax and property structure of the largest copper mines in Chile. The president wanted Korry to know that his motivations and intent differed substantially from those of the Peruvian military dictatorship and that, on the contrary, he wished to maintain the best relations with the U.S. government. He was still convinced of the soundness of the "Chileanization" accords signed a few years earlier but was now "morally convinced and politically persuaded that the reaction against him and against the U.S. would become overwhelming if he were not to rectify a situation that had changed radically since the signing of the agreements."[40]

Although he was not yet set on a specific course of action, Frei had decided that his government had to tackle two fundamental issues. First, taxes paid by the copper companies had to be somewhat indexed to the fluctuations of the price of copper in the world market. Second, and more important, the government had to seek some kind of agreement with Anaconda, owner of Chuquicamata. Unlike Kennecott, owner of the El Teniente mine, Anaconda had not sold part of its producing mines to the Chilean government under the policy of "Chileanization." Instead, it had established a joint company with the Chilean government for the exploitation of a new copper mine, Exótica, whose operation began in 1970. Consequently, the company had made remarkable profits off the higher prices of copper after 1965.

According to Frei's reasoning, considering the mounting political pressure for some form of nationalization, it was in the best interest of Anaconda to pursue in good faith a deal with the Chilean government. Frei, who wanted to approach this matter as discreetly and cautiously as possible, told Korry that he was informing him of this decision before approaching the companies, particularly Anaconda, and even before apprising his party and several members of his cabinet.[41] The day after his meeting with Korry, Frei sent a personal letter to President Nixon telling him about his intentions.[42]

The negotiations between the Chilean government and Anaconda began officially on 2 June 1969. As reported by Ambassador Korry, the positions of both parties seemed at first irreconcilable. Richard Sims, vice-president of the Chilean branch of Anaconda, told Korry that the company did not see favorably the establishment of a partnership with the Chilean government in the manner of the Kennecott agreement and preferred outright nationalization with proper compensation. If the Left were to introduce a full-nationalization bill in terms unfavorable for Anaconda, the executive thought the company could successfully lobby for the votes of enough senators of the National and Radical parties to allow Frei to veto the proposed legislation. The Chilean government, for its part, wanted an accord similar to that agreed upon with Kennecott a few years earlier, as Frei and his economic team were convinced that the Chilean state did not have the wherewithal to offer proper compensation for full expropriation. The company wanted one dollar per each ton of unexploited copper reserves lying on the Anaconda reserves—about $2 billion, according to Korry's calculation. The Chilean government, on the other hand, was not willing to pay Anaconda more than the book value of its assets, intentionally understated for tax purposes.[43]

Since direct negotiations between the Chilean government and Anaconda executives seemed to be going nowhere, both parties agreed that the participation of Ambassador Korry in the conversations could help bridge the positions initially held by the two sides. To a large extent because of Korry's counsel, Anaconda negotiators came to realize that their bargaining position was much weaker than the Chilean government's. The political support they thought they could obtain from Nationals and Radicals was largely illusory; if the situation were to come down to a full-blown confrontation between the Chilean government and Anaconda, no smart politician would side with the U.S. company.[44] Furthermore, Anaconda's assets in Chile were too important for the company to let them go in unfavorable terms only as a result of its executives' mistaken reading of the domestic political situation. Consequently, the company representatives rapidly gave up some of their earlier points and began to negotiate in terms that were largely set by the Frei administration.[45]

The loudest opposition to any concession among Anaconda executives came from Guillermo Carey, one of the company's vice presidents, a Chilean citizen of far-right political views whose analysis of the political situation in Chile was, according to Korry, "so far-fetched as to be ludicrous." Carey, whose office was in the Anaconda headquarters in New York, had been feeding his peers with his own, warped view of Chilean politics, thus making the company's negotiating team think they could ask for much more than was realistic to expect from the Chilean government. More important, Carey and other "upper-middle class Chileans" had convinced many Anaconda executives that the National Party and many Radical senators would stand by the company if its interests were threatened and that the State Department and the embassy in Santiago would always take the side of the Chilean government.[46] If Anaconda executives had initially considered it logical to trust their Chilean colleague's judgment on the politics of his country of birth, only a few days in Santiago and a couple of hours of conversation with Ambassador Korry thoroughly dispelled the illusions they harbored when they arrived in Chile in early June.

Eventually, it was Korry who presented both negotiating parties with the basic structure of the final agreement. In essence, it was based on the general views of the Frei administration. Contrary to their original hopes, Anaconda executives had to agree to sell 51 percent of the shares of their assets in Chile, with the exception of Exótica, and form a joint company with the government— basically, the same arrangement as between Kennecott and the Chilean government. Less than that was for the Frei administration unacceptable and politically suicidal; more than that was for the Chilean state materially impossible. The final agreement, however, went a little further than the Kennecott model. Not only would the Chilean state immediately buy 51 percent of the company's shares, paying with twelve-year bonds, it would also commit to buy the remaining 49 percent after a minimum of three years, as per Korry's suggestion. The value of the shares acquired by the Chilean state was set at $198.5 million, much below what was originally considered fair by the Anaconda representatives, who were thinking of amounts well above a billion dollars for their assets in Chile.[47]

Eduardo Frei announced the agreement to the Chilean public on 26 June 1969. The reaction in the United States was favorable. The State Department viewed the negotiation and its successful result as a step forward in the removal of an "abrasive historical legacy" marked by Anaconda's character as a "state within a state dominating Northern Chile."[48] Nevertheless, the State Department's assessment of the agreement noted, correctly as it turned out, that its consolidation after the end of the Frei administration in November 1970 was still uncertain. The *New York Times* and the *Washington Post* devoted editorials to the "negotiated nationalization" and praised it as a possible model for other countries and U.S. companies with holdings abroad. Both newspapers, moreover, extolled Frei's moderate approach to the matter, explicitly different from the way the Velasco Alvarado dictatorship had handled the nationalization of the International Petroleum Company in Peru.[49] Korry himself received warm congratulations from the Chilean government, Anaconda representatives, and Secretary of State William Rogers for his key role in the negotiations.[50] Even high-rank Anaconda executives ended up recognizing that they got almost as much as they could realistically hope for. Charles Brinkerhoff, chair of the company's board of directors, took the situation, in Korry's words, "very philosophical[ly]." "We had a good run for some 40 years," Brinkerhoff told the ambassador, "[and] now we much [sic] adjust to the new realities."[51]

In Chile, however, the "negotiated nationalization" did not earn Frei any significant political gain. The Left, as could be expected, maintained its line on the matter, calling for outright expropriation through legislation.[52] The issue would be an important point in the program of Salvador Allende's presidential bid in 1970 and would, in fact, come to fruition in the manner preferred by the Left in 1971. The Right also opposed the deal, although with much less intensity. For PN President Sergio Onofre Jarpa, nationalization was essentially simpler than and, therefore, preferable to the model of joint state-private companies. The ideological roots of such conviction, however, were much shallower than those on which the Left based its opposition to the negotiation. The U.S. embassy officer who talked with Jarpa while the negotiations between the government and Anaconda were still ongoing got the impression that the PN opposed the deal mainly because it could entail a triumph for the Frei administration.[53]

After some persuasion, Jorge Alessandri, the most likely presidential candidate of the Right in the 1970 presidential election, conceded to Ambassador Korry that the agreement, indeed, took out of the picture the biggest political problem regarding copper and that Frei's successor could have wide latitude in deciding how to proceed with the next stages of the nationalization. Alessandri, however, still held doubts about the matter, especially as it highlighted the tensions between the worlds of politics, which he ostensibly despised, and business, in which he thrived. He criticized Frei for "breaking a contract," and, in his rather idiosyncratic manner, reiterated his deep contempt for all politicians, no matter what their affiliations or sympathies.[54]

Even in circles closer to Frei, the "negotiated nationalization" received criticism and even opposition. Former finance minister Raúl Sáez thought the deal undid everything he had worked for in the previous years when he had played an important role in the accords signed under the "Chileanization" framework. Sáez took the situation virtually as a personal affront and quite bluntly told Korry that the United States should have stood its ground more forcefully and should have invoked the Hickenlooper amendment, which mandated curtailment of foreign aid to countries that expropriated U.S.-owned properties without proper compensation, after the military dictatorship confiscated the assets of the IPC in Peru in 1968.[55]

More galling for Frei and the Christian Democratic Party, however, was the position taken by Radomiro Tomic, the most likely presidential candidate of the party in the 1970 election. Tomic's views on copper were known to everyone, and his opposition to the deal struck between the Chilean government and Anaconda should not have taken anyone by surprise. Nevertheless, his stance on the matter reflected a much deeper division in the PDC and greatly diminished the favorable political impact the agreement could have had on the party. To Frei's chagrin, Tomic's program as a presidential candidate, endorsed by the PDC, called for the immediate nationalization of the main foreign copper corporations. According to the program's disingenuous wording, such full nationalization would "complete the process started by the [Frei] government." Even though Tomic and the PDC attempted to show their proposals regarding copper policy as a continuation of the work done by the Frei administration on this matter, it was clear that the PDC candidate for the 1970 presidential election had no intention to continue the gradual approach symbolized by and implemented through the policies of "Chileanization" and *nacionalización pactada*.[56]

In a broader sense, Tomic's reaction to the agreement demonstrated that the matter of the property of the largest copper ores in Chile, the *Gran Minería*, was far from settled. Contrary to the hopes and expectations of Frei, Korry, Anaconda executives, and State Department officers, the "negotiated nationalization" did not remove the issue from the political arena—not least because even within the party of the president the agreement did not receive unanimous approval. The environment of Chilean politics, moreover, had changed significantly since Frei took office after his landslide victory in 1964. The Christian Democratic Party, to a large extent because of its internal divisions, was no longer the undisputedly strongest force in Chilean politics. Ultimately, given the state of the political competition in Chile in 1969 and regardless of the character of the policy, no initiative undertaken by the Frei administration regarding copper could have effectively removed the issue from the public debate. Public opinion in general seemed to drift ever closer to the position long promoted by the Left.

In 1970, Salvador Allende campaigned on the promise to nationalize all the U.S.-owned copper assets in Chile and, once in office, he delivered. In July 1971, all the PDC and PN parliamentarians joined their leftist colleagues in approving a constitutional amendment that nationalized all the remaining holdings of the U.S. copper companies of the so-called *Gran Minería*. Furthermore, the amendment assigned to the president the task of calculating the compensation to be paid to the U.S. corporations. Thus, less than a year after Frei left office, his entire copper policy, one of the tenets of his political project, was swiftly undone by the revolutionary and anti-U.S. Allende government—with the votes of all the political forces of the Chilean spectrum, including Frei's own PDC.[57]

Chapter 5

The Presidential Candidacy
of Radomiro Tomic

Shortly after assuming the presidency, Eduardo Frei Montalva appointed his old friend and fellow Christian Democratic leader Radomiro Tomic to the ambassadorship in Washington. The decision, apparently made after consulting with the appointee, clearly looked toward the 1970 presidential election.[1] Tomic, as it was widely known, was second only to Frei in the Christian Democratic leadership, and his nomination as the candidate of the party for the next presidential election was all but preordained. As the country's representative in the most important center of power in the Western Hemisphere, Tomic's image and standing in Chile would be shielded from the potentially negative consequences of being actively involved in domestic politics. At the same time, Tomic would be able to forge links with the Washington establishment, a more than precious asset for someone whose main political goal was to become president of Chile. Last but not least, the exposure from the foreseeable public appearances with renowned U.S. and international personalities would, undoubtedly, help boost his prestige.

Tomic was one of the historic leaders of the Christian Democratic Party. Born in 1914 in the city of Calama, next to Chuquicamata, the largest copper mine in the world, Tomic was elected deputy in 1941 and 1945, representing the northernmost districts of the country (Arica, Iquique, and Pisagua). In 1950, he won the by-election held in Tarapacá and Antofagasta to replace Senator Pablo Neruda, who was kicked out of Congress after the Communist Party was outlawed in 1948. Tomic and the other parliamentarians of the party, then called Falange Nacional, voted against the anti-communist legislation pursued by Radical President Gabriel González Videla, for they viewed this measure as an unacceptable infringement of political rights inherent to a democratic society.[2] After a temporary retirement from active politics in 1953, he returned to Congress in 1961, this time as a senator for the provinces of Aconcagua and Valparaíso. As one of the founders and most respected leaders of Falange Nacional, Tomic had become a figure of national prominence, especially as an advocate of a more significant presence of the Chilean state in the business of copper and ever closer to the Left's position in favor of outright nationalization.[3]

Although he identified himself with the principles of Christian Democracy, Tomic's position was significantly to the left of Frei's. He spoke much more openly and much more fiercely against capitalism than Frei and other Christian Democrats, dreaming of a structural transformation that would usher in communitarianism, the new social order—or utopia—toward which the Christian Democrats aimed but were never able to articulate into a readily identifiable ideology or set of principles. In reality, communitarianism was more easily explained in negative terms than presented as a clearly defined political goal. Trying to describe what the term meant, Tomic told Sydney Weintraub, director of the Agency for International Development mission in Santiago in July 1968, that "everybody knows what capitalism is . . . everybody knows what communism is; communitarianism is neither."[4]

Besides his left-leaning political position, what identified Tomic and distinguished him from most politicians of his generation was his charisma. A fiery and compelling orator, Tomic's speeches projected a mystique not unlike that of contemporary revolutionary movements. This distinctive feature of Tomic's, however, was simultaneously his main asset and his worst defect. If his oratory, his charisma, and his wholehearted devotion to the Christian Democratic cause—as he rather idiosyncratically understood it—earned him a respectable level of popularity in Chilean politics, his grandiloquence and somewhat unrealistic views and expectations led him to take positions that sometimes, especially toward the end of the 1960s, put him at odds with his own party, especially with Eduardo Frei.[5]

A large ego is a common and mildly healthy feature among politicians in positions of leadership, but Tomic seemed to have a self-esteem that bordered on the messianic. The PDC leader certainly loved to receive attention, not only from large followings but also from individual interlocutors. Conversing with him required a high degree of patience, as Tomic was known to go on and on about a subject of his interest without regard for the person who had to listen to him. In one of the many dispatches Korry devoted to his interactions with the PDC stalwart, the ambassador described the experience of

Figure 7. Eduardo Frei and Radomiro Tomic, shaking hands enthusiastically in this 1964 photo, grew apart toward the end of the 1960s, mostly as a result of Tomic's insistence on a political strategy at odds with Frei's deepest convictions about the country and the doctrine of Christian Democracy. *Courtesy of Archivo Fotográfico Casa Museo Eduardo Frei Montalva.*

talking with Tomic as an "exquisite torture."[6] It is said that on many occasions he got so carried away that he started his tirades with the phrase "Tomic says."[7] Observers who did not share Korry's personal animosity toward Tomic were also struck by the high opinion the Christian Democratic leader held of himself. Besides pointing out this fact explicitly in one of his communications to Washington, AID official in Santiago Sydney Weintraub portrayed Tomic as "a man who feels that his destiny is to lead his country."[8] Another U.S. embassy officer reported to Washington that the most likely PDC candidate for the 1970 presidential election saw himself "as a heroic figure capable of evoking sacrifice from a bourgeois-oriented Chilean people."[9] Tomic, in sum, aimed at the highest summits of power because of his strong, if somewhat fuzzy and unrealistic, conviction about the road to development that Chile should follow but also because reaching those heights was the realization of his deepest personal ambitions. One unidentified member of the PDC who spoke with Ambassador Korry in mid-1969 about the incipient presidential race put it in the most precise terms: "Tomic has a steel fragment imbedded in his heart, his desire to be president. If it is removed, he dies; if it is left, he is killed."[10]

Tomic and the "Popular Unity" Strategy

Tomic wanted, as did a sizeable number of his fellow Christian Democrats, to form some sort of political alliance with the parties of the Left. For Tomic and the significant left-leaning wing of the PDC, the *rebeldes,* the core purpose of the party was to bring about substantial economic and social transformation, and its goals did not differ significantly from those of the Marxist Left. A coalition between the left-wing parties and the PDC would constitute a broad and formidable alliance of the truly progressive forces in Chilean politics and would be able to carry out the structural reforms the country, according to the most widespread conviction in Chilean politics, so badly needed.[11] In 1967, one of the most prominent figures of the *rebelde* wing of the PDC, Rafael Agustín Gumucio, won the presidency of the party.[12] Furthermore, the National Junta of the PDC in the same year approved a programmatic document whose title aptly sums up the spirit of the more left-leaning members of the party: "Propositions for Political Action in the 1967–1970 Period for a Non-Capitalist Road to Development."[13]

Although Tomic did not endorse the *rebelde* faction of the party, nor was he recognized as its leader, he tried to build bridges between the PDC and the Left. As early as April 1967, when he was still ambassador in the United States,

Tomic let it be known that he considered seriously the idea of an alliance between the Christian Democrats and the left-wing parties, which he had termed
"Popular Unity." In a conversation with Ambassador Ralph Dungan in Santiago, Tomic asked the U.S. diplomat what he thought of collaboration between
the PDC and the "Marxists." Dungan, who in his report of the talk said that
Tomic was "as fuzzy and unrealistic as ever," rejected outright this possibility
and chastised the presidential hopeful for even entertaining such an idea.[14]

Tomic also shared his idea of a broad coalition of Christian Democrats, So-
cialists, Communists, and even Radicals with Frei, Foreign Minister Gabriel
Valdés, and other members of the PDC in July 1967. Frei was appalled. The
Christian Democratic project had little in common with the vision of the
Marxist Left, so there was no ideological and programmatic basis for the alliance
Tomic considered. Frei, whose friendship with Tomic went back decades,
expressed his disappointment in kind but nonetheless strong terms: "If you
[Tomic], the one who must lead the party in the next few years, think this way,
I frankly don't see a destiny for the country or the party. I know of your recti-
tude, your good faith, and your capacity, but I sincerely believe that your political scheme has no real chance in Chile." In fact, for Frei the sole expression of
such an idea betrayed an "unbelievable" lack of knowledge on the part of the
Chilean ambassador in Washington.[15] If anything, Frei told Tomic in December 1967, the Christian Democrats should consider some sort of understanding with the Right, as had occurred without any concessions from the PDC
in 1964.[16]

In actuality, the chances the Communist and Socialist parties would sub-
scribe to Tomic's plan and support him in the presidential election were at best
slim. Communists and Socialists had opposed the Frei administration with
great alacrity. One Socialist senator, Aniceto Rodríguez, had told one of his
PDC colleagues in 1964 that the Socialist Party would try to block the Frei
administration every step of the way—the Socialists would deny the PDC "the
salt and the water," in the infamous assertion of the Socialist leader.[17] In addition, by the time Tomic began to think about coming back to Chile and start
his work toward the 1970 election, the parties of the Popular Action Front
were already approaching the Radicals with the intention of building a coalition similar to the Popular Front that had carried Pedro Aguirre Cerda to the
presidency in 1938—with the significant difference that now Socialists and
Communists would be the major partners in the alliance.

Moreover, the incipient rapprochement between the Radical Party and the
Left had already yielded concrete results; in December 1966 the votes of
Radical, Communist, and Socialist senators had made Salvador Allende presi-

dent of the upper chamber. The Socialists, and especially the Communists, might have welcomed—as they did in 1969 when the Unitarian Popular Action Movement split off from the PDC—a Christian Democratic opening to the Left and might have entertained the idea of a limited political pact but only with them in the saddle. The strength of the PDC, still the largest in electoral terms as attested by the 1965 parliamentarian and the 1967 municipal elections, rendered the possibility of the PDC participating in an alliance as a junior partner all but null. Furthermore, the *rebelde* PDC leaders had heard insinuations from the PC that the latter might consider supporting Gumucio if he were to win his party's nomination but would not do the same regarding Tomic.[18] Indeed, Tomic's grand vision seemed unrealistic. The PDC leader, however, would not easily give up his convictions.

The PDC's drift to the left and Tomic's dreams of a coalition between his party and the parties of the Left unsettled those who saw Christian Democracy as a worldview and a political project incompatible with Marxism. In January 1968, the PDC held an extraordinary national assembly called ostensibly to assess the legislation on wages then about to be discussed in Congress. The real purpose of the meeting, however, was to straighten up the relations between the government and the party, somewhat strained since Rafael Agustín Gumucio assumed the presidency of the PDC in mid-1967. A few days before the assembly took place, Ambassador Korry, still a newcomer in the Chilean political scene, met with President Frei to talk about the current situation. "The conversation," Korry stated in his report to the State Department, "was a blunt effort by the ambassador to influence the president to adopt a less tolerant view of the leftist rebels in his own party [and] of the Communist party of the Soviet Union on the eve of Mr. Frei's confrontation with his Christian Democrats at a junta."

Korry told Frei, with whom he had developed a friendly relationship almost instantly, that Chile could become a target of real interest and little cost for the foreign policy of the Soviet Union, as the left-wing faction and some leaders of the PDC (for example, Tomic and Foreign Minister Gabriel Valdés) had abetted the Communist Party's strategy by openly speaking of and even pursuing an alliance between the PDC and the parties of the Left. Korry tried to drive his point home by referencing one of the men most admired by the Christian Democrats: "It was one thing for a Foreign Minister to seek to cater or emulate De Gaulle while in Paris; it was another thing to forget that De Gaulle, whatever else his objectives, never lowered the barrier between the French people and the Communist Party of France." Korry argued that all those Christian Democrats who seriously considered "the amateur undertaking" of a political alliance with the Communists "had contributed greatly to the erosion if not destruction of the fundamental psychological barrier separating those in Chile who believed in democratic principles, parties and processes from those who did not."[19]

Frei did not need to be apprised of the concerns of Korry or the United States government to worry about the PDC's drift to the left. In fact, he agreed with Korry's assessment of the situation almost entirely. Frei, according to Korry's report, assured the ambassador in the most emphatic terms that he was "philosophically an anti-communist because he could never accept anti-democratic principles." Valdés' and Tomic's comments on the possibility of an alliance with the Communists were "nonsensical" and "absurd."[20] As to the *rebelde* wing of the PDC, he had told Korry in December that he would deal with that issue in the upcoming assembly. Frei delivered a powerful speech at the PDC gathering a few days after his talk with Korry in a move to reassert his leadership within the party and, by explicitly inveighing against the Communist Party, stall any chance of a rapprochement with the Marxist Left. As a result of Frei's maneuvering, the *rebelde* party chief Gumucio stepped down and was replaced by someone more amenable to the *oficialista* (Frei) line, an intellectual stalwart of the PDC, Jaime Castillo Velasco. This reshuffling in the highest echelons of the party dealt a hard blow to the *rebelde* faction.

The internal wrangling between *oficialistas*, *rebeldes*, and *terceristas* (a faction that did not identify itself with any of the other wings but leaned to the left) continued until the end of the Frei administration and ended up with the *rebeldes* leaving *en masse* to create a new party, the Unitarian Popular Action Movement, in 1969. However, with Gumucio stepping down from the role of president of the party, the faint chance that the PDC might have moved decisively to the left of the political spectrum suffered a huge setback. Korry was, of course, very pleased with the result of the assembly and, rather exaggeratedly, claimed personal credit for the stance taken by Frei.[21]

From Frei's and Korry's viewpoint, the situation within the PDC improved significantly after the January 1968 meeting. Tomic's ideas about his probable presidential candidacy and the future of Chilean politics, however, did not change. Concerned about his friend's stubbornness, Frei asked Ambassador Korry that the U.S. government do something about it. Since Tomic had decided to come back to Chile in March 1968, Frei thought a word from Vice President Hubert Humphrey or even President Johnson himself showing their coldness to the prospect of an understanding between the PDC and the Left could help convince Tomic to disavow his idea.[22] Interesting, when informed of this, Undersecretary of State Nicholas Katzenbach did not react unfavorably to Tomic's vision. At the bottom of the memo in which he was told of Frei's request, Katzenbach wrote a remarkable comment: "I have heard that Chilean Communists are less radical than the Socialists. Tomic's idea of a coalition of the left may not be all that bad. At any rate, it is worth further investigation."[23]

Eventually Tomic met with Secretary of State Dean Rusk on 19 March 1968, just a few days before Tomic's departure from Washington. In the conversation, held in the friendliest terms, Tomic exposed his views with frankness—in fact, quite boldly, considering that he was speaking with a high representative of the government that had given the most financial and political support to the administration he had represented diplomatically since 1964. The outgoing ambassador told Rusk that "the government of President Frei had reached the limit in its ability to carry forward its program of economic and social reform within a democratic framework." The only way around this hurdle, according to Tomic, "was a new alignment of forces and a re-definition of social and economic goals to coincide with this realignment." Such reconfiguration contemplated almost surely an alliance between the PDC and the parties of the Left. Rusk responded mildly but in the terms that had been suggested by Frei. The secretary said that "he could not speak on Chile, but that the pattern of Communist Party activities in South East Asia and the Middle East clearly [indicated] that they had not [abandoned] their goals of world domination." To this rather predictable argument, Rusk added a question that went to the core of the polarization of forces then occurring in Chilean politics: Why could not an alliance between Christian Democrats and Radicals be worked out? The question remained for the most part unanswered, as Tomic was personally more inclined to an alliance with the left-wing parties.[24]

Shortly after arriving in Chile, Tomic met with Korry to discuss the prospects of a presidential candidacy in 1970 and the U.S. view of a possible alliance between the PDC and the Left. Korry tried to dissuade Tomic from his plan by pointing out the subservience of the Chilean PC to Moscow and their probable preference for a candidate with a weaker personality—Gumucio, among the Christian Democrats, or Alberto Baltra, of the Radical Party, for instance.[25] Korry used flattery generously to try to talk Tomic out of his obsession. "We, unlike the Communists, appreciate [your] honesty, [your] strength and [your] intelligence," the ambassador told the PDC leader. In addition, Korry said the Communists would expect him to break with or at least make some distance from the United States if the pretended alliance were to work properly. Tomic tried to assure his interlocutor in the strongest terms that he would not agree to a break with the United States, as his extremely ambitious political project could not be carried out without U.S. support.

Tomic thought, however, that the current international context allowed for an alliance such as the one he conceived, for neither the United States nor the Soviet Union wanted the rise of another Cuba. The conversation between Korry and Tomic ended without either men attaining fully what they had hoped for. Korry could not persuade Tomic that his idea was unfeasible. Tomic, for his part, could not get U.S. approval of his vision, which he had been seeking in his last months in Washington.[26] This, however, would still not be enough to discourage the PDC leader in his ever more quixotic intent.

The Communist leadership rebuffed Tomic's and other Christian Democrats' overtures bluntly, which pleased Frei and Korry quite a bit.[27] It proved that the position of the left wing of the PDC and the most likely candidate of the party for the next presidential election was untenable. Throughout 1968, Korry had deliberately tried not to antagonize Tomic, even though the well-publicized vision of the PDC leader ran counter the most basic principles of U.S. foreign policy. On the contrary, according to Korry's depiction, his outwardly friendly attitude had successfully projected the impression that Tomic might well receive active support from the United States for his race to the presidency, thus making him unacceptable, or at least suspicious, to the Communists.[28]

The ambassador's reasoning was more than a little self-serving, but it underscores the undeniably relevant presence of the U.S. embassy, and particularly of Korry, in the play of Chilean politics. In fact, Frei himself attributed the attitude of the PC partly to the "magistral" U.S. embassy's policy toward Tomic—a most telling sign of how much leverage the U.S. mission had or was perceived to have in Chilean politics. Frei, just as Julio Durán and others in 1964, had no qualms about drawing a U.S. diplomat into the most delicate internal and even intra-party affairs. In a meeting on 7 November 1968, the Chilean president informed the U.S. ambassador that Jacques Chonchol, one of the intellectual leaders of the *rebelde* wing of the party, would be fired as head of the Institute for Agrarian Development (INDAP), one of the agencies in charge of the agrarian reform then being carried out by the Frei administration.[29] Not only did Frei keep Korry well-apprised of developments within the government and the PDC, he also asked the U.S. ambassador for his help in shaping the presidential race still over a year and a half ahead. The president requested that Korry "continue to give Tomic his due and that the embassy not provoke him by criticism into adopting a hostile posture." Korry, of course, assured Frei that he would act accordingly.[30]

The Communists' rejections notwithstanding, Tomic insisted on his vision. In a conversation with Korry in December 1968, Tomic expressed in the most emphatic terms, as was his wont, that he would not run for president in 1970 unless he could get broad support for his program of structural change at least within his own party. Although the PDC leader thought this was as unlikely as the possibility of the Communists supporting him, he remained convinced that only his program, based on the construction of a "communitarian" system, could save Chile from an impending catastrophe. Tomic, a man given to apodictic statements and dramatic gestures, even compared his prognosis about the future of Chile to Churchill's early warnings against Hitler in the 1930s.

In his report of the meeting, Korry described the PDC leader as someone with "a propensity for spouting hot air" and presented Tomic's position as very far on the left—in fact, almost the same as the position of one of the main intellectual leaders of the *rebelde* wing of the Christian Democratic Party, Jacques Chonchol. Nevertheless, Korry asserted that Tomic was still the most likely and the best possible Christian Democratic candidate for the election of 1970—better, for instance, than Bernardo Leighton, a man, in the assessment of the U.S. ambassador, of inferior intelligence and less able to lead.[31] Furthermore, despite the foreseeable emergence of a few problems in the relationship, the U.S. government could develop an effective modus vivendi with an eventual Tomic administration. Korry, in sum, was not opposed to some type of substantial political understanding between the U.S. government and Tomic, which could even entail support for the latter's candidacy in the 1970 election. It would certainly not be the same kind of close partnership developed between the Johnson and Frei administrations, but it could still be an amicable and mutually convenient relationship.[32]

If Tomic's vision were to materialize, Frei's support (or at least his silence on the matter) was indispensable. A few days after the congressional elections of 2 March 1969, Tomic met with the president. He tried to expose his point of view and attempted to convince Frei of the convenience of his popular unity strategy. The meeting, which Frei described in detail to Korry, was a perfect representation of the battle between the two hearts of the PDC. One heart, represented by Tomic and the *rebelde* and *tercerista* wings of the party, felt the Revolution in Liberty promised in 1964 had not been revolutionary enough and more radical steps had to be taken to bring about "communitarianism." The other, that of Frei and the *oficialista* wing of the party, believed the administration had delivered as much as it could on the promises made during the 1964 campaign, effectively substantiating some of the structural changes needed in the country, and that the Christian Democratic philosophy was inherently incompatible with Marxism.

Frei's and Tomic's differing views on some particular but important policies embodied the distance between their ideological and strategic positions. Tomic talked about the need for nationalizing the largest copper mines owned by U.S. corporations. Frei replied that such an action, coming after the "Chileanization" policy carried out years earlier, would only scare away foreign investors and, therefore, was, for him, out of the question. Tomic argued for the nationalization of foreign trade to block the flight of capital. Frei, ever the realist, responded that this measure would be counterproductive, and he even sympathized with big capitalists in his response to Tomic's argument. According to Korry's report, Frei told his old friend that "he understood perfectly why the Augustín Edwardses and the Yarurs of Chile [kept money abroad] when the country had such a history of inflation and other unstabilizing [sic] elements."[33]

The main topic of conversation in the meeting between the two main PDC leaders was, however, the party strategy for the 1970 presidential election and, especially, Tomic's idea of a grand coalition of their party and the Left. Tomic laid out his vision simply. First, the prosperity of the country in the future depended on the capacity of the government to implement hard measures to foster growth and curb inflation. Second, those decisions could be taken only by a government supported by all the popular forces, including the parties of the Left. Frei, whose relationship with Tomic was still cordial, told his friend that he would oppose such a strategy by all means at his disposal. The president, more than a little irritated by Tomic's insistence on his scheme, even made a somewhat theatrical pitch to show his interlocutor the foolishness of his idea. According to Korry's report, Frei tried to talk Tomic out of his vision by describing how a government of the desired coalition of the popular forces would work out: "Adonis Sepulveda [one of the most extremist Socialist leaders] would become Director of Investigaciones, Castroite Senator [Carlos] Altamirano would become Minister of Foreign Affairs or even the Director of Social Security. [Do you] believe such a government could last more than a fortnight? [Don't you] know Chilean history?" The president suggested a party strategy for the near future aimed at mending fences within the PDC and, thus, strengthening Tomic's position for the 1970 presidential election. If Frei's ideological argument did not make any significant impression on Tomic, his capacity to understand the day-to-day workings of Chilean politics and articulate a clear strategy for acting in such a context did. "Ah, Eduardo, that is the difference between us. You see things clearly always. I cannot. I have so many different pulls and tugs on my mind," said Tomic, as per Korry's dispatch.[34]

On 19 March 1969, the weekly news magazine *Ercilla* published an interview with Tomic in which the PDC leader announced he would not run for president unless he received the support of all the forces of the Left.[35] A few days later, the former ambassador to the United States sent a letter to the president of the PDC, Renán Fuentealba, reaffirming and explaining his decision. In the letter, Tomic described his desired popular unity coalition as the alliance of "all the political forces committed to the substitution of the capitalist regime" and presented it as the political vanguard of a "true revolution." Tomic had first proposed this scheme in 1963, and the experience of the Christian Democratic government had, to Frei's chagrin, only strengthened his conviction. Nevertheless, none of the fundamental requisites for the formation of the popular unity coalition, as they were understood by Tomic, could be met at the time. The PDC would not unanimously support the strategy; the Frei government would by no means get behind such a scheme; and the Left had already manifested quite explicitly its absolute rejection of entering an alliance with the PDC.[36]

The popular unity idea, as conceived by Tomic, was stillborn. One cannot but wonder why the PDC leader, an experienced and successful politician and an intelligent man, thought his will alone could bring about such a substantive overhaul of Chilean politics. Since his return to Chile from Washington in early 1968, only the left wing of the PDC had manifested a position convergent with Tomic's, but the PDC leader had carefully tried not to identify himself with a faction that could (and actually did) break the unity of the party. All the other significant actors who would have had to get behind his strategy—Frei and the Communists, for instance—had manifested in the strongest terms their absolute refusal to endorse Tomic's idea.

Tomic's announcement did not cause much of a fuss in Chilean politics. It was widely known that there was no other Christian Democrat who could garner the same level of popular support as the former ambassador to the United States and that Tomic himself wanted to be president too much to give up his opportunity so easily and so early. The announcement was more likely an attempt on Tomic's part to provoke a reaction within the PDC and maybe force the party to endorse his thesis about the need for an alliance with the parties of the Left.[37]

Frei, of course, did not like this move and told Korry, who had become something of a political confidant of the Chilean president. In a lengthy conversation with the U.S. ambassador on 24 March 1969, Frei spoke of his frustration over Tomic's attitude. For Frei, the actions of the PDC presidential hopeful amounted to a "ridiculous spectacle" that in any other country would have ended Tomic's political career. Frei resented deeply the position taken by his old friend since the latter's return from the United States because it had hurt the party and its chances in the 1970 presidential election. Moreover, there seemed to be more than just abstract ideas and political considerations behind Tomic's stance. In Frei's telling words, "Tomic was the victim of his own ego-centricity."[38]

Tomic and the 1969 Copper Agreements

In late June 1969, the Frei administration ended negotiations with the copper company Anaconda for the nationalization of the firm's assets in Chile.[39] The approach of the Frei administration, hailed as a model for other underdeveloped countries in the United States, was supported by the majority of the Christian Democratic Party.[40] Radomiro Tomic, however, did not approve of the deal and expressed his opposition to the so-called *nacionalización pactada* (negotiated nationalization)—an expression coined by none other than Edward Korry—within party circles. Tomic, who had been one of the main proponents of nationalization in the PDC, manifested his anger at the fact that he had not been considered at all during the negotiations with Anaconda. His most important concern, however, was that the Frei administration had chosen to negotiate with the U.S. company instead of pursuing nationalization through legislation. Tomic's position regarding this policy, besides annoying Frei and Korry, threatened to deepen the crisis of the Christian Democratic Party, which had just suffered the loss of a number of members of the *rebelde* wing who created a new party, MAPU.

A few days after the agreement was signed, Korry met with Carlos Massad, president of the Central Bank. The events that took place on that evening illustrate the importance that Korry had acquired as an actor in Chilean politics and his ability to influence, albeit to an extent not easily discernible, some of the decisions made at the highest levels of the Chilean government. One of the reasons Tomic had not given up his idea of an alliance between the PDC and the Left was that the Socialist Party had not yet rejected this vision as explicitly as the Communists. The PDC presidential hopeful still harbored the illusion that the Socialists could get on board with his strategy. The always well-informed Korry, however, broke the news to Massad, who in turn informed Foreign Minister Valdés, that the Socialists had just reached an understanding with the Radicals. The broad left-wing coalition, including the Radicals, wanted for so long by the Communists and some Socialists, was about to come to fruition.

The ambassador, Massad, and Valdés agreed that this news was a crushing blow—one more—to Tomic's hopes.[41]

During his conversation with Massad, Korry learned that, at the same time, Frei was with Tomic at La Moneda. The ambassador asked Massad to call Frei at once. According to Korry's report, Massad had to call five different numbers to finally reach Frei; when communication was established, he put the president on the phone with the U.S. ambassador. Korry, more than a little angry at Tomic's opposition to the copper accords, told Frei that he "would use whatever influence [he] had to make sure that if Tomic upset the accord there would be no . . . 'understanding' of his position or for Chile's in the United States." Although the copper accords, brokered by the ambassador, were important in and of themselves, Korry's frustration at Tomic stemmed from a larger concern about the future of the country. The ambassador told Frei about his conviction that "Tomic could destroy the center of Chile, could ease the strategy of the Communists and could destroy democracy" and that to "stick [Frei's] head in the sand would be to encourage Tomic in his pig-headedness." Korry went on to advise Frei on the possibility of a showdown within the PDC, a fight the president "had to be determined to win." According to the ambassador's dispatch, Frei's curt but telling response to his remarks and advice was "*Muchas gracias*, Ed."[42]

As Tomic did not change his mind on the issue of the copper accords, the PDC and the government faced another tense situation. Three of the top government officials who had conducted the negotiations with Anaconda—Minister of Mines Alejandro Hales, Finance Minister Andrés Zaldívar, and Central Bank President Carlos Massad—threatened to resign if the terms of the agreement were in any way modified because of Tomic's opposition to it. Undoubtedly, Korry's active participation in the negotiations in his capacity as U.S. ambassador had given the agreement between the Chilean government and Anaconda the character of a virtual diplomatic accord. Any change in the deal, which for all practical purposes would be unilateral, would upset not only Anaconda but also the U.S. government, already involved in a nasty disagreement about nationalization of U.S. assets with the Peruvian military government.[43]

This could, in turn, imperil the position of the Frei administration, and particularly the PDC, before the United States—a most undesirable outcome, especially considering that 1970 was an election year. In addition, changing its terms would also send a negative message to foreign investors. In the minds of those who had negotiated the agreement, including Korry, any further modification would badly hurt the country, so they were convinced they had to stand firm to prevent any such development.[44] Needless to say, the fact that Korry felt the deal was to a great extent struck because of his brokering and, therefore, considered it a personal achievement, played its part, too, in shaping the ambassador's attitude.

Korry's frustration at Tomic turned into spite. The PDC leader's insistence on his idea about a coalition between his party and the parties of the Left had already irritated the ambassador. Tomic's opposition to the copper accord, which threatened to overturn the policy and further divide the PDC, made Korry lose his cool. On 11 July, Korry told Massad, one of his closest interlocutors in the Chilean government, "that he was prepared to resign to lead the fight against [Tomic] and to have printed [in Chile] in a private capacity millions of copies of Tomic's speeches in the last 10 years to show what a charlatan he [was]."[45] The gap between Tomic and the U.S. ambassador had become all but unbridgeable.

Eventually, Tomic's position regarding the agreement with Anaconda lost out within the PDC, although not without leaving an impression. The PDC directorate decided to set up a committee to study Tomic's and other members' suggestions for modifying the accords. Few believed the committee would propose changes to the accord or that, if that was the case, the government would follow through with them. Nevertheless, the different approaches to the issue of copper that came to the fore in the wake of the negotiations between the Chilean government and U.S. companies in mid-1969 represented clearly the ideological, strategic, and even personal divisions that had increasingly bedeviled the PDC since Frei's accession to power in 1964.

Tomic and Frei

Eduardo Frei had become almost as indignant at Tomic as Korry. From Frei's viewpoint, instead of showing unity of purpose behind a project that went far beyond anything any other government in the past had done, the PDC, mostly because of Tomic, was projecting an image of division that could only hurt its electoral performance in the near future. In a letter written a few days after the congressional election of 2 March 1969, a saddened Frei expressed his disappointment at his friend's attitude toward the achievements of the Christian Democratic government. The president told his old comrade what everyone could notice in Chile: Tomic did not consider the Frei government as really different from its predecessors; the real change would only come about with

Tomic.[46] As Tomic's attitude did not change and, in fact, became even more distant from Frei's when the government struck the accord with the Anaconda copper company in June 1969, the president became plainly angry at his preferred successor.

Frei told Korry on 24 July that he had gone as far as to threaten Tomic and two leaders of the National Party with "[provoking] a constitutional crisis by resigning, dissolving Congress, and going to the people asking for new elections" if the Anaconda agreement could not be carried forward.[47] Frei, who had been drifting apart from Tomic since the latter returned from Washington in March 1968, had also crossed a threshold in his personal relationship with his old friend.

Notwithstanding the chasm separating the two men, the president still thought that his old comrade, as the candidate of a united and still strong PDC, was the best prospect for Chile in the near future. On 6 August 1969, Frei sent Tomic a lengthy and deeply emotional letter—as transparent and telling a primary source as can be found among the personal papers of Chilean politicians—in which he outlined his position regarding the presidential election of 1970 and the attitude of the most likely PDC candidate in that contest toward his administration. "It is truly dramatic that you have not wanted to accept the fact of this government; that you have lived in permanent contradiction with it," Frei wrote. The president's bitterness at Tomic's position stemmed from a sense of disappointment that went beyond the circumstantial matter of the assessment of his administration. Frei felt profoundly distressed that Tomic's vision of Christian Democracy differed so much from his. The president's conviction about the Christian Democratic project of reform for Chile may have been more moderate and conscious of the limitations imposed by the institutional and political realities of the country than Tomic's but it still was a deep and strong conviction. "I believe," Frei wrote in his eleven-page letter to his old friend, "that we are defining a character, a way and a political practice that project a style of action and a philosophy very different from the one wanted for Chile by the Marxist groups, whose triumph I would consider . . . a historic catastrophe with no return."

While Tomic spoke openly of the insufficiency of capitalism and called explicitly for its substitution by means of a "Chilean Revolution," thus very much coinciding with the political discourse of the Marxist Left, Frei's foremost concern was the maintenance of the liberties that only a democratic system such as the one sanctioned by the Chilean constitution could protect and promote.[48] For the president, "[Christian Democracy was] the alternative that can carry out change in the country without violating the freedom and the essential rights of mankind and without destroying the values that the Marxists do not appreciate and for which we should give our lives so that we do not have to give it later as in the cases of Czechoslovakia and Hungary, so that we do not live threatened as in Romania or subjected as in Cuba." Frei summed up his position and the reason he could not understand—let alone support—Tomic's vision in a short yet eloquent sentence: "To me, Christian Democracy is an alternative to the Right and to Marxism."[49]

Tomic's reply was just as heartfelt and showed as much anguish and sorrow as Frei's letter. The former ambassador did not address the ideological points made so forcefully by the president in his letter. Tomic preferred to devote most of his communication to arguing in favor of his views on copper and to reiterating his specific criticisms of the Anaconda accord, the matter that concerned him the most through 1969. He would not change his mind as to this question and would not shut up; his conviction was unmovable. He knew, however, that Frei would not move from his stance either, so the letter was, more than anything else, a requiem for a position that had already lost the fight within the PDC—although only for the time being. It was also a representation of the heavy toll the experience of governing and the divergences in ideological matters had taken on the close friendship between the two Christian Democratic leaders. Tomic's finishing lines were dramatic, and sincerely so: "I feel sad, truly and deeply sad about our disagreements at a time that could be so beautiful for our lives and on a matter of such a profound transcendence for our fatherland. I don't know what to do."[50]

Frei wrote one more time to Tomic in August 1969. The president still resented Tomic's insistence on his criticism of the *nacionalización pactada* and his unwillingness to support the government line on this matter. For Frei, Tomic's reluctance to conform to the position of the majority of the party on the specific matter of copper and, more broadly, the political strategy for the upcoming presidential election spelled doom for the short- and long-term hopes of the PDC. "You are the only one erecting hurdles for yourself," Frei told Tomic, still in cordial terms. And to Tomic's finishing line, Frei answered forcefully: "It is very clear what you have to do. Accept the nomination; seek the popular unity, not as a specific coalition of parties, but of all the social and economic forces of Chile around the Christian Democratic Party and yourself . . . Give the country the clear impression that you are a second phase, which can be much better, and much brighter than the first one."[51]

Unfortunately for Frei, Korry, and all those who pursued a path of profound reform of Chile's social and economic structures yet were opposed on principle to the Marxist Left, Tomic did not follow his old friend's sad and desperate advice. The program proposed by Tomic in the 1970 campaign did not differ much from the Left's on matters such as copper and agrarian reform. It did call for measures to curb inflation and promote the accumulation of capital in Chile that in some ways seemed more socialist than the expansionary economic policies proposed by the left-wing coalition.[52] Moreover, it did not build on the achievements of the Frei administration, much less on the highly popular image of the Christian Democratic president.

Tomic's choice had its consequences. As Enrique Krauss, one of the managers of the Tomic campaign, explained in a retrospective analysis, between two left-wing candidates, the electorate chose the one clearly placed on the Left.[53] The reasons for Tomic's poor performance in the 1970 election were multidimensional, and many of them did not depend on him or his party. However, his personal traits and convictions, so different from those of the victorious Frei of 1964, certainly played a part in the defeat, and this was something no one could ignore or overlook. Reflecting on the 1970 presidential election a few years later, PDC President Renán Fuentealba—no friend of Frei's—told one U.S. embassy officer that Tomic's "idiosyncrasies and messianic vision of himself made it impossible to put together a winning coalition." Someone in the room concurred, joking that in 1976 Tomic would have much brighter prospects as the candidate of the Left. Fuentealba did not laugh, but he did not object either.[54] Tomic had certainly strayed too far from the line that had allowed the PDC grow, in a quarter of a century, from a small movement of young upper- and middle-class intellectually oriented politicians to the broad-based political machine that had managed to win a presidential election and successfully implement a project of ambitious social reform within a framework of relative political stability.

The experience of governing had taken its toll on the PDC. Frei won the 1964 presidential election as the main leader of a party that had showed a great deal of unity in the pursuit of its political objectives—much more so than the Radicals and the Socialists, for instance. After 1964, the soul of the party gradually but rapidly became a prize over which factions of quite different ideological sensibilities fought decidedly and, to the dismay of the president, publicly. The breakup of the party in 1969 was the crowning moment of a process of erosion that had begun in earnest almost immediately after Frei assumed the presidency. Many thought, Frei among them, that the defection of the *rebelde* faction would help clear the PDC of its most troublesome cadres without a great quantitative loss. This should, in turn, contribute to solidify the unity of the party behind the project represented by the Frei administration. It would not be so. Tomic kept talking unfavorably about the depth and the pace of the policies pursued and implemented by the Frei administration, and he even opposed some of them, such as the deal with Anaconda. The PDC was not broken, and it would continue to be the largest individual party in electoral terms until 1973; however, it was clear that the sense of common purpose shown in 1964—which to a large extent was due to Tomic's restraint at the time—did not exist anymore and that the strongest candidate the party could present for the 1970 election would not receive the unconditional and enthusiastic backing Frei had received in 1964.

Chapter 6

The United States and the Last Two Years of the Frei Administration

The congressional election of 1969 took place in a landscape substantially different from that of 1965. Most political forces, had endured transformative changes that led to the birth of new organizations, further internal polarization, or outright fragmentation. The Christian Democratic Party had suffered a predictable decrease in its popularity after four and a half years in government, during which many promises had been delivered on but no truly revolutionary change had been implemented. As shown by the internal fights of 1967–1968 and the attitude of its most likely presidential candidate for 1970, Radomiro Tomic, the PDC had lost the unity of purpose that had accounted for so much of its electoral success a few years earlier.[1] The landslide victory in the congressional election of 1965, in which the party won an unheard of 42 percent of the vote, was little more than a fond memory. Nevertheless, Frei's personal popularity and the party's electoral following—the largest in the country as attested by the 1967 municipal election, in which it obtained over one-third of the votes cast—still allowed the PDC to stand as the strongest party in Chilean politics.

The Radical Party had also been weakened by internal divisions. Since 1967 the party had moved decisively, although not without conflict, to the left.[2] The Conservative and Liberal parties, after failing dramatically in the 1965 election, had ceased to exist. The right wing of the political spectrum had been represented since 1966 by the National Party, a composite of former Conservatives, Liberals, and politicians of nationalist persuasions, and had already shown some vigor in the 1967 municipal elections. The Socialist Party had adopted a radical platform in 1967, accepting the legitimacy of violent means to achieve political objectives—although no clear change in its political strategy followed this rhetorical hardening.[3] In addition, one of the most important Socialist leaders, Raúl Ampuero, created a new political movement in 1968, the Popular Socialist Union (USOPO), generously funded by the CIA.[4] The only party that had not endured any transformative crisis or substantial change in the years after the election of 1964 was the best organized and most united of all, the Communist Party.

The 1969 Congressional Election

Even though Chilean politics had become more polarized in the previous years, in 1969 the election process went on as usual. Considering the widening ideological gaps then separating the different political sensibilities and the widespread sense of crisis that characterized the political debate, the campaigns and the electoral contests were carried out in a remarkably peaceful manner, as was the custom in a society where the practice of democracy had become deeply entrenched. Counting presidential, congressional, and municipal elections, Chileans had gone to the polls twenty-six times since the victory of Arturo Alessandri in the presidential election of 1932. To be sure, women did not attain full enfranchisement until 1949, and many citizens of poorer backgrounds had remained outside the electorate until the reforms of the end of the 1950s and beginning of the 1960s.[5] However, the process of expansion and improvement of Chilean democracy throughout the twentieth century did not lag too far behind the state of affairs in the countries considered to be advanced in this regard. In fact, in terms of enfranchisement, Chile had made more progress than the United States, where African Americans effectively gained access to the vote only after passage of the Voting Rights Act in 1965. Chileans were accustomed to the content and practice of an ever more inclusive democracy in a way few other polities in the continent, and maybe even in the world, could match.[6]

As expected, the PDC suffered a severe drop from the extremely high 42 percent of the vote obtained in the 1965 election. In fact, counter to Ambassador Korry prognostications a few weeks before the election, the PDC fell slightly below the 30 percent mark that made so much of an impression in the public. The ambassador, a man given to making flamboyant and emphatic statements—not unlike one of his nemeses, Radomiro Tomic—had reported to Washington on 20 February that "anything below 30% would be a disaster for

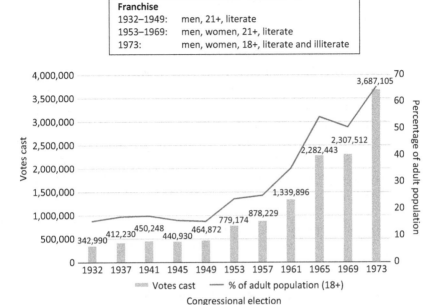

Franchise	
1932–1949:	men, 21+, literate
1953–1969:	men, women, 21+, literate
1973:	men, women, 18+, literate and illiterate

Figure 8. Participation in congressional elections, 1932–1973. Data from Díaz, Lüders, and Wagner, *La República en Cifras*, pp. 744–745.

the [PDC] that would transform the political direction of Chile and render very fluid the landscape for the 1970 presidential race."[7] Korry's words were exaggerated, as the PDC remained the strongest single party in Chilean politics, a position it would occupy until the end of the twentieth century. Nevertheless, the decreasing share of the vote was an unmistakable sign that the PDC, as the ambassador aptly put it, "[was sliding] farther down the greasy pole of power."[8]

The Right, represented by the PN, did well in the election. As forecast by the political staff of the embassy, it earned a solid 20 percent of the vote. The vote of the PN fundamentally consisted of the base right-wing constituency that had voted for Frei in 1964—estimated at a 16 percent to 18 percent by the embassy—and part of which had supported the PDC in 1965.[9] Despite being a party with no "intellectual coherence," according to Korry's assessment, and still unable to "bridge the gaps between [its] component parts of ex Liberals and ex Conservatives," the PN had successfully exploited, to its advantage, the personal charisma and popularity of former president Jorge Alessandri.[10] The Right, pronounced dead by many after the epic failure of the traditional Conservative and Liberal parties in the 1965 election, had regained much of the ground it had lost in the first half of the decade. Equally important, Jorge Alessandri seemed to be the early leader in the incipient presidential race.[11]

Much like the Liberal and the Conservative parties, albeit without falling as dramatically, the PR lost much of its historic influence and prestige during the 1960s. The forecast of the embassy assigned the PR a maximum of 16 percent in the election.[12] The PR, the quintessential center party of Chilean politics for much of the twentieth century, had become "a party without principles," as a CIA report bluntly put it, and was being depleted of their right-wing constituency by the rise of the PN and, more so, by the prospect of an Alessandri presidential candidacy in 1970.[13] The CIA station in Santiago, however, still feared that a Radical share of the vote between 15 percent and 20 percent that bested the PN could entail a serious danger for U.S. interests in Chile. Such a result, the CIA reasoning went, "would breathe new life into [the] party's left-wing leadership." Worst of all, an outcome that could be presented as a success for the party's drift to the Left would "boost the popular front presidential chances for 1970" and "would go a long way towards assuring that a Radical (Baltra, specifically) gets the nomination." This scenario was considered by the CIA station in Santiago as the most dangerous for U.S. interests, "since the Communists, Socialists and Radicals in a good race could come close to 45 percent."[14]

The Radicals' final tally barely reached 13 percent, putting them behind the Communists—but electing more deputies—and a paltry twenty thousand votes ahead of the Socialists. Both because of its declining electoral strength and its inability to articulate a project that could effectively serve as the axis of an alliance, in any coalition the PR would be inevitably a junior partner. Ambassador Korry's harsh words for the Radicals and one of their leaders in the wake of the 1969 election sums up only a little too sensationally the state of affairs in that centennial political movement at the time: "*Radicales* such as newly elected Senator [Anselmo] Sule have regressed from their pre-electoral call-girl status to common street-walking, openly soliciting the favor of the Socialists." The paragraph, which also shows the kind of personal animosity Korry could develop toward some characters in Chilean politics, continued in the libelous style: "This tactic is simply doing what comes natural to [Sule] and it will be some time before he and other Radical bosses decide where they can best pander."[15]

Once the main column of a vigorous democracy and a functioning political system, the PR had, by the end of the 1960s, shrunk to a fading shadow of its past stature and glory. In the ever more likely alliance between them and the left-wing parties, the Radicals would neither be able to impose their candidate nor significantly influence the political program of the coalition. For the first time in decades, no Radical candidate would run for the presidency and, more important, no political program would bear the ideological imprint of the PR.

The Communist Party—"the most disciplined, most dedicated, best led of all," in the words of Korry—earned a respectable 16 percent of the vote, its best result ever in a parliamentary election. The single highest vote in the senatorial races fell on Luis Corvalán, secretary general of the PC. This was achieved in part because the Communists, by far the best tacticians in Chilean politics, generally ran small lists, so that the strongest candidate presented by the party in a given district would concentrate a high number of votes—in some cases high enough to be the most voted among all the candidates. This tactic suited the PC very well. Whereas other parties comprised different sensibilities and, consequently, presented numerous candidates, often with opposing views, the PC did not allow for any dissension from the official line, so there was little room for diversity, let alone competition, within its ranks.

The Socialists obtained slightly less than 13 percent of the vote. The result was not very impressive, as all the other major parties (the PDC, the PN, the PC, and even the PR) polled better. Moreover, the nearly fifty thousand votes lost to the splinter USOPO cost the PS about seven seats in Congress, according to the estimate of the U.S. embassy.[16] Nevertheless, the outcome could still be considered favorable for the party and even more so for its most popular leader, Salvador Allende.

As a share of the electorate, the vote of the PS in the 1969 election grew with respect to the party's performance in the 1961 (11 percent) and 1965 (10 percent) elections. It did fall two points from the 14 percent obtained in the 1967 municipal elections, but this decrease roughly corresponded with the vote gained by the splinter USOPO. More important, the vote of the PS was high enough to place the party in a position of parity with the declining Radical Party. As the added vote of Communists and Socialists reached a robust 29 percent, it became clear that any other party that might join the leftist coalition still known as FRAP would necessarily have to do it in a secondary position. Since the PR, the only major party that could enter an alliance with the Marxist Left, was on the wane and the Communists could not realistically hope for one of their own to be elected president, the position of the PS toward the 1970 election was strengthened by the result of the 1969 election.[17]

Although not widely realized or recognized at the time, partly because he was not as popular within the higher echelons of his party as he was among

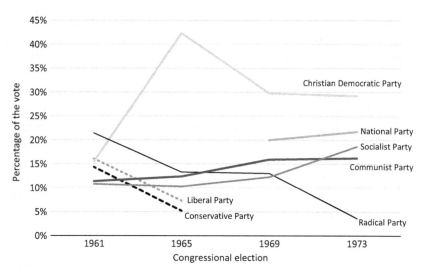

Figure 9. Share of the vote of the major parties in congressional elections, 1961–1973. Data from *Elections in the Americas*, edited by Nohlen, pp. 272–273.

the people, Salvador Allende was the main victor in the 1969 election. Besides the position of the PS vis-à-vis the PR in an eventual Popular Front-type coalition, Allende's electoral result was a personal triumph of significant proportions.[18] Allende, who had already served terms as senator for three different districts, got the highest vote in the southern provinces of Chiloé, Aysén, and Magallanes. In the 1969 race, which involved fewer than seventy thousand voters but was, nonetheless, very important because of the candidates in competition, Allende beat, among others, Juan Hamilton, a handsome young politician who enjoyed Frei's favor and, according to one high-rank government officer, was "absolutely the most attractive PDC candidate in [the] parliamentary races."[19]

Even more significant, at least in symbolic terms, Allende also defeated Raúl Ampuero, who ran on the list of the party he had founded after his ejection from the PS in 1967, USOPO. Allende and Ampuero, both members of the PS since the 1930s, had usually been on opposite sides within the party. By the mid-1960s the gap between them had turned into outright rivalry, even though there was no substantive ideological difference between their positions. Both were convinced Marxists and pursued the construction of a socialist order in Chile. However, important matters of tactics and style set them apart. Allende was a politician of the people, not a theoretician, and was mostly concerned with national rather than partisan affairs. Ampuero, on the other hand, was a thinker and, above all, a party leader, devoting the bulk of his efforts to strengthening the PS. Whereas Allende always wanted to draw the PR into a grand coalition of the Left—a kind of resurrection of the Popular Front of the 1930s and 1940s, this time with the Socialists and the Communists at the helm—Ampuero refused the idea of striking any deal with the largely opportunistic Radicals.[20] Allende was very close to the Communists; Ampuero rejected many of the assumptions and ideas of the PC and even engaged in a public argument with some of its leaders in 1962.[21]

The two Socialist leaders also differed in how they conducted their private affairs. In an interview with an embassy officer in 1964, Socialist historian Julio César Jobet pointed to the stark contrast between Allende's "strictly bourgeois background" and his habit of "[having] mistresses and chasing women," with Ampuero's more modest "middle class background"—his parents were primary teachers from Chiloé—and his proven devotion to his wife and children. Although he was a supporter of Allende, "a man of real stature and prestige among Chileans," Jobet credited Ampuero with keeping the PS together. If he were gone, Jobet told his U.S. interlocutor in 1964 somewhat presciently, "there would be no one to replace him as effective leader of Chilean Socialism."[22]

In 1964, a few months before the election of his successor, President Jorge Alessandri also expressed his contrasting opinions about Allende and Ampuero to a U.S. interlocutor, in this case Ambassador Charles Cole. For Alessandri, Allende was not "a true Marxist, but merely an opportunist whose campaign was considerably less violent than that of Gabriel González Videla in 1946," while Ampuero was a "real extremist" and, therefore, the political leader whom the president feared the most.[23] The rivalry between the two Socialist leaders applied even to the issue of the presidential election of 1970 years ahead of the contest. A few weeks before Ampuero's ejection from the PS in 1967, Salvador Allende publicly proposed that both he and his adversary should renounce their presidential ambitions, so as to mend bridges within the party. Ampuero rejected Allende's proposal, arguing that he had never been offered the presidential nomination of the party.[24]

Allende's triumph over Ampuero in 1969 was widely anticipated. USOPO never got off the ground and did not become a significant challenge or alternative to the other Marxist parties. Nevertheless, the race in Chile's southernmost senatorial district still warranted close attention. After all, it is not common to see two politicians of national standing who have served multiple terms as senators moving to other districts and running for reelection against formidable adversaries. More significant, the outcome of the election brought about an event that, given what happened in later years with Chilean democracy, has been largely forgotten. In retrospect, however, it must be considered of the utmost importance. For all practical purposes, the 1969 election in the southernmost provinces of the country put an end to the political career of one of the most intelligent, skillful, and charismatic leaders of the Chilean Left in the twentieth century.[25]

Although the outcome of the 1969 congressional election could be considered favorable for the prospective presidential candidacies of Jorge Alessandri and Salvador Allende, no party or coalition could claim a decisive victory, as the PDC did in 1965. As Korry put it, only slightly overstating the point, "the results can be read as again providing an anti-communist vote of 85 [percent] or an anti-Right vote of 80 [percent]." Indeed, the outcome of the election indicated that the Chilean political spectrum was divided into three largely irreconcilable sectors—the infamous *tres tercios* (three thirds) of Chilean politics. To Korry, "Chile, like [the] Yankee Stadium, [is] divided into left, right and center with the latter having the largest field but with the edges blurred."[26] The center, however, was occupied by two parties unwilling to work toward a programmatic understanding, much less enter a coalition. The PDC could be partially forgiven for this, as it had a distinct and more or less coherent ideological identity and presented the country with a political project that differed significantly from the projects offered by the other major parties. The PR, on the other hand, was playing "a tired game of opportunism," in the words of Ambassador Korry, and its main leaders were thinking they could "temper any 'Popular Front' of the Left and thus indirectly serve the center and preserve democracy."[27]

In 1964 the PR had chosen not to join the Popular Action Front, despite the explicit invitation to do so from Allende and others on the Left. The U.S. diplomat Joseph John Jova had played a role in persuading some Radicals, especially Julio Durán, to stay in the presidential race and fend off the overtures coming from the Allende camp. In 1969, the embassy could no longer contemplate a similar course of action, since no one in the political staff had the close acquaintance with PR members that Jova had developed. The lack of connections with the PR, a severe handicap for the embassy, was a consequence of the decisions made by Ambassador Dungan a few years earlier, bitterly resented by Korry, of the PR's drift to the left and, last but not least, of the more prosaic but not less relevant fact that Jova himself was not in Chile anymore.

President Frei saw the results of the election in much the same way as the embassy, and the CIA station in Santiago. Frei, as reported by Korry, thought the PDC had suffered a severe setback in the congressional election. The field was now divided in three more or less equivalent parts, and the PDC had no real chance of making alliances. Significantly, Frei considered the Socialists, not the Radicals, the natural partners of the Christian Democrats in an eventual political coalition, but such a possibility could not be entertained at the time as the PS was even further left than the PC. The president said he could talk to and reach an understanding with such Radicals as Humberto Aguirre Dolan and Julio Durán, but none of them carried much weight within the PR at the time. As to the presidential election of 1970, Frei thought Tomic would be the PDC candidate, since no other party leader seemed to be quite up for the task. Men of his liking, such as former ministers Juan de Dios Carmona and Bernardo Leighton, did not have the "required political clout," while recently elected Senator Juan Hamilton "was too young and had not defeated Allende." A leader of the *rebelde* wing of the PDC—the president had Rafael Agustín Gumucio in mind—would become the party's standard bearer only over Frei's "dead body."[28]

U.S. Covert Operations in the 1969 Congressional Election

Edward Korry understood early on in his tenure as ambassador in Chile how important the congressional election of 1969 would be for the future of Chilean politics and, consequently, U.S. interests. In July 1968, Korry and the CIA requested of the 303 Committee, in charge of approving covert actions, that an operation aimed at influencing the outcome of the 1969 congressional election be authorized and funds made available for its implementation.[29] The operation proposed by Korry consisted of supporting a number of moderate candidates of the non-Marxist parties. The outcome of the 1969 election was especially important considering that, in all likelihood, Congress would have to choose the president for the 1970–1976 term among the two highest pluralities in the election scheduled for September 1970. Furthermore, the Congress elected in 1969—half of the Senate and the entire Chamber of Deputies—would serve during the first half of the administration of Frei's successor, so its composition was as important for the future of Chilean politics as the 1970 presidential election. Largely agreeing with Ambassador Korry's assessment of the situation, the 303 Committee gave its approval for the operation on 12 July 1968. Further down the road toward the election, the scope of the operation was expanded to include funding for anti-Marxist propaganda and a new movement that split from the PS in 1967, Raúl Ampuero's Popular Socialist Union.[30] Under another ongoing operation, the CIA was also providing funds for members of the PR, which would, in turn, suffer a split in mid-1969.[31]

The operation was carefully planned and tailored to the specific state of political affairs in Chile at the time. Korry, supported by the political staff of the embassy, and the CIA station in Santiago, decided the funding provided through the operation, which in the end amounted to about $175,000, could not be channeled directly to political parties. In the PDC, the PR, and the PN there were "extreme elements for whom support should not be provided," according to a CIA report issued a few days after the election. Both the PR and the PDC had left wings that, especially in the former case, seemed to be winning the upper hand in the intra-party competition for hegemony. Assisting the PR and the PDC in institutional terms, then, was out of the question. In the PN, on the other hand, some members leaned too far to the other side of the spectrum, although this was certainly less of a concern for those involved in the planning of the operation. Consequently, funding went directly to twelve individual candidates of the PR, the PDC, and the PN selected by a team of embassy political officers and CIA agents under the active leadership of Ambassador Korry.[32]

Besides the financial assistance given to individual candidates, the operation consisted of the creation of anti-communist propaganda and placement thereof in the media—a low-intensity reiteration of the anti-Allende "scare campaign" of 1964—and funding for the splinter USOPO, which presented candidates in a great number of districts. The money was channeled to USOPO through a Jewish businessman who explained his support for the party on the grounds that it had expressed its "moral support to Israel's right to existence" in opposition to the outright pro-Arab position taken by the PS since the 1967 war. The specific amount of money given to USOPO has not been disclosed, but, according to the CIA's final assessment of the operation, it covered about half the party's campaign costs. It is impossible to assert with total certainty that the main leader of the party, Raúl Ampuero, knew of this CIA support; however, considering how significant the amounts of money involved in this operation were, it is unlikely that their origin was entirely unknown to the recipients.[33]

The covert operation carried out by the embassy and the CIA to influence the outcome of the congressional election was quite successful. Of the twelve candidates whose campaigns were partly underwritten by U.S. money, ten were elected (five Christian Democrats, four Nationals, and one Radical), thus denying those seats in Congress to members of the Communist and Socialist parties. Support for USOPO also yielded positive results. Ampuero's party obtained a meager fifty-two thousand votes across the country, less than 3 percent of the national vote. However, it was enough to deny the PS six seats in the

Chamber of Deputies and one in the Senate. The CIA's final evaluation of the operation estimated that the PS could have won between twenty-six and thirty seats in the Congress if it had received the fifty-two thousand votes obtained by the USOPO candidates; as it was, the party got only nineteen.[34]

The victories of CIA-backed candidates in some specific races, however, were not enough to substantially alter the general balance and alignment of forces in the big picture of Chilean politics. The PDC lost its majority in the Chamber of Deputies, but it was still the strongest party in the lower chamber, with fifty-six seats. Socialists and Communists, still aligned in the FRAP, elected, together, thirty-seven deputies. The National Party, for its part, obtained thirty-three seats in the Chamber of Deputies, nine more than the Radical Party. As Frei, Korry, and others stated after the election, the political spectrum was divided into three big sections and there was little room for understandings and accommodations between them. Counter to Frei's preferences and U.S. interests, but very much in the way it was expected beforehand, the Marxist Left came out of the congressional election in a strong position toward 1970. The Right had also repositioned itself as a viable alternative for the race of the following year, especially because its most likely standard-bearer, Jorge Alessandri, still carried a great deal of popular support. The PDC had won the largest share of the vote and elected the most parliamentarians, but in comparison with the extraordinary results of the election of 1965, the congressional election looked like a setback to the party in government. Still, even though the Right showed a reckless optimism toward the immediate future, no one could at the time predict with solid certainty which way the 1970 presidential election would go.

The Chilean Political Landscape in 1970

As events unfolded, the presidential election of 1970 became even more crucial than the election of 1964. Although the Frei administration's record showed many significant achievements (the "Chileanization" and subsequent negotiated nationalization of copper, a meaningful agrarian reform, a substantial expansion of elementary and secondary education, multiple housing programs, and a relatively healthy fiscal situation, among others), the PDC did not manage to build a base of popular support large enough to assure it a new victory in 1970. The PDC was still the party with the largest electoral following but, as the Christian Democrats refused to enter any coalitions with other political movements, that base was the only support they could surely count on. Furthermore, the presidential candidate of the party, Radomiro Tomic, distanced himself from Frei on a number of matters, the most important being the negotiated nationalization of copper. Tomic dreamed of becoming the candidate not only of the PDC but of all the forces of the Left, including Communists and Socialists. Although Tomic outwardly stood by the record of the Frei administration, in actuality his stance as presidential candidate meant a disavowal of the reformist character of the Christian Democratic program. The personal support enjoyed by Frei, widely believed to be larger than the electoral support gained by his party in the 1969 congressional elections, could not be passed on to Tomic.

Tomic's position entailed a significant challenge to the ability of the PDC to act as a thoroughly unified movement, but it did not prompt any organizational reshuffle. Toward the end of the Frei administration, however, the party did suffer a schism as a consequence of the position taken by its left wing, the so-called *rebeldes*. In mid-1969, a number of left-wing Christian Democrats, discontent with the tone and the pace of the reforms implemented by the Frei administration, bolted from the party and founded a new political movement, the Unitarian Popular Action Movement. The new party, small by any quantitative measure, included some of the brightest young politicians of the time and soon became an important force in Chilean politics. In late 1969, MAPU joined the leftist coalition, which in an ironic twist of history had adopted the name Popular Unity (UP). MAPU did not have any real leverage within the alliance. Nevertheless, as a party of intellectuals rather than political operatives, it became a powerful voice for the cause of the Left and contributed to the expansion of the coalition's ideological scope.[35]

The PR, after purging some of its most conservative members, also joined the left-wing coalition in 1969. The Radicals had done poorly in the 1969 parliamentarian elections and had endured a split because of this turn to the left. Some prominent leaders, Julio Durán among them, had founded a new party after being expelled from the Radical Party. The new movement, Radical Democracy (DR), received financial support from the CIA during the critical months in which the organization had to gather the ten thousand signatures required by Chilean law to establish formally as a party.[36] DR supported the right-wing candidate Jorge Alessandri in the 1970 presidential election, joined the opposition to Allende, and survived until the 1973 coup, but it did not drain many militants from the PR. Nevertheless, the PR that joined UP in 1969 was not the strong—even hegemonic—middle-class party that had been the key actor in Chilean politics for decades. Its role in the coalition would be, therefore, secondary to the axis of Communists and Socialists that constituted the ideological core and the organizational backbone of UP. The presence of the PR, however, did allow UP to claim that it was not an exclusively Marxist coalition but, instead, a broad-based alliance of left-wing forces.

The enlargement of the left-wing coalition in 1969 posed some problems for the nomination of the UP's candidate for the 1970 presidential election. The left-wing Radicals who promoted their party's joining the coalition of Socialists and Communists were pushing for the candidacy of Senator Alberto Baltra, an economist whose ideas were very close to Marxism. MAPU, for its part, presented Jacques Chonchol, one of the main designers of Frei's agrarian reform, as their own prospective candidate. Even the founder and leader of tiny Independent Popular Action (API), Rafael Tarud, was actively, openly, and somewhat bizarrely pursuing the dream of becoming the presidential candidate of the Left.[37]

Within the PS, the process of choosing a candidate did not go as smoothly as appearances may have indicated. Even though Allende performed very well in his senatorial race, and was undoubtedly the most popular leftist politician in the country, his three failed previous presidential bids were an undeniable handicap for his aspirations. As a result, Allende did not have much support among his fellow Socialist cadres. The Central Committee of the PS nominated Allende as the candidate of the party in August 1969 in a split decision: thirteen members voted for him, while the remaining fourteen—heavyweights such as Clodomiro Almeyda and Carlos Altamirano among them—preferred to abstain.[38]

The Communist Party, for its part, presented famed poet Pablo Neruda as its candidate for the 1970 presidential election. This proposition, however, was only a shrewd move by the Communists aimed at strengthening their bargaining position and, thus, gaining the ability to impose their truly preferred candidate, Salvador Allende. Neruda, an obedient but sensitive Communist, played dutifully his assigned role in the scheme; however, he harbored many doubts as to the wisdom of the strategy of the Left and expressed to some of his political acquaintances that, in his view, Frei's Foreign Minister Gabriel Valdés should run as the candidate of a broad coalition including Communists, Socialists, and Christian Democrats.[39] It may be that Neruda's idea was seriously considered early on by the Communists if Korry's reports to the Department of State are to be believed. According to a retrospective account by the ambassador, based on multiple sources, in 1968 Communist Senator Volodia Teitelboim discreetly probed Valdés' willingness to run as the candidate of a broad progressive coalition that would include all the major forces of the political spectrum except the National Party.[40] As per Korry's account, Valdés may have seriously considered the Communists' presumptive offer, which certainly did not help improve the already poor opinion of Frei's foreign minister held by the temperamental U.S. ambassador.

In the end, the strategy favored by the Communists prevailed within UP, which nominated Allende as its candidate in January 1970. The Left could feel reasonably optimistic as to the chances of its standard-bearer in a three-way election. Adding up the electoral support of all the parties comprising the coalition, UP could realistically expect to get over one-third of the popular vote. This was far from the majority obtained by Frei in 1964 in what, for all practical purposes, was a two-way race but close to the plurality that yielded Jorge Alessandri the presidency in a more populated contest in 1958. This time, no single candidate was expected to get a majority of the vote. Furthermore, as the precedents of 1946, 1952, and 1958 had shown, the victor in the popular election had the upper hand in the runoff in Congress. Winning on 4 September might be all Allende needed to become, after three failed attempts, president of the Republic of Chile.

The Right, which had recovered much of its electoral strength after the foundation of the PN in 1966, would present its own candidate: former President Jorge Alessandri, a man whose personal popularity was at the time matched only by Frei's (and maybe Allende's). According to the few polls conducted in the months before the election, the conservative candidate had the lead in the race.[41] The expectation of victory, founded on the results of polls conducted mainly in Santiago, ended up being a curse for the Right and all the forces opposed to the Left. In March, the Right rejected almost instantly a constitutional amendment proposed by MAPU providing for a second round if no candidate obtained a majority in a presidential election.

It must be noted, however, that the PDC and the major parties of UP also rejected such a possibility, as they all understood that their own candidate's best chance lay on the parliamentarian runoff prescribed by the constitution.[42] In July, Alessandri asserted publicly that if the election went to Congress, the candidate with the highest vote in the popular election should be elected president.[43] Alessandri's statement bespoke a shortsightedness that would severely affect his standing after Allende's triumph on 4 September. If the Right and its candidate drew any lessons from the Naranjazo, the by-election that shocked the Chilean political landscape in the early stages of the 1964 presidential race, the acquired knowledge and experience did not show at all in their conduct of the 1970 campaign.

Chapter 7

The United States and the Presidential Election of 1970

Paradoxically, Chile was an emblematic Cold War battlefield on account of the uniqueness of its political system and culture. In few other countries in the world was the competition between Marxism and anti-Marxism so evenly matched and maintained through the means provided by the institutions and the political culture of an open society.[1] While other countries and regions of the world had endured or were enduring turmoil, violence, and destruction because of the ideological and geopolitical conflicts of the Cold War, political divides in Chile had, in general, remained within the limits set by the institutional framework.[2] Consequently, as the Marxist Left had a good chance of winning, the 1970 election stood as a rare opportunity for a nation to head toward socialism by freely choosing an avowedly Marxist leader and an explicitly revolutionary project—albeit not one to be thoroughly implemented in the course of one presidential term.[3]

The implications of such a choice, everyone understood, were enormous. From the viewpoint of Allende and the Left, the so-called "Chilean road to Socialism" would eventually lead to a thorough renovation of Chile's political framework and economic system and realize the goals of social justice long sought by the parties representing the true interests of the working class. From the viewpoint of anti-Marxist sensibilities, especially in the Christian Democratic Party, a government of Popular Unity could transform Chile's fine democracy into an authoritarian or dictatorial system like those of Cuba or Eastern Europe. Furthermore, on its way toward that goal, an Allende government could wreck Chile's economy and would certainly further the process of political polarization underway since at least the 1964 election.

On the international scene, an Allende victory would also have profound repercussions. If socialism, as understood by the Marxist Left in Chile and elsewhere, were to be successfully implemented through the means offered by the electoral politics of a democratic system, revolutionary projects of the same vein would gain new vigor and legitimacy in many other places in the world. This was especially true for the Southern Cone, where only Chile and Uruguay remained under democratic governments and the military dictatorships of Brazil, Argentina, and Paraguay professed militant anti-communism. In European countries such as France and Italy, where political alignments closely resembled Chile's, a victory of UP in the 1970 election would most certainly give new impetus to the already vigorous local Communist parties.[4] In the larger scheme of international Cold War politics, the victory of a Marxist revolutionary project in Chile was bound to challenge U.S. hegemony in the Americas and, thus, upset the geopolitical balance of the Cold War. As Richard Nixon himself put it in his memoirs, a government of the Left in Chile along with the revolutionary regime in Cuba would envelope the whole of Latin America in a "red sandwich."[5]

Even though the metaphor is wildly exaggerated, it shows the extent of the preoccupation of the United States with the possible regional effects of an Allende government in Chile. Finally, and more important from the point of view of the United States, a victory of the Chilean Left's revolutionary project through electoral means called into question the conventional narrative on the incompatibility between revolution and democracy underlying the ideological position of the opponents of communism in the context of world politics. In sum, an Allende victory in the presidential election of 1970 would be a huge triumph for the cause of world revolution and, consequently, a crushing blow for the standing of the United States in the global Cold War.

The Nixon Administration and Allende's Chances

Unlike the election of 1964, the United States did not throw its support behind any candidate in 1970. The Nixon administration did not want to embrace a political project in the same way the Johnson administration had in 1964 under the spirit of the Alliance for Progress and the choice in this case was not self-evident. Tomic did not seem to have a real chance to win or even to get the second highest vote. In addition, his position did not differ significantly from

that of the Left on many matters, and his personality and somewhat demagogic style made U.S. diplomats and policymakers—many of whom knew
him from his time in Washington—uncomfortable. Korry, as has been shown,
had no sympathy whatsoever for the PDC candidate. Still, some policymakers
in Washington thought it would be wise for the United States to support his
campaign through the same kind of covert operations that had been used to
help Frei in 1964.[6]

The Alessandri candidacy, on the other hand, seemed the best card in the
anti-Allende game. Not only did the right-wing candidate have a strong
popular following and the backing of powerful industrial, commercial, and
landed elites in Chile, he also enjoyed the active support of influential U.S.
businessmen. Charles Jay Parker, head of the copper giant Anaconda, asked
Assistant Secretary of State for Inter-American Affairs Charles Meyer to have
the United States provide funds for the Alessandri campaign or else it would
be the end of private enterprise in Chile and the Nixon administration would
have to confront a "Castroite situation."[7] Of course, Anaconda and other U.S.
corporations with interests in Chile, ITT among them, supported the Alessandri campaign regardless of the attitude taken by the Nixon administration.[8]

Alessandri, however, represented a political project to which some important U.S. diplomats involved in Chile, especially Edward Korry, were unsym-
pathetic. The ambassador advised explicitly against support for Alessandri. A
victory of the right-wing candidate—a man who exuded "all the warmth of an
Easter Island Moai monolith," according to Korry's unflattering description—
could polarize Chilean politics and society even further, thus opening the way
to an even more delicate and volatile situation.[9] The usefulness of any help
coming from the U.S. government was questionable, too. Since the conservative candidate seemed to be leading anyway, it was doubtful that U.S. financial
aid would make a significant difference. Conversely, if such aid became
known, it would do more harm than good to the anti-Allende cause.

Furthermore, since Alessandri was the candidate of the entrepreneurial
class, he could certainly run a generously funded campaign without U.S. monetary help. As Korry put it, "one thousand Chileans each donating one thousand dollars could supply [$1 million] without any contribution from any US
quarter." Since the wealthier Chileans were not supporting the Alessandri campaign as generously as they could and, on the contrary, were shipping money
abroad, the U.S. ambassador saw no reason for the United States to step up and
fill in for them. Korry argued against the prospect of the U.S. government
funding the Alessandri campaign as "the very antithesis of what I understand to
be the Nixon Doctrine."[10]

Without support for any of the candidates in competition, the U.S. strategy for the 1970 Chilean election focused on courses of action exclusively aimed to oppose Allende. The plan, as approved by the 40 Committee (formerly the 303 Committee), contemplated two stages. Phase I consisted of the creation of anti-Allende propaganda and support for Chilean groups dedicated to the same task, in a reiteration of the tactics used in 1964 in the so-called "scare campaign."[11] Phase II was a two-legged operation to be carried out in the interlude between the popular election of 4 September and the runoff in Congress scheduled for 24 October, in case the Socialist candidate advanced to that stage of the electoral process. The first part of the operation was a continuation of the anti-Allende propaganda campaign; under the second part of the plan, the CIA would dispose of money to pay Radical and maybe some Christian Democratic members of Congress so that they would cast their votes for Alessandri—or Tomic, in the least likely scenario—in the presumed runoff against Allende.[12] Phase II of the plan, however, was conceived under the conviction, firmly espoused by Korry, that Alessandri would finish first, ahead of Allende.[13] The prospect of a sizeable number of PDC members of Congress voting for Allende in the runoff, even if the Socialist candidate finished second in the popular election, was quite plausible, especially if the margin of an Alessandri victory was short. Consequently, some sort of financial persuasion could be necessary to make sure Alessandri obtained enough votes in Congress to assure his election.[14]

Polls conducted in Santiago in early 1970 showed Jorge Alessandri ahead, and the general impression was that the former president would win a plurality in the election scheduled for 4 September. That outcome, however, might not result in his election as president. Despite the much-vaunted tradition of Congress choosing the first plurality if no candidate won a majority of the vote in the popular election, the composition of the Chilean parliament at the time could allow for an alignment of forces favorable for either Allende or Tomic in an eventual runoff election. In March 1970, as the campaign was starting to intensify, Korry reported from Santiago that UP had a more than even chance to get its candidate elected—much higher than in 1964, for instance. Should Allende finish second in the popular election by a margin less than 5 percent behind Alessandri, Korry reasoned, it was conceivable that the PDC could splinter along the ideological lines that had divided the party in previous years. Given the correlation of forces in Congress, Allende would need only twenty Christian Democratic votes to win.[15] The scenario of Allende becoming president of Chile even without winning the popular election, a nightmarish prospect for the U.S. foreign policy apparatus, seemed plausible.

Other signals gave the Left reason for moderate optimism. The military leadership, especially in the army, had no intention of intervening to overturn the result of the election—whatever the result. The head of the army, General René Schneider, had been appointed by President Frei in the wake of the Tacnazo in October 1969, and his was an agreeable choice for the officers behind the mutiny. For the U.S. officials who met him, however, Schneider clearly stood out among his colleagues. Political officer Harry Shlaudeman thought Schneider was "an impressive cut above his predecessor [General Sergio Castillo] in terms of personal style," mostly on account of the fact that he was "cultivated, broad-gauged and intelligent."[16]

In another report, Shlaudeman described the Chilean general as a man with a "range of interests and a degree of tolerance unusual for a Latin American military officer." Such interests included, for example, modern literature, especially the works of writers such as Julio Cortázar and Mario Vargas Llosa, for they portrayed "very well the social ambient in Latin America."[17] Ambassador Korry himself considered Schneider an "astonishingly urbane and cultivated gentleman."[18] To be sure, the opinions of Shlaudeman and Korry reflected not only a high regard for Schneider but also a thinly veiled contempt for the Latin American and, more specifically, the Chilean military. Nevertheless, the contrast between Schneider and his colleagues gave the head of the Chilean army a degree of respectability among his U.S. interlocutors that few other officers enjoyed at the time.

Schneider, indeed, seemed to be a different kind of army officer. Unlike many of his colleagues in Chile and Latin America, he did not espouse rabidly anti-communist views. Furthermore, he thought the military should stay out of politics and be content with carrying out their constitutional duties. In May, Schneider stated publicly that the army would not intervene in the political process should Congress have to elect the new president.[19] One of the implications of that assertion was that the military would not prevent an Allende presidency if the Socialist candidate won the election in Congress. Historian Joaquín Fermandois has noted that, for all its republican zeal, Schneider's announcement was a reaffirmation of what was, indeed, a basic constitutional obligation for the armed forces. The fact that the highest military authority in the country felt he had to make such a statement was a sign that things were not entirely quiet within the army.[20] Nevertheless, Schneider's assertion contributed to the development of an electoral process situated within the norms of the institutional framework established by the constitution and without the shadow of a looming military intervention. For Allende and the Left, along with the fact that the election pitted three relatively even forces, this setting was the best scenario they could expect.

Notwithstanding Schneider's assurances, rumors of military intervention and other schemes to avoid an Allende victory circulated profusely in the months and weeks before the election. As it became increasingly clear that Tomic would finish third, the PDC parliamentarians would in all certainty decide the final result of the election. Considering the ideological divide then bedeviling the PDC, Allende's way toward La Moneda might well remain open even in case of an Alessandri win on 4 September. Enough PDC parliamentarians could choose to vote for the Socialist leader in the runoff in Congress even if he finished second in the popular vote. A less likely but still plausible scenario was an Allende victory at the polls. In that case, few PDC parliamentarians would be willing to vote for Alessandri in the runoff, making an Allende final victory all but secure. Frei, aware of this situation, apparently told some people weeks before the election that if Allende or Tomic won a plurality the military would stage a coup. The U.S. embassy in Santiago, with input of well-connected Defense Attaché Paul Wimert, had reached the conclusion that the heads of the navy, the air force, and the Carabineros (Fernando Porta, Carlos Guerraty, and Vicente Huerta, respectively), as well as army generals Carlos Prats and Camilo Valenzuela, were "opposed to the idea of an Allende government," but it was doubtful that they would autonomously decide to intervene to stop the electoral process. Frei, however, did not indicate that he would lead an unconstitutional movement to stop Allende.[21]

President of the Senate Tomás Pablo, a staunchly anti-Marxist Christian Democrat, thought about a different way to stop Allende in case the left-wing candidate won the election of 4 September over his right-wing opponent and, unsurprisingly, spoke frankly about it with Korry. According to Pablo's scheme, Congress could elect Alessandri even if he finished second in the popular vote. The right-wing candidate, who had stated during the race that the winner of the popular election should be the next president, would deliver on that vow by resigning, thus paving the way for a new election. In this new electoral contest, Frei, supported by the PDC and the Right, would win handily. Although Pablo's plan was perfectly legal, it would run against the precedent set by the presidential elections of 1946, 1952, and 1958 and would be viewed by the Left, not without reason, as an illegitimate maneuver meant to deprive the winner of the popular election of what he rightfully deserved.

Consequently, the PDC senator understood that the move would not succeed without the full backing of the armed forces, especially the army. Pablo's purpose in discussing his ideas about the election with Korry was to ask for the help of the embassy in persuading the Chilean military to go along with the scheme if the situation reached that point. Korry, without being too committal, assured the president of the Senate that he was convinced the election of Allende would result in the establishment, sooner rather than later, of a Marxist-Leninist state in Chile. Although no specific commitments were made, Korry's strong words successfully carried the message of support that Pablo was looking for and the ambassador could not express openly.[22]

After 4 September, the scheme discussed between Pablo and Korry on 9 August became the only constitutional way to block Allende's road toward the presidency, and Alessandri embraced it a few days after the election. It is very likely—although impossible to assert with certainty—that there was a direct link between Alessandri's decision to remain in the race after Allende's victory at the polls and Pablo's conception and discussion of the idea in the weeks prior to the election. In any case, the circulation of rumors of a coup in case of a UP victory, voiced by none other than President Frei, and the discussion between Pablo and Korry of a scheme devised to deny Allende the presidency clearly illustrate the extent to which the prospect of a government of the Left frightened some important political and military actors in Chile. Whatever the results of the election, the fifty-day period between 4 September and the runoff in Congress, scheduled for 24 October, was bound to be tense. Despite Schneider's explicit assurances, as Election Day approached the shadow of an institutional crisis loomed ever larger over the horizon.

"An Irreversible Road"

On the eve of the presidential election of 4 September 1970, Ambassador Korry and Frei met at the house of Raúl Troncoso, one of the president's closest men in the cabinet. Frei's mood was bleak. Radomiro Tomic, the candidate of his party, offered a road that diverted significantly from the project he had tried to realize during his tenure. The two Christian Democratic stalwarts, formerly close friends, had grown apart in the past two years as a result of the deep chasm between their ideological visions and strategies. Frei, however, still thought Tomic offered a better prospect for the country than either of the other two choices the Chilean people had before them. According to the much anguished president, an Alessandri government would further the polarization of Chilean politics and would push the PDC to the left; an Allende government, on the other hand, would set Chile on an "irreversible road" toward the imposition of a Marxist-Leninist state and it would spell "the end for Chile . . . for him [Frei] and for everything he had labored." If Tomic were to finish third, Frei thought, "it would be universally interpreted as a rejection of all that he

Figure 10. President Frei and German Chancellor Willy Brandt walking through the streets of downtown Santiago, followed by a large and respectful crowd, in 1968. Frei's positive international standing stemmed to a large extent from the favorable image projected abroad by Chilean democracy. *Courtesy of Archivo Histórico Gabriel Valdés—D&D Consultores, http://www.ahgv.cl.*

and his government had sought to accomplish." The likelihood of such an outcome, ever higher as election day approached, deeply saddened and baffled Frei. He had received only positive comments "from all over the non-Leninist world . . . from countries as different as Yugoslavia and Japan, Israel and France, Spain and the United States, West Germany, Britain, Italy and all the others. How could anyone explain that good government and personal popularity resulted in such a defeat and in such frightening perspectives for the country?"[23]

The results of the election matched Frei's and Korry's worst nightmares— and gave the lie to the ambassador's optimistic prediction (see Table 4). Allende won a plurality of the vote (1,070,334; 36.2 percent), slightly ahead of Alessandri (1,031,159; 34.9 percent). Tomic obtained a little less than 28 percent of the vote, two points below the mark set by the PDC in the 1969 congressional election.[24] Popular Unity wasted no time and proclaimed Allende president the same night of the popular election, even though the final vote in Congress would take place seven weeks later. Allende's victory shook the Chilean politi-

Table 4. Presidential Election of 1970

Candidate	Votes	Percent
Salvador Allende (UP)	1,070,334	36.2
Jorge Alessandri (Independent, PN-backed)	1,031,159	34.9
Radomiro Tomic (PDC)	821,801	27.8
Invalid votes	31,505	1.1
Total	2,954,799	100

Source: Nohlen (editor), *Elections in the Americas*, p. 287.

cal environment to its core and sent shockwaves through the Americas all the way to Washington. As it was abundantly reported worldwide in the days after 4 September, for the first time in history an avowedly Marxist politician had won a free, competitive election for the post of head of state or government.[25]

The day after Allende's victory, Korry duly sent a lengthy report on the political situation in Chile. Korry's words betrayed his deeply felt frustration at the results of the election and a pessimism about the future of the country that closely mirrored Frei's. "Chile voted calmly to have a Marxist-Leninist state, the first nation in the world to make this choice freely and knowingly," informed Korry, echoing the headline of most reports about the election then circulating throughout the world. While he extolled the Chilean Communist Party's strategic skills, Korry complained bitterly about the way the PDC, especially Foreign Minister Gabriel Valdés, had handled things throughout the year. Just as Valdés, "no. 1 grave-digger of Chilean democracy," had chosen to appease Castro in the international scene, the PDC had "ceded on every issue . . . to the PC and the Socialists" and had foolishly "played the card of anti-Americanism." Once again showing his tendency to conflate political views with personal feelings, Korry ended his tirade against the Christian Democrats who had supposedly chosen to go soft on the Left with the damning recommendation that "they should be given neither sympathy nor salvation." No more sympathy was deserved by the Chilean Right, which had "blindly and greedily pursued its interests," and had "preached vengeance against the Christian Democrats whom they regarded as a more justifiable enemy because of its betrayal of class than their class enemy, the Communists."[26]

Korry's emotional and personal tone notwithstanding, his concerns about the future of Chilean institutions were as genuine as Frei's. The U.S. ambassador could not entertain the idea that Allende and his coalition pursued a form of socialism that differed significantly from the socialism practiced in Cuba or Eastern Europe. In this regard, Korry's fears did not relate exclusively to the strategic interests of the United States in the context of the Cold War. After all, those interests stemmed to a large extent from an ideology founded on the conviction that liberal democracy is the best system of political and societal organization. The ambassador, in many ways an archetypical Cold War liberal, held Chilean democracy in the highest esteem because it represented quite faithfully the founding principle of the U.S. ideology. Thus, it is only logical that Korry identified the U.S. interests in Chile with the maintenance of the institutional democratic order in which Chileans used to pride themselves.[27]

The political project of the Marxist Left ran against the most basic tenets of such an order. In fact, even though Allende and his followers carefully avoided explicit calls for a rapid revolutionary transformation throughout the presidential race, Communists and Socialists—and Allende himself—had always been frank about their final goal, a socialist order and, in their political discourse, references to Chilean democracy were usually accompanied by derisive adjectives such as "formal" or "bourgeois." Furthermore, they had consistently refused to condemn Cuba or the Eastern European regimes as dictatorial and even looked to them admiringly.

Not only did the Chilean Left pursue a goal that would entail the destruction of Chilean democracy, according to Korry's and Frei's assessment, but, more worrying, they had a good chance of reaching their ultimate goal. In the wake of Allende's victory on 4 September, the ambassador presented the State Department with a list of ten reasons why Chile offered a unique setting for the establishment of a communist state without resort to violence. From the strong power the president enjoyed under the Chilean constitution to the weakness of the Right and its main press outlet, El Mercurio, through the fact that "no [other] country on Earth [was] so far from the two superpowers and Red China," conditions seemed to be favorable for the realization of the Marxist Left's project for Chile.[28]

A Threat to Chilean Democracy?

The Chilean Communist and Socialist parties officially adhered to Marxist ideology. Consequently, most of their members subscribed to the conventional Marxist teleological vision of history and its derived epistemology, albeit applied to the reality of an underdeveloped country like Chile. This is especially true of the elites that occupied positions of leadership in both parties. These elites, however, responded to grassroots party members and larger electoral constituencies that, even though sympathizing with the Left, its ideology, and its program, did not necessarily share the most elaborated and theoretical views of those in positions of political leadership. Most of the Left's popular support came from working class men and women who wanted a better, more comfortable life experience, especially in a concrete, material sense. Arguably, for most of the Left's voters, socialism was the best way to improve their lot as rapidly as possible.[29]

That socialism, as practiced in all the countries in the world to which the Chilean Left looked admiringly, entailed not only a state-run economy and universally guaranteed social rights but also the effective suppression of most political rights and the ruthless crushing of dissent, was probably not fully grasped by most of the Marxist Left's constituents. Furthermore, when the opponents of the Left pointed to the harsh reality of socialist countries elsewhere, Communists and Socialists responded by pointing to the profound and shameful inequalities that still characterized Chile's social order. From the perspective of the left-wing parties and many of their followers, the abysmal injustices of Chilean capitalism—dominated by a small oligarchy whose interests converged with those of U.S. imperialism—stripped the political and civil rights guaranteed by Chile's "bourgeois democracy" of much of their substance. The question of the supposed incompatibility between a Marxist revolutionary project and the institutions and political culture of Chilean democracy was simply not as important to the parties and the following of the Left as it was for many of its opponents.

Along with the ideological convictions of Communists and Socialists, an issue that greatly concerned the opponents of the Left and reinforced their misgivings about the possibility of an Allende victory both in 1964 and 1970 was the position taken by Chilean Communists on the international Cold War divide. The PC held the Soviet Union as the true leader of world revolution, and its members never made any attempt to conceal their admiration for the way the leaders of the Communist Party of the Soviet Union handled matters both domestically and internationally. One of the most shocking instances of such devotion was the reaction of the PC to the invasion of Czechoslovakia carried out by troops of the Warsaw Pact in 1968. On 21 August 1968, the Orwellian main headline in the front page of El Siglo, the party newspaper, read: "Czechoslovakia requested armed help from Socialist countries."[30] For those who opposed Marxism out of an ideological commitment to the practice of liberal democracy, the attitude taken by the Chilean PC toward the sad ending of the Prague Spring should have proved conclusively to the Chilean people the inherently anti-democratic nature of the Left's political project.

It would not be so. Even though the Communists certainly did not project a kind image in the wake of the Soviet invasion of Czechoslovakia, especially as the Socialists took a more critical position toward the issue, in the congressional elections of March 1969 the PC reached the peak of its electoral performance. For many of those who supported the Left's radical platform of social and economic change, events occurring elsewhere could always be rationalized into a sufficiently acceptable narrative of Cold War politics; for most of them, the realities of faraway places simply did not have a perceivable impact on their own experiences and, consequently, were not a major factor in their political choices.

The Socialist Party had, in general, shown a more independent attitude with regard to international affairs. One of the main issues addressed in the 1962 public exchange of letters between Raúl Ampuero and Luis Corvalán, secretary general of the PC, was the role of the Soviet Union in the international revolutionary movement. For the PC, the Soviet Union was the "center" or "vanguard" of world revolution; the PS rejected such a notion outright.[31] This defiant attitude toward what Ampuero caustically called "ideological Vaticans" did not imply, however, major disagreements between the PS and the PC over the proper features of a socialist system.[32] For both parties, especially at the grassroots level, socialism meant fundamentally an economy run by the state—the only effective way to end Chile's oligarchical order—and universally guaranteed social rights. As has been said, the question of why socialism in Chile would not adopt the authoritarian character it had elsewhere was left largely unaddressed, partly because it was strategically convenient but mostly because the issue was not as pressing for the Left's constituencies as it was for politicians of other persuasions.

The Marxist Left historically had acted within the limits set by the institutions of Chilean democracy. For Communists and Socialists, such behavior—finely exemplified by Salvador Allende's long career—proved their commitment to the institutions and political culture of Chilean democracy better than any statement of principles. Furthermore, the Communists could argue that they had disavowed violence even while banned from legal politics between 1948 and 1958. Nevertheless, by the mid-1960s many in the higher echelons of the PS, certainly influenced by the experience of successful anti-colonial or left-leaning revolutions in other Third World countries such as Vietnam, Cuba, and Algeria, had reached the conviction that violence was eventually inevitable in the unfolding of the revolutionary process. This view was even recognized as the official party line in 1967.[33] Although the adoption of this plank was not followed by an equally radical change in party strategy, the open rejection of the institutional and peaceful channels for incremental change offered by the constitutional order could not but reinforce the fears of those who loathed the prospect of violence and feared for the survival of Chilean democracy under a government headed by the alliance of Communists and Socialists.

Yet for all the ideological and rhetorical polarization of Chilean politics, a cold analysis of the general situation in 1970 should have shown to anyone that a revolutionary takeover and a thorough transformation of Chilean society from the springboard offered by government was, to say the least, improbable. Neither the PC nor the PS, in spite of the heated rhetoric of many of the latter's leaders, had the material and human resources necessary for the successful realization of a violent revolution. Even the Revolutionary Left Movement (MIR), the only significant political organization that explicitly stood out of electoral politics, made an eleventh-hour call to vote for Allende in the 1970 presidential election. Furthermore, it was very unlikely that, in the absence of a foreign threat, a government of the Left could coopt the armed forces and turn them into an instrument for the eventual establishment of a socialist system. Even though there was a tradition of left-leaning nationalism within the army going back to the military movements of the 1920s, the officer corps in all branches of the armed forces was, as was typical among the Latin American military, averse to Marxism.[34] Moreover, the Chilean armed forces were highly dependent on U.S. supplies, so high-rank officers in all the branches of the military were naturally reluctant to support a project that could risk the material standing of their institutions. In sum, the odds for a complete seizure of power by a government of the Left and, hence, a thorough transformation of the country into a socialist state were decidedly low.

The structural and circumstantial reality of the country in 1970 did not seem to amount to a pre-revolutionary situation either. After all, Chile in 1970 was neither Cuba in 1959 nor Czechoslovakia in 1948—the two models of successful revolutions most frequently pointed out by the opponents of the Marxist Left. No Chilean politician aspired to be what Castro had become for Cuba, even though many admired the Cuban revolutionary leader and the system he and his followers had put in place since their victory in 1959.[35] More important, Chile's democratic system offered an institutional way for change that a majority of the population, even many of those who most radically criticized it, considered legitimate. Chile in 1970 had probably more in common with post-World War II Italy than with Fulgencio Batista's Cuba. And although the Chilean political system was populated by plenty of politicians of the Masaryk type and the Chilean PC was, indeed, pursuing a truly revolutionary program through institutional means, Chile had not suffered the material consequences of the bloodiest war in history, and no Red Army was stationed near the country. The differences between Chile's reality in 1970 and the historic situations in which communist revolutions had succeeded—Russia, Eastern Europe, Yugoslavia, China, North Vietnam, Cuba—were too many and too significant. Contrary to the historic interpretations of the most fervent ideological opponents of the Marxist Left, the experience of the successful communist revolutions of the twentieth century showed that the situation in Chile in 1970 was not propitious for a swift and thorough transformation of the country into a socialist state.

Frei, Korry, and other civilian and military opponents of the Left were certainly far off the mark in believing that Allende and his coalition would be able to turn Chile into a socialist state in the course of a presidential term and, possibly, even in their apocalyptic certainty that they would be able to successfully carry out their project at all. This is not to say that their philosophical understanding of the Chilean Left's ultimate goals was mistaken. Chilean Communists and Socialists were fervently committed to a revolutionary transformation of Chilean society and institutions. They embraced the ideas of Cold War Marxism, albeit in different ways, and looked to countries such as Cuba, East Germany, Yugoslavia, and the Soviet Union as models for the organization of the economy, social relations, and political institutions. On an academic level, Frei and Korry were right. On the more significant political level, they were betrayed by their fear. Communists and Socialists had made great efforts to adjust their strategies to the institutional framework of Chilean politics and sought to accomplish their short- and long-term objectives through lawful means.

Unlike many other countries in the world, Chile did not experience situations of violence as a consequence of the revolutionary pursuits of the Marxist parties and organizations. The PC and PS had become regular and normal participants of the electoral game of Chilean politics, and their leaders gained prominence and respectability before public opinion just like politicians of all the other persuasions. Furthermore, the situation in Chile, especially regarding the military, was not favorable for a complete revolutionary takeover. Last but not least, no foreign power was willing to sustain with its economic prowess or its military muscle the establishment of a socialist system. A UP government, although a significant challenge, was not a mortal threat for Chilean democracy—precisely because Chile's was an advanced democracy. Unfortunately, Frei's and Korry's worst and decidedly exaggerated fears, echoed by many in the Americas and Europe, led them to reach the conviction that an Allende government would spell the end of the Chilean institutional order as it had existed under the Constitution of 1925 and, consequently, it was necessary to act to avoid such an outcome.

Chapter 8

Eduardo Frei, the U.S. Embassy, and the Election of Salvador Allende

The Nixon administration, after choosing not to involve itself in the 1970 presidential race to the extent the Johnson administration had in the 1964 election, reacted with great alacrity to Allende's victory in the popular election of 4 September.[1] The prospect of a government headed by a coalition of avowedly Marxist parties with ideological and sentimental ties to Cuba was utterly unacceptable for Nixon, as it probably would have been for any Cold War U.S. president. On 15 September, Richard Nixon himself instructed CIA director Richard Helms to conduct covert operations in Chile, behind Ambassador Korry's back, to prevent Allende from attaining the presidency.[2] The story of those operations, whose only tangible consequence was the death of the commander in chief of the Chilean army, René Schneider, has been widely treated in reports issued by the U.S. Congress in the 1970s and by numerous scholars and other authors, so it will not be reiterated here.[3]

The covert operations carried out by the CIA without informing the ambassador, however, were not the only efforts against Allende in the weeks before the runoff election of 24 October. Chilean politicians, particularly Christian Democrats of the Frei line, tried or at least explored, ways of averting an Allende victory and sought for that purpose the support of the U.S. embassy in Santiago. Korry's correspondence with the State Department and the White House, a good deal of which has been recently published in the *Foreign Relations of the United States* series, shows the dejected mood that took over President Frei and some of his closest advisers in the days and weeks after the 4 September election and the courses of action they considered to block an Allende presidency.[4] Though many of the documents that tell this part of the story have been available to researchers since at least the early 2000s, only one scholarly work has treated these attempts by Chilean politicians, especially Eduardo Frei, in depth.[5] This lack of attention can be partially explained by the character of the covert operations carried out by the CIA at the same time. The dramatic consequences of these operations and the particulars of the decision-making process that spawned them, with the added seasoning of Nixon's and Kissinger's style of foreign policymaking, have overshadowed almost every other development that was unfolding simultaneously. In addition, the tendency of scholars of U.S. foreign relations during the Cold War to assume rather un-critically that the only decisions that mattered were taken in Washington has narrowed the perspectives from which the history of Cold War Chilean politics has been studied and interpreted—especially, but not exclusively, in the Anglo-Saxon world.

Waiting for Alessandri

Since no candidate reached a majority in the popular election and Congress had to choose between the two highest votes, the constitutional path still of-fered an opportunity for those who loathed the prospect of a Popular Unity government. If enough Christian Democratic and Radical members of Con-gress could be persuaded to vote for Alessandri in the runoff, the former presi-dent (Alessandri served from 1958 into 1964) could return to La Moneda in a perfectly constitutional manner. Though the formal legitimacy of such an op-tion was unquestionable, in substance, the election of Alessandri would have dealt a serious blow to Chilean democracy. Alessandri had forcefully asserted during the campaign that the winner at the polls should become president.[6] His election in Congress would have been a flagrant betrayal of those words. In ad-dition, even though there were only three precedents, the election of the largest plurality in the popular vote had become something of a tradition in Chilean politics. Alessandri himself had been elected president in 1958 after receiving only 31 percent of the votes cast.[7]

If Congress elected Alessandri on 24 October, Allende and the Left would have felt cheated out of what they had fairly earned. The Socialist and Com-munist parties, although devoted to the realization of a revolutionary project, had always acted within the institutional system and pursued their radical goals through legal and democratic means. Allende and the Left had run their cam-paign—as they had done in the three previous presidential elections—on the conviction that they were participating in a contest with rules that applied to and were equally understood by all the competitors. Now, they had won an election, just as the Right and Alessandri had done in 1958. The prize they deserved for that triumph had to be the same as the one obtained by their opponents twelve years earlier. If Congress elected Alessandri, why should Allende and the Left stick to a constitutional and peaceful strategy that, even at the peak of its success, was getting them nowhere?

Traditions, promises, and practices notwithstanding, Alessandri, Frei, Korry, and others considered that no blow would be worse for Chilean institutions than a government of the UP parties, and they attempted to prevent that development. The plan designed prior to the election by the United States foreign policy apparatus—Korry included—contemplated attempts to influence the runoff in Congress through propaganda and by bribing parliamentarians into voting for Alessandri. The plan, known as Phase II, was based on the presumption that Alessandri would win the popular vote by a slim margin, which might not be enough to guarantee his election in the runoff. Allende's victory at the polls radically altered the scenario. On 5 September, Korry told the CIA headquarters in Langley that he considered it improbable that Phase II could be carried out as originally conceived. Nevertheless, he had already begun working toward the goal of blocking Allende. In the hours after the popular election, the ambassador had "already taken steps to 'condition' Frei, to persuade Alessandri not to issue any cession statement re Allende . . . and to keep [Roberto] Viaux from precipitating ill-calculated actions."[8] The first tactical objective in the effort to avoid an Allende presidency was to prevent any acknowledgment of the triumph of the Left by any of those who could do something about it.[9]

Radomiro Tomic was certainly not among those who feared the prospect of an Allende government. On 5 September Tomic called Allende and recognized him as president elect. This meant a lot, as it made clear that a section of the Christian Democratic caucus was decided on voting for Allende in the runoff. However, President Frei still commanded a great deal of support within the PDC, and it was conceivable that his active leadership could steer the party parliamentarians into officially, if not unanimously, deciding to cast their votes for Alessandri. If this were to happen, though, it was necessary that the runner-up in the popular election hold on to the still existing chance of becoming president—a most uncertain possibility given his strong statements regarding a runoff during the campaign. An unnamed source who had spoken with the candidate in the wake of the popular election told a CIA agent that Alessandri was despondent and thought that Chile was finished, unless the military intervened—a reiteration of an idea he had shared with Ambassador Korry the very first time they had met, in December 1967.[10]

Nevertheless, the former president would not publicly or privately acknowledge Allende's victory, "because it [was] not simply in his character to do so."[11] Alessandri's personality may have played a role in his unwillingness to concede to Allende. The night of the election, after he learned the results, he went to bed without making any public statement, not even to his supporters.[12] The real reason behind Alessandri's attitude, however, was his stated conviction that a UP government would mean the end of the Chile he knew. Whether this Chile was mainly characterized by its fine democratic system, its unequal social order, or its still elite-oriented cultural mores, it is impossible to know for sure. In any case, as Alessandri's publicly stated hopes for a military coup in 1967 and again in the wake of the 1970 election show, any doctrinal adherence to democracy found its limits in the prospect of a government of the Marxist parties.

On 6 September, one of the managers of the Alessandri campaign, Enrique Ortúzar, issued a statement asserting that the electoral process was still on.[13] The implication of that declaration was that Allende should not claim victory yet because Congress could still choose Alessandri. Behind the scenes, PDC leaders Bernardo Leighton and Edmundo Pérez Zujovic, both of whom had occupied the position of minister of the interior in the Frei administration, were negotiating with representatives of the Alessandri camp. Leighton was not much liked by the National Party, and his position regarding a possible Allende government was not decidedly negative, so Senator Julio Durán quickly took his place in these talks. Frei, according to an unnamed source who spoke with the ambassador in the wake of the election, was in a deep state of depression. Korry, also in the bleakest of moods, derisively reported that "the man positively delights in playing Hamlet in moments like this." According to this informant, although Frei would not take a step in that direction, he strongly believed the military "had to do something."[14]

In the meantime, the heads of the armed forces met to discuss the situation. General Camilo Valenzuela, chief of the Santiago garrison, attended the meeting and informed Ambassador Korry and the Army Attaché Paul Wimert that the generals had approved of his idea of supporting a constitutional process whereby Frei could run against Allende in a new presidential election. This scenario could be brought to fruition, as President of the Senate Tomás Pablo had already suggested to Korry a few weeks earlier, if Alessandri, after being elected by Congress, resigned. General René Schneider, the commander in chief of the army, expressed his absolute disapproval and unwillingness to participate in a coup but confirmed his previously stated position that the army would back the constitutional process, whatever its outcome was. Schneider reaffirmed this position in a meeting with army generals on Monday, 7 September. Fully aware of the close relationship between the ambassador and the president, Valenzuela asked Korry to persuade Frei to go along with the proposed scheme.[15]

On Monday, 7 September, President Frei met with Salvador Allende at La Moneda. The conversation, as narrated by Frei a few days later—and recorded by Korry—highlighted the insurmountable political and ideological chasm that separated the two leaders. The chat, which Allende requested explicitly be held as old colleagues and friends rather than political adversaries, was tape recorded, an issue that Frei took care to underline in his account. Allende expressed his preoccupation about the "rightist machination" to create a widespread perception of crisis and panic in Chile with the purpose of stalling his ascension to the presidency. Frei responded that the situation was not the result of a plot but a natural reaction to the radical platform set forth by UP during the campaign. Still, Allende asked Frei to issue a public statement "to calm the Chileans and get them back to work." The president replied that the situation that so concerned Allende had not been provoked by the government and that he had already taken measures to keep things functioning more or less normally.

Frei also asked Allende about the international situation of Chile under a government of the Left, especially regarding the country's dependence on some specific sources of foreign currency, spare parts, technical assistance, and aid. The president pointed out that U.S. legislation limited the provision of aid to countries that officially recognized the governments of Cuba and North Vietnam, as UP advocated. Chile, in Frei's view, could not forsake political and, above all, economic relations with the United States and other capitalist countries. Chile, the president told Allende, was very different from Cuba: "In Cuba . . . it was only sugar, tobacco and cattle; in Chile there is considerable industrialization, a great need for foreign exchange and a dependence on foreign supplies."

Allende, to Frei's bafflement, said that it would take approximately six years to find other sources for the state power companies. "Say only three years," Frei retorted, "but do you realize what would happen in Chile in those three years and the political consequences of such changes as the Communists hardened their control?" According to Frei, Allende had not really thought about these matters. This assertion, which was not too exaggerated, described the other cause of deep concern for many of Allende's opponents. Besides the fact that UP sought to build, in the medium- or long-term, a socialist system that few cared to clearly differentiate from the regimes then in place in Eastern Europe or Cuba, there seemed to be no detailed and all-encompassing plan to deal with the very specific, immediate, and inevitable consequences of the radical measures required to implement the proposed revolutionary project.

The main purpose of Allende's visit was to ask Frei for a formal PDC recognition of his triumph, as this would greatly diminish the uncertainty and the sense of crisis that was already taking over the country. Frei flatly rejected the request. The exchange that followed—as reported by Korry—portrays vividly and accurately the unbridgeable gap between the visions and convictions of the two leaders: "But why," Allende protested, "I have been a democrat all my life . . . I believe in free elections and in free opinion." For the president, this guaranteed nothing: "I believe you, Salvador and if it were you alone, there would be no problem." The real problem for Frei was Popular Unity: "[at least half of the] Socialist Party detests you; the Radical Party is a collection of corrupt hacks; and there are a few other minor hangers-on." The only real force on which a government of UP could depend were the Communists, "who are cold and calculating and who will convert Chile into something quite different than [Allende's] conception." The Socialist leader, who seemed closer to the Communist Party than to his own, strongly affirmed his will to oppose that possibility: "I would resign if they did that." That meant very little, Frei replied, as the case of Manuel Urrutia, the first president of Cuba after the triumph of the revolution, had already demonstrated: "Who remembers [Urrutia] today . . . and had Cuba become any less of a Communist state?" Reiterating what he had already told Korry and other advisers, Frei concluded his argument with a deeply pessimistic remark: "Wherever the Communists had the power it was an irreversible road."[16]

Even though Frei shared Korry's conviction that an Allende government would spell the end of Chilean democracy as it had functioned under the Constitution of 1925, the president was undecided as to what he should do at that crossroads. This indecisiveness provoked a deep frustration in the always emotional and often mercurial Korry and led him to conclude very early that the chances of blocking an Allende presidency were almost null. In a dispatch of 8 September, the ambassador complained, "neither the president nor the armed forces have the stomach for the violence they fear would be the consequence of intervention." No one, according to the ambassador, seemed as determined in the pursuit of their interests as the awe-inspiring PC. In his caustic view, "the military talks and talks; the president and his cronies talk and talk; but the Communists, who have prepared themselves so diligently for this opportunity, act and they act with dexterity, determination and the dread they inspire."[17]

Korry was especially angry at the way Frei had handled things throughout the campaign and in the wake of the popular election, so his harshest words were directed at the outgoing president: "[Frei's] caution permitted Tomic, an all-time loser, to win Frei's party. A man without pants does not feel the shirt being removed from his back."[18] However, Korry's anger, markedly present in his report of 8 September, had vanished by the next day. One of his dispatches of 9 September read: "I believe [Frei] is playing his cards with extraordinary astuteness in the circumstances."[19]

On 9 September, six days before Nixon gave the agency explicit orders to carry out covert operations in Chile without informing Ambassador Korry, the CIA had already decided the only way to block an Allende presidency was a military coup.[20] The very same day this strategic decision was communicated to the station in Santiago, the institutional way opened up again. Jorge Alessandri came out of his silence and publicly declared that, in case Congress chose him over Allende, he would resign, thus forcing a new presidential election. The maneuver coincided precisely with the idea suggested by President of the Senate Tomás Pablo a few weeks before the election and the plan set forth by General Valenzuela in the wake of Allende's victory at the polls.

Alessandri's declaration, according to Korry, had been cleared with Frei. The ambassador also claimed partial credit for the statement, on which he had "been working since before the election."[21] Korry still thought the Alessandri formula was a long shot, but he felt a little more confident about the possibilities of stalling Allende than he had a few days earlier, when he had stated that "the US must begin to plan now for the reality of an Allende regime."[22]

Alessandri's statement presented the PDC with a legal chance to defeat Allende. Nevertheless, despite Frei's preferences, a good many members of the party had no intention of backing the proposed scheme and, as it was widely known, some of them preferred Allende over Alessandri under any circumstance. On 10 September, one of the most respected PDC leaders, Bernardo Leighton, made known his refusal to support the Alessandri formula, thus weakening even further its already slim prospects of success. Other renowned Christian Democrats—Radomiro Tomic, Foreign Minister Gabriel Valdés, party chair Benjamín Prado, Senator Renán Fuentealba, and Deputy Luis Maira, among others—were also of the opinion that the party should respect Allende's plurality and that its parliamentarians should vote for him on 24 October. On the other hand, an unnamed PDC source told a U.S. embassy officer that President Frei was decidedly in favor of the maneuver and that he would try to influence the party into supporting it.[23] Eventually, the final battle over the position of the party regarding the runoff in Congress would take place in a national assembly to be held in the first days of October. In the meantime, Ambassador Korry would be a privileged witness to the ideas conceived by Christian Democrats and military officers to make the Alessandri formula win and, if that attempt failed, provoke an institutional crisis and a subsequent military takeover to prevent the election of Salvador Allende.

Ministers, Parliamentarians, and Generals

On the night of 11 September, three men of high standing in Chilean politics—two of them Christian Democrats—visited Korry in his house, "each barely missing the other," according to the ambassador's account. Minister of Defense Sergio Ossa, President of the Senate Tomás Pablo, and former Finance Minister Raúl Sáez stopped by Korry's residence "seeking information . . . and indirectly asking for advice."[24] Sáez, a man with no party affiliation, who had held the post of finance minister briefly in 1968, had been designated as a liaison between the embassy and the anti-Allende camp within the government. Any meeting between Korry and government officials or members of Congress would surely draw the attention of interested observers and give the impression of undue intervention in Chilean politics on the part of the embassy. Sáez, a good personal friend of the ambassador, was an effective and sufficiently secure go-between.

Minister of Defense Ossa confirmed that Frei had decided to go along with the Alessandri formula and run for president again if the situation got to that point. All but two incumbent ministers also supported the scheme, and thirty-eight of seventy-five PDC members of Congress were decided on voting for Alessandri in the runoff election. Ossa sought to involve Korry and the U.S. representation in Chile directly in the effort to block Allende—much like General Valenzuela had done a few days earlier. The minister of defense requested Korry's help on several counts. First, he wanted some assurance from the U.S. government that, should the maneuver fail, all those involved in it and their families could get out of the country rapidly to avoid retaliation from the Left. Second, as he distrusted the intelligence he could get on the views and attitudes of the military in the weeks preceding the runoff, Ossa asked Korry to share with him any information the U.S. diplomatic and intelligence corps could garner from Chilean officers. Third, the minister asked the ambassador to do what he could to get Guillermo Carey Jr., son of one of the highest executives of Anaconda, out of Chile, as he was a hothead and was "feeding [retired General Roberto Viaux's] pathetic Peronist ambitions." Fourth, Ossa wanted the embassy's help in "listing and locating those key individuals in the Marxist camp whose absence from Chile might be desirable if it comes to [the] point of [a] possible violent leftist reaction to [a] congressional decision against Allende." Finally, the Christian Democratic envoy told the ambassador that press reports from abroad telling about supposedly ominous moves already being made by the Left to encroach on their opponents would help the anti-Allende cause.[25]

Senator Pablo, for his part, discussed with Korry the situation of the relations between Chile and the United States in the event of an Allende presidency. This input was critical for the decision the PDC had to make regarding the election in Congress. Tomic was telling everyone that the United States would not cut credits or aid if Allende was elected, as "old Cold War standards no longer [applied]." In addition, Tomic was flaunting his important connections in Washington, particularly Senators J. William Fulbright and Ted Kennedy, as a sort of guarantee of a continuing and largely undisturbed relationship between the U.S. government and Chile.

Not everyone bought this line, and many in the PDC feared an Allende government would mean the end of the favorable relationship between Chile and the United States and, consequently, an inevitable drift toward the Soviet bloc. Korry spoke his mind on the matter and told Pablo what the senator most probably wanted to hear: the ambassador was opposed to any U.S. bailout of Chile under an Allende government. Furthermore, the likelihood of significant Soviet aid was extremely low, as the current attitude of the Soviet Union toward Cuba and the military government in Peru was showing. As a result, the economic situation of the country did not look good under the prospect of a UP government.[26]

Coincidentally, in those days an OAS meeting on education was taking place in Viña del Mar (eighty miles northwest of Santiago) and Assistant Secretary John Richardson was among the attendants. Frei requested to meet with Richardson with the purpose of passing a message directly to President Nixon about the situation in Chile. Other than the fact that he might be able to meet personally with Nixon—and no record shows that such an encounter occurred—no substantial factor made Richardson a better interlocutor for Frei than Korry, so it can be assumed with a high degree of certainty that the president's real intention was to speak freely, without raising suspicions, with the ambassador. Korry, in fact, had rushed from Santiago to make the meeting on time. Frei basically gave Richardson the same line he had shared with Korry, who in turn had communicated it abundantly to the State Department and the White House. In fact, Frei went as far as to assert that his views coincided

100 percent with those of the ambassador. He thought there was a 98 percent chance that Chile under Allende would become a communist state; that the armed forces would do nothing to prevent such an outcome, as they were convinced that politicians should find solutions to the problems that belonged in the realm of politics; that the small economic crisis caused by reactions to the victory of Allende at the polls would contribute to a higher level of inflation and, thus, would further deteriorate the political situation; and that the people of Chile, convinced by the long history of participation in regular politics of the revolutionary parties and Allende himself, believed they deserved a chance in the presidency without really understanding the consequences for the country of a government of the Left.

Even though he wanted to highlight the delicacy of the situation that Chile was going through, Frei explicitly asked that the United States not make any public statement or gesture that could be interpreted as an attempt to influence the outcome of the still ongoing electoral process. In the same vein, Frei praised the attitude and actions of the embassy throughout the year, which he deemed "impeccable." The president then told Richardson and Korry about his conversation with Allende a few days earlier. Finally, Korry asked the president about his thoughts on a number of efforts the United States could make to try to help him and the anti-Allende bloc in the weeks ahead. Basically, Korry proposed an international propaganda campaign through reputable media outlets informing about the supposed encroachment of opponents by Communists, the economic situation of the country in the wake of the popular election, and the difficulties the military would encounter in replacing old equipment or buying weapons under an Allende government. "Stupendous," was Frei's short but eloquent response on all three counts.[27]

While the situation in Chile was still filled with uncertainty, in Washington two Chilean men—Agustín Edwards, owner of *El Mercurio*, and an unidentified aide of his—met successively with National Security Advisor Henry Kissinger and Director of the CIA Richard Helms. The occurrence of these meetings has long been known; however, no record of them had been declassified until 2014, when the *FRUS* series volume dedicated to Chile during the Nixon administration published a redacted transcript of the memorandum of the conversation between the two Chileans, Helms, and the president of Pepsi Cola Company, Donald Kendall. Edwards told his interlocutors what he knew about the situation in Chile, much along the same lines as Korry had been reporting since the popular election. Edwards confirmed that the issuing of Alessandri's statement of 9 September had been the result of the maneuvers made behind the scenes by Frei's envoys, particularly Bernardo Leighton. (The specific reference to Leighton in this context is rather perplexing, as he had already made known his rejection of the Alessandri formula a few days earlier).

The Chilean tycoon, however, did not think the Alessandri formula stood much of a chance given the correlation of forces in Congress. If the congressional path did not work, there would remain little room for maneuvering in the interlude between the runoff and Allende's inauguration. Edwards and his companion manifested their outright preference for a military coup but saw little hope for it, as only Director General of Carabineros (the Chilean police force) Vicente Huerta seemed willing and determined to act against the election of Allende. The heads of the navy, Fernando Porta, and the air force, Carlos Guerraty, were apparently opposed to Allende and the Left but had no intention of intervening to block a UP government. Schneider had already stated emphatically that he would not lend himself to an unconstitutional effort. Edwards' companion told Helms that the "key to a coup would be to get General Carlos Prats, chief of the National Defense Staff, to move." Such a maneuver, this unknown man continued ominously, "would involve neutralizing Schneider." The only high-ranking army officer who seemed determined to act was General Camilo Valenzuela. Edwards, though convinced of the necessity of a military intervention led by the army, spoke bluntly of the danger entailed by any plot headed by the retired Viaux or "some other nut."[28]

On 14 September, the same day Edwards met with Kissinger and Helms in Washington, Korry reported that Frei had begun to make some moves to prevent the election of Allende. An undisclosed source who had recently spoken with the president informed Korry that Frei told Generals Camilo Valenzuela of the army and Vicente Huerta of Carabineros, the two men in uniform most determined to prevent a UP government, of his intention to resign after the upcoming national holidays (18–19 September). President of the Senate Tomás Pablo would then assume the presidency and appoint a military cabinet, with the exception of two posts, in which the incumbents would stay. Frei hoped, according to Korry's account, that "under Pablo and a military cabinet steps [could] be taken to neutralize the Communist Party." After this task was finished, Frei would agree to run in the elections that would follow. The president recognized, however, that for the plan to be successful some important hurdles had to be overcome. The most significant of those obstacles was the immutable unwillingness of General Schneider to go along with any course of action that deviated from the constitutional electoral process. Frei, the man who loathed the prospect of a left-wing government because of his deep attachment to the substance and the forms of Chilean liberal democracy, said more than a little angrily to Korry's informant that Schneider had "constitutional sickness and [was] therefore a problem."[29]

Korry met again with Minister of Defense Ossa on 15 September. The ambassador deliberately showed his anger at Frei's indecision to his well-placed Chilean interlocutor. "We were prepared to give appropriate support if Frei could decide his own course," Korry told the minister, "but if he preferred to live interminably the Hamlet role, if he preferred to cite all the reasons he could not act, there was no justification for anyone else to be concerned about his fate or that of Chile." The ambassador, using strategically the frustration that was taking him over viscerally, went on to say that "if [Frei] chose immobility, [he] would regard him personally . . . as a pathetic castrate unworthy of either sympathy or sustenance." He even dared to put forth an ultimatum of sorts. If Frei had not made up his mind by the last week of September, Korry stated somewhat melodramatically, he "would take that indecision to mean that [Frei] had opted for a Communist Chile."[30]

On 16 September, Viaux issued a public declaration in which he stated his intentions and views regarding the current situation. Although he made no particular commitment as to his future actions, and, of course, he did not announce he was plotting to provoke a military coup, his statement made clear that he considered himself a leading voice within the military.[31] With some exaggeration, it was widely believed at the time that Viaux had a large following among low-rank and noncommissioned army officers—"the men who really control the troops," per Korry's description. Frei considered the statement an asset in the still incipient operation aimed at preventing Allende from becoming president as it had "served to bring the army in line at the same demonstrating that Chilean generals are not for sale." This line, which Korry got from an unnamed source, was a reference to the attempts of API senator and former candidate for the UP nomination Rafael Tarud, to persuade Viaux to stand still as the electoral process went on.[32] In his reports to Washington, Korry said he had convinced Ossa to let Viaux issue his statement without interference, as it would help galvanize the armed forces into a more determined stance. Coupled with a statement by Finance Minister Zaldívar about the deteriorating situation of the economy after the popular election, the Viaux declaration could contribute significantly to the creation of an atmosphere of crisis that might drive the military to intervene.[33]

Some ministers close to Frei shared the president's conviction about the grim future of Chile under a UP government and considered acting on their own initiative to block Allende's path toward the presidency. Korry informed

Washington on 17 September that the ministers of finance, Andrés Zaldívar, and the economy, Carlos Figueroa, were "determined to resign," as they wanted "to provoke the crisis and push the military and Frei to action." The ambassador had developed very close relationships with the two men. Indeed, they were the "only two ministers in whom [he had] absolute confidence and with whom [he had] maintained the most special of friendships." For the anti-Allende camp, that sort of move was becoming ever more urgent, as the chances of the Alessandri formula were narrowing rapidly. Frei himself had recognized, as reported by Korry, that he could at best be able to get a quarter of the PDC members of Congress to vote for Alessandri in the runoff, not enough to defeat Allende. At that point, according to the sources Korry relied on to report to Washington, Frei had made up his mind: "It was the army or nothing."[34]

Ambassador Korry obtained more details about the steps to be taken by Frei and some members of his cabinet at the traditional opera night in honor of Chile's independence day on 18 September. Given how delicate the Chilean situation was since Allende's victory at the polls, Korry had avoided direct contact with Frei. Only when Frei met with Assistant Secretary John Richardson in Viña del Mar on 12 September could Korry discuss the ongoing situation with the president. That night, the intermission offered an almost cinematographic opportunity for the two men to talk about the current state of affairs in Chile. As reported by the CIA station in Santiago, the brief conversation was held in whispers and "under [the] watchful eye [of the] diplomatic corps including Soviet ambassador." Frei told Korry that he should see Ossa as soon as possible and that the "important date" would be Tuesday, 22 September. Although not stated explicitly in the CIA cable, Frei was, in all likelihood, referring to the report then being prepared by the economic team of the government, including former minister Raúl Sáez. The ambassador also had the chance to speak briefly with Minister of the Economy Carlos Figueroa, who asked Korry for a meeting too. Figueroa wanted Korry's political advice as well as his help with the economic report then in the making.[35]

On 19 September, the holiday in honor of the Chilean army, the CIA station in Santiago sent a report to Langley elaborating on the likely course of action to be followed by the military should the armed forces step in and take over the government. The plan included the appointment of an all-military cabinet and Frei's departure from Chile. The rationalization for the takeover, at least as it would be stated publicly, was that the two-thirds of the Chilean electorate who had not voted for Allende should be given an opportunity to decide by themselves, and not through Congress, between the Marxist coalition and a "democratic regime." The highest-rank officer involved in the planning of such a move, and the man who informed the embassy and the CIA station in Santiago about it, was General Camilo Valenzuela. According to Valenzuela, the military takeover would entail the arrest of about two hundred UP militants. Frei talked about these developments with René Silva, director of *El Mercurio*, and told him that he thought that after Zaldívar's speech about the state of the economy, which would be delivered in the following days, most of his ministers would resign and the army would depose him. Consequently, there would be no need for him to take specific measures, such as appointing a military cabinet or tendering his resignation. In fact, the CIA station's source emphasized that, during his conversation with Frei, the president had at no point committed himself to a specific course of action and had contented himself with describing what he thought others would do in response to the unfolding of events.[36]

As arranged at the opera, Korry met with Minister of the Economy Carlos Figueroa on the morning of 20 September. Figueroa reassured Korry that he and Zaldívar were willing to step down and, thus, trigger the resignation of the entire cabinet. However, he doubted Frei would follow along and pointed out, with noticeable resentment, that the president preferred others make the hard decisions and take the decisive steps—a view shared by Korry. Figueroa also asked that Korry, through the means the ambassador found suitable, pass the word to the military that an Allende government would mean the end of the relationship between the Chilean armed forces and their U.S. counterparts and suppliers. In exchange, Korry convinced Figueroa that it was in the best interest of the whole anti-Allende operation to have the heads of the armed forces, particularly Schneider, informed of Frei's lack of faith in the Alessandri formula and his conviction that the only way to avoid an Allende government was for the military to step in.[37]

Later in the evening of 20 September, Korry met with Minister of Defense Sergio Ossa. Confirming what Figueroa had told the ambassador earlier, Ossa said that several members of the cabinet were determined to resign so as to provoke an institutional crisis and, thus, open the door for a military intervention. (Besides Figueroa, Zaldívar, and Ossa, a CIA document of 21 September includes among the ministers involved in this plan Minister of Interior Patricio Rojas and Secretary General of the Presidency Raúl Troncoso).[38] However, Ossa did not know whether Frei would step down, too, or what exactly he would do after the resignations were tendered, even though the president knew and approved of his ministers' plans. Ossa had also spoken about the eventuality of a cabinet crisis with General Schneider, who said that he, as head of the army, would be willing to fill some ministerial posts but only with the purpose of sustaining the constitutional process. According to Ossa's assess-

ment, Schneider was the most influential and respected man among the officer corps, which, in general, shared the constitutionalist view of the head of
the army. Nevertheless, Ossa thought, and assured Korry, that one of the
generals who could take the post of minister of the interior, Carlos Prats,
"could be depended upon [for] any effort to stop Allende." On the contrary,
Schneider, either as minister of the interior or head of the army, "would continue to be a problem." If the unfolding of events required, Korry and Ossa
agreed, the commander in chief of the army "would have to be neutralized,
by displacement if necessary."[39]

Minister Ossa also agreed to deliver a message from the ambassador to Frei.
Korry wanted to push Frei to act resolutely by blaming him for the situation
that Chile would inevitably confront if Allende became president. If Frei did
nothing, history would "judge him harshly, (and not Allende or Tomic) as
mainly responsible for Chile's loss to communism." Echoing a line that had
already been voiced from some ultra-conservative quarters, Korry said Frei
would be considered "the Kerensky of Chile."[40] Even worse, not only Frei's
image would be damaged, but the country would have to endure untold suffering if the Left was not stopped. "Once Allende comes to power," threatened the ambassador, "[the U.S. government] shall do all within [its] power to
condemn Chile and the Chileans to the utmost deprivation and poverty, a
policy designed for a long time to come to accelerate the harsh features of a
communist society in Chile." Frei, concluded Korry, should harbor no illusions that there would be "much of an alternative to utter misery" if Allende
was elected president. Ossa agreed fully with Korry's words and promised he
would convey them to Frei.[41]

On 23 September Minister of Finance Andrés Zaldívar delivered his
speech about the state of the economy. The report was prepared by Frei's
economic team and was meant to provoke an atmosphere of crisis in Chile.
Zaldívar spoke about the runs on banks, the drop in demand, and the government recourse to the printing presses to deal with the problems of liquidity
that arose after 4 September.[42] Purportedly, the report would be followed by the
resignations of the ministers who wanted to block Allende. The combination
of a cabinet crisis and the dire state of the economy, the reasoning went, would
create the conditions for an army takeover. The plan, however, had not been
coordinated among all the participants. On the contrary, it seemed that all the
relevant actors interested in preventing Allende's ascent to the presidency—Frei,
the ministers and Christian Democratic leaders closest to the president, military
officers such as Valenzuela—were acting under different assumptions. The
ministers—Zaldívar and Figueroa, among others—spoke with Korry about

their determination to resign so as to provoke a cabinet crisis that would force the military to step in and fill some of the ministerial positions left vacant. Figueroa and Ossa, Korry's direct interlocutors in those days, did not know if this would be followed by Frei's resignation. Frei, for his part, did not tell anyone what exactly he would do. He apparently thought the military would move on their own initiative after Zaldívar's economic report. In fact, Frei met with Schneider on 23 September to tell him about the presumed dangers of a UP government for the military and the country and hint at the necessity of direct action by the armed forces to prevent Allende's election. Schneider, as reported by the CIA station in Santiago, got the opposite message: the constitutional process and his personal attitude toward it would be respected.[43] The officers who wanted to act, in turn, hoped for some specific indication in that direction from Frei. Lacking that indication and, more important, being under the command of a general totally opposed to any unconstitutional intervention, Valenzuela and the other officers committed to the anti-Allende initiatives had no real chance to act in representation of the armed forces.

The same day Zaldívar delivered his speech about the state of the economy, a cohort of Christian Democratic members of Congress met with Allende and other representatives of UP to open negotiations for the PDC vote in the runoff. Some of the PDC parliamentarians were already determined to vote for Allende; others, probably a majority, needed some sort of reassurance by Allende and his coalition that the institutional framework of Chilean politics would be respected under a UP government. The conversations were not unanimously approved of within UP.[44] Some members of the coalition did not think any reassurance was necessary, as they were participants of the democratic game in no different terms than all the other political forces. The talks, nevertheless, continued and would eventually yield an agreement acceptable to both parties.

After the PDC opened negotiations with UP, the already low likelihood of success of the Alessandri formula decreased substantially. At that point, after a rough journey of half a century through the hilly roads of Chilean politics and at the very doorsteps of power, it was unlikely the Left would adopt an intransigent stance and reject the demands of the PDC. Frei understood the chances of defeating Allende in the runoff had dimmed almost to the point of nonexistence and told General Schneider so in their meeting of 23 September. The president, even though he believed the military could block Allende, informed Schneider that he would not ask the armed forces to intervene, for that would be an act of cowardice.[45] As reported by Minister of Defense Ossa, the meaning of Frei's message to the head of the army was purposefully ambiguous. On the one hand, the president pointed out the dire situation that would befall

Chile if Allende were to succeed him and stated explicitly his conviction that the military could do something about it. On the other, Frei complimented Schneider's rigorously constitutional position and ostensibly asked him to maintain that course—while lamenting that he, as a politician, could do nothing to prevent Allende's taking the highest office of the republic.[46] Whatever Frei's intentions were, and it seems clear he did want the armed forces to move on their own, Schneider would not deviate from his constitutional stance and would not lend himself for any irregular maneuver. With Schneider in command, neither a bloody nor a bloodless coup was an option.

In the weeks following 4 September 1970, the economic situation and the social climate in Chile did not take a dramatic turn for the worse, to the chagrin of Frei, Korry, and others in the anti-Allende camp. Such deterioration was an almost indispensable condition for a successful move, constitutional or not, to block Allende's presidency. That was Ossa's understanding, as on 25 September, the minister of defense explicitly asked Ambassador Korry to do "whatever [he] could to help create the proper bearish climate," including requesting that the United States not complete any pending delivery of military material to the Chilean armed forces.[47] Korry, for his part, even though largely pessimistic, still clung to the hope that something could happen. On a dispatch of 25 September, the moody ambassador expressed his conviction that "if one large enterprise hero were to shut its doors next week, if one bank were to fail, if one savings and loan association were to collapse, we would still have life before October 24th and we would be contributing to the chaos that has its natural yeast in any case."[48] The CIA staff in Langley and Santiago, working under orders given by President Nixon to Richard Helms on 15 September and largely away from Korry's radar, also reached the conclusion that only a deteriorated situation in Chile would galvanize the military or Frei into action. On 28 September, the CIA headquarters instructed the station in Santiago to "employ every stratagem, every ploy, however bizarre," to create the necessary climate for a coup, either by Frei or the armed forces on their own. As the CIA headquarters' blunt message to Santiago put it, for the anti-Allende endeavor to succeed, "the key [was] psych [sic] war within Chile; we cannot endeavor to ignite the world if Chile itself is a placid lake."[49]

Nixon, Korry, and the CIA largely overestimated the extent to which U.S. actions could contribute to the creation of a serious economic crisis in the short term. Any decrease in the flow of money from the U.S. government to Chile in the form of credits or aid could (and did) materialize only in the medium term. Curtailment of funds from international financial organizations such as the World Bank or the Inter-American Bank could not make a significant difference in the short term, and it was uncertain that they could do it in the longer term. Banks and businesses with assets in Chile could not be forced by the U.S. government to cease their activities in the country. A public announcement by the Nixon administration regarding the future of the official economic relations between the United States and Chile under an Allende government might have provoked the desired panic and subsequent crisis. Such a move, however, had to be discounted, as it would have amounted to overt interference in the ongoing Chilean electoral process, something the Nixon administration was anxious to avoid.

On 30 September the State Department informed Ambassador Korry of the actions taken by the U.S. government in the economic realm to try to create the critical situation necessary for the desired defeat of Allende in the runoff or, what at that point was the more likely course, a military coup. The actions listed by the State Department communication could hardly do significant damage to the current state of the Chilean economy, let alone provoke widespread social chaos. Up to the last day of September, the U.S. government, through the concerned agencies, had secured the temporary suspension of a loan for cattle development, the downgrading of Chile in the ranking of credit worthiness of the Export-Import Bank, and the deferral of any new loans by the Inter-American Bank. Talks with officials of businesses with assets in Chile, such as Ford Motor and the Bank of America, had yielded no concrete results other than the acknowledgment on the part of the representatives of the companies that the future in Chile under an Allende government did not look good.[50] The ability of the U.S. government to wreak havoc on the Chilean economy in the short term was at best limited, considering that the one course of action that could have brought about significant results, the adoption of a publicly hostile position such as the one taken on Cuba since 1960, was out of the question.

The situation did not deteriorate as the Allende opposition and the United States desired because the majority of the Chilean population did not fear the prospect of a UP government in the same way Frei, Korry, and others did. The "psychological warfare" of the CIA, which sought to create a pre-coup climate through propaganda and support for groups engaged in small-scale terrorism, did not attain its goal. Furthermore, after some internal wrangling, on 2 October UP expressed its willingness to negotiate the terms of the constitutional reform demanded by the Christian Democratic Party in exchange for its votes in the runoff in Congress. Korry made one last pitch in the night of 3 October to convince Frei to attend the PDC assembly the next day and attempt to swing the party, by way of his leadership, into supporting the Alessandri formula. Massachusetts Institute of Technology economist Paul Rosenstein-Rodan, who also spoke with Frei trying to persuade him to lead the anti-Allende cause with determination, aided the ambassador's effort. Former Venezuelan President Rómulo Betancourt and one of the philosophic mentors of the international Christian Democratic movement, Jacques Maritain, wrote to Frei in those days remarking on the perils of handing over the presidency to an avowedly Marxist leader.[51] Eventually, Frei decided not to attend the assembly in which the PDC would decide its position regarding the runoff. His leadership within the PDC would be greatly imperiled if his appearance at the assembly failed to achieve its goal, so senators Juan de Dios Carmona and Patricio Aylwin led the anti-Allende effort instead. On 4 October, the majority of the PDC delegates to the party convention then meeting in the outskirts of Santiago voted for supporting Allende in the runoff. On 8 October, a group of UP and Christian Democratic congressmen introduced the agreed-upon constitutional amendments in the Chamber of Deputies. The lower chamber approved the amendments on 16 October; the Senate followed through on 22 October, the same day General Schneider was shot.[52] In the interim, Jorge Alessandri had publicly withdrawn his name from the runoff, effectively killing any lingering chances of success for the anti-Allende forces within the constitutional frame.

On 22 October one of the groups aided by the CIA, whose leader was the notorious retired army general Roberto Viaux, carried out its ill-conceived plan to provoke a military coup. (The other group supported by the CIA, it must be noted, was headed by none other than General Camilo Valenzuela.) A gang of young men, without any experience on operations of this nature, attempted to kidnap General Schneider, and the attempt failed miserably. The general tried to defend himself from the attack and reached for his gun, and the kidnappers opened fire on the army chief. As the perpetrators lost the little nerve they had, Schneider's driver managed to get through and took the general to the army hospital, where the commander in chief of the army died on 25 October. The CIA headquarters, mistakenly expecting a military coup, even sent a commendatory message to the station in Santiago the day after the attempt.[53] The attack on Schneider, however, brought about the opposite effect. The military, under the leadership of General Carlos Prats, closed ranks behind the constitutional process, and elites across the political spectrum understood that no move against Allende, legal or not, would bear any legitimacy after the events of 22 October. In fact, later that same day, the Senate approved the constitutional amendments agreed on by the PDC and UP as a condition for the former's votes for Allende in the runoff. On 24 October, as Schneider still fought for his life in the army hospital, 153 of the 195 parliamentarians cast their votes for Salvador Allende in the runoff held by Congress, as the constitution mandated, fifty days after the popular vote. Chile had become, now without any shadow of a doubt, the first country in the world to vote into power a coalition of parties whose avowed goal was the establishment of socialism according to the Marxist understanding of the concept.

The United States and the Election of Salvador Allende

Although the covert operations ordered by President Nixon to forestall by any available means a definitive Allende victory in the runoff election are only marginally addressed in this work, any assessment of the U.S. involvement in Chilean politics must include at least a few comments about those actions, as they had a great impact on the course and atmosphere of Chilean politics—albeit not in the manner desired by the Nixon administration. The covert operations carried out by the CIA to prevent an Allende presidency, generally known as Track I and Track II, undoubtedly constituted the apex of U.S. involvement in Chilean politics during the Cold War. They amounted to an imperial attempt by the Nixon administration to radically reshape the course of Chilean politics, for no alliance with significant Chilean actors was established or even sought. This was a sharp departure from the way the United States had engaged in Chilean politics previously. It is no accident that U.S. policies toward Chile—and particularly those against the Left—functioned better when they converged with and complemented the actions of Chilean partners capable of working within the system or, as in the case of the military in 1973, of becoming masters of the system should they decide to act in a united way.

On the contrary, in the weeks between the popular election of 4 September and the runoff in Congress of 24 October 1970, CIA agents in Chile, circumventing Ambassador Korry by President Nixon's express order, conspired with Roberto Viaux, a retired general whose ability to garner support from the people, the political establishment, and even the armed forces was minimal, and with fringe groups embarrassingly unprepared, to put it mildly, to carry out the critical operations necessary to redirect the course of political developments at such an important crossroads. As a consequence, the eleventh-hour attempt of the Nixon administration to avoid the dreaded outcome of a Marxist politician assuming the presidency of a democratic republic by constitutional means failed dramatically, leaving in its wake the death of René Schneider, one of the ablest generals in the Latin American scene, and inflicting a wound on Chilean democracy that has not yet healed.

Even though the political responsibility for the U.S. covert actions in Chile in September and October of 1970 unquestionably rests with Nixon and National Security Advisor Henry Kissinger, the CIA bears the greatest operational responsibility in the tragic events that ended with the murder of General René Schneider. After Nixon instructed Richard Helms to conduct covert operations in Chile on 15 September, the CIA station in Santiago set out to support the plots organized by Viaux and General Valenzuela. The CIA pursued the Viaux route even though Korry warned that such an operation could become the Bay of Pigs of the Nixon administration and Agustín Edwards had advised explicitly against it.[54] Even Henry Kissinger instructed the agency on 15 October to send a message to the retired Chilean general through the station in Santiago asking him to suspend any action before the runoff in Congress.[55] The CIA, probably because of the urgent tone of the orders given by Nixon and its natural propensity to take advantage of existing assets that might serve the U.S. interest at a relatively low cost, assumed that any action that could contribute to the effort of provoking a coup before the runoff was worth pursuing.

This assumption eventually worked as a blindfold that prevented the agency staff in Langley and the agents stationed in Santiago from seeing what many others had noticed and noted quite emphatically: any conspiracy led by Viaux was bound to fail and, therefore, would probably be counterproductive. Not only did the CIA not heed that advice and even Kissinger's instructions, it also failed to realize that the Viaux plot lost any little chance of success it may have had the moment the would-be kidnappers opened fired against General Schneider. In a remarkable demonstration of ignorance of the state of affairs in Chile, the day after the attack on Schneider the CIA headquarters congratulated the station in Santiago on the "excellent job [done] of guiding Chileans to point today where a military coup is at least an option for them."[56] By partnering with local assets who had no substance in Chilean politics and conducting covert operations in which intelligence—in all its connotations— was largely absent, the CIA agents at Langley and Santiago, along with the plotters and perpetrators themselves, bear the most direct responsibility for the death of General Rene Schneider.

The murder of Schneider and the CIA complicity in the conspiracy have understandably overshadowed almost every other aspect of the U.S. involvement in the presidential election of 1970. The attention received by the CIA operations and Schneider's death is certainly warranted, as they, indeed, were extraordinary events. The interpretation that usually comes with that attention, however, is a different matter. The urgent and conceited tone of Richard Nixon's orders to Richard Helms on 15 September certainly bespeak the imperial attitude of a man occupying an imperial office, as the U.S. presidency was described with only a little too much exaggeration by historian Arthur Schlesinger Jr. in 1973.[57] Moreover, the broader ideological vision from which Nixon's decisions stemmed, largely shared by Henry Kissinger, was founded on the premise that the United States was the natural and even rightful hegemon in the Americas and had to act as forcefully as circumstances allowed to protect its interests in the region against real or perceived threats. This vision, not significantly different from the ideas and attitudes historically held by U.S. political elites and society, was compounded by the ideological cleavage of the Cold War, an especially prominent factor in the Chilean presidential election of 1970. In addition, Richard Nixon's idiosyncratic personality and Henry Kissinger's seemingly amoral understanding of international politics contributed to make both men's attitudes toward the election of Allende all the more scandalous. When told in isolation, with little reference to other important aspects of the U.S. involvement in Chilean politics, the story of the covert operations ordered by Richard Nixon to prevent Allende's election as president looks like a textbook case of the inexorably unilateral and imperialistic character of the relations of the United States with its Latin American neighbors.

A scholarly assessment of the U.S. involvement in the Chilean presidential election of 1970, nevertheless, must widen the focus of the analysis and stop making the CIA covert operations that led to the murder of General Schneider the only subject worth exploring in this context. As this and previous chapters have shown, U.S. involvement in Chilean politics had begun several years earlier. The commanding strategic objective had always been the same: to keep the Left out of power. In this sense, the covert actions precipitously ordered by Richard Nixon fit well into the larger picture, since they pursued the same goal as the overt and covert policies toward Chile carried out in previous years. However, those covert actions deviated sharply from the operational pattern of U.S. involvement in Chilean politics set since the presidential election of 1964. Until Nixon gave his much-quoted orders on 15 September, the operations of the CIA had been subordinated to strategic plans carefully devised and had been generally carried out under close supervision from the embassy. In fact, the political staff of the embassy and the ambassadors themselves had arguably played the largest role in the pursuit of U.S. interests in Chilean politics, as demonstrated by the cases of political counselor Joseph John Jova's involvement in the 1964 presidential race and Ambassador Korry's conception and direction of the covert operations carried out in the 1969 congressional election. Furthermore, the United States had attempted, rather successfully, to influence the course of the political competition in Chile by supporting the autonomous actions of Chilean politicians, parties, and other organizations with a strong footing on the institutional framework. The politicians and parties aided by the United States since 1964—Frei, the Christian Democratic Party, Julio Durán and the right-wing Radicals, and even Ampuero's USOPO—were active participants in Chilean politics by their own will. Even more significant, those Chilean actors were not ideologically or programmatically beholden to the United States. Until the CIA established its notorious association with Viaux and Valenzuela in September 1970, the United States put its weight behind insiders whose relative and particular successes within a robust political system could contribute to the protection or promotion of U.S. interests. The CIA association with plotters who had no significant support from political parties or the armed forces and who sought to subvert the normal functioning of Chilean politics was a significant departure from the way U.S. policies toward Chile had been conducted theretofore.

The course Chilean politics had begun to follow in 1964, and would follow until 1973, was largely the result of the decisions of Chilean politicians and organizations acting within the possibilities offered by the institutional framework. Until 1970, the United States performed effectively its chosen supporting role in the play of Chilean politics. In the wake of the popular election of 4 September, Korry recognized that any successful attempt to block Allende's rise to the presidency required the committed participation and even the initiative of Eduardo Frei. The United States could provide only limited assistance in the form of promises for the future or political advice to those engaged in the constitutional and unconstitutional maneuvers acted upon or only thought of to prevent Allende's final victory in the runoff in Congress.

Korry gave that assistance and did as much as he could to convince Chilean and foreign interlocutors that a UP government would be a catastrophe for Chile. However, he understood that the outcome of the electoral process depended on the autonomous decisions and actions of Chilean politicians and military officers who thought in almost the exact terms he did regarding the prospect of an Allende government. In fact, it was the Chileans—Frei, some of his ministers, Senator Pablo, General Valenzuela—who approached the ambassador to ask for his help in their rather uncoordinated pursuits.

Frei and other Christian Democrats subscribed to an ideological view of the Marxist Left almost identical to that of U.S. liberalism. They reached the conclusion that something must be done to prevent a UP government because of their own philosophical convictions and decided to act upon that conclusion without any prodding from external actors. Their strong intellectual inclination to act, however, was not matched by an equally strong determination to break with the institutional rules and the traditions of Chilean politics. More-over, neither Frei nor his ministers really knew what exactly they should do to create the institutional crisis of which they spoke so much. They all had been politically educated within the framework set by the continuous practice of democracy, so they had no experience whatsoever in the irregular moves nec-essary to provoke a crisis, let alone a full-blown coup d'état. In addition, they were deeply afraid of a situation of widespread violence and the prospect of a civil war, so their own fears acted as a deterrent for their extraconstitutional intentions.[58] In the end, it was the inertia of Chilean politics that kept Frei and his ministers from taking the fateful decisive step toward an institutional crisis and, maybe, a military takeover. The United States, through Korry or the CIA, could offer and provide help to the Chilean political and military actors whose interests converged with those of U.S. foreign policy. To Nix-on's frustration, however, it could not shape unilaterally the general course of Chile's political system and culture.

Conclusion

The Influence of the United States in Chilean Politics

Since the dynamics of Chilean politics replicated very closely the ideological divide of the global Cold War, the overarching goal of the U.S. strategy toward Chile between 1964 and 1970 was to keep the Marxist Left from taking power. Arguably, the most important part of that strategy was the considerable support provided to the reformist political project of the Christian Democratic Party, as it constituted a viable alternative to the growing appeal of the revolutionary Left and offered a path toward economic and social modernization that coincided with the ideological outlook of the Johnson administration's foreign policy. In particular circumstances, the U.S. foreign-policy apparatus, especially the embassy and the CIA station in Santiago, partnered with political actors of other sensibilities to promote and advance the interests of the United States in the autonomous scene of Chilean politics. With the exception of the covert operations ordered by Richard Nixon in the wake of Salvador Allende's victory in September 1970, the United States followed the operational lead of Chilean parties and politicians acting within the parameters established by the regular functioning of the Chilean political system. In other words, despite an imbalance of power, the U.S. foreign policy apparatus did not determine the motivations or intentions of the Chilean political actors with which it established relationships, nor did it shape the political debates on which the U.S. interests in Chile could be at stake. The United States established itself as a relevant and even powerful informal actor in Chilean politics but only as an ally of forces whose interests and goals, though convergent with U.S. interests, were independent.

In 1964, the United States supported Eduardo Frei's presidential candidacy by providing generous funding for his campaign through a smoothly run CIA covert operation. The political program of the PDC, however, remained unaltered, even when some issues ran against the preferences of the United States, such as the promise of diplomatic relations with the Soviet Union and other communist countries. Not only did the United States help Frei run a well-funded and successful campaign, it also contributed to shaping the race by supporting the ill-fated presidential bid of the leader of the right wing of the Radical Party, Julio Durán. Even though Durán's candidacy was doomed to failure after the coalition that supported him imploded in March 1964, from the point of view of the PR's right wing it was worth keeping him in the race because his candidacy would prevent a split in the party along ideological lines, a more than probable risk considering that many Radicals wanted the party to join the Communists and Socialists in the Popular Action Front. Durán's candidacy would also keep many of the PR's constituents, doctrinally indisposed to the PDC because it was still perceived of by many Radicals as a religious party, from voting for Salvador Allende, the FRAP standard-bearer. The interests of the right wing of the PR, thus, coincided with those of the United States. Consequently, the U.S. embassy in Santiago, mostly through the backroom maneuvers of political officer Joseph John Jova, actively and successfully supported the efforts of the PR's right wing and of Durán himself to stay in the race.

Eventually, Eduardo Frei won the election by so wide a margin (17 percentage points) that Durán's final tally (5 percent) became largely irrelevant in quantitative terms. However, the reasoning behind the effort to keep Durán in the race, both from the perspective of the PR's right wing and the U.S. embassy's view, was rendered accurate by developments throughout the campaign and the final election results. The PR preserved its unity and independence through 1964 and for most of the Frei administration, avoiding for the time being a schism along the ever wider ideological gap dividing the party. Furthermore, even though an important number of Radical voters cast their ballots for Allende in September 1964, Durán's staying in the race prevented any formal deal between the PR and the FRAP. Such union of forces would have significantly boosted Allende's chances and could have had a significant impact on the election.

Toward the end of the Frei administration, three of the five major parties endured splits as a result of their ever more intractable internal divisions. The causes and terms of these schisms were rooted in the Chilean political system and culture, yet the hand of the U.S. foreign policy apparatus showed in all these intra-party crises. In the case of the PDC, Korry directly approached President Frei to persuade him to fight the left wing of the party in 1967 and early 1968. To be sure, Frei did not need such prodding to understand that the success of his government and the historic project of his party required him to stand firm against the *rebelde* wing of the PDC. Eventually, a significant number of radical Christian Democratic members left the party in 1969 and founded the Unitarian Popular Action Movement. In the other two cases, the splits in the Radical and Socialist parties, the U.S. foreign policy apparatus played an even more direct role. Between 1967 and 1969, the CIA, under a plan largely conceived by Ambassador Korry, provided funds for the formation and survival of the breakaway parties, Julio Durán's Radical Democracy and Raúl Ampuero's Popular Socialist Union. Tactical support for these political organizations contributed to the overarching U.S. goal in Chilean politics, in these cases by keeping a small but still consequential number of voters from supporting the FRAP parties in the 1969 congressional election.

As an alignment shaped by the core ideological confrontation of the Cold War, the partnership between the Johnson administration and the PDC went far beyond the immediate common goal of defeating the Marxist Left. After Frei took office, Chile received a good deal of aid from the United States, even as the Frei administration took steps to partially nationalize the assets of U.S. copper corporations and opposed specific decisions of the Johnson administration, such as the invasion of the Dominican Republic in 1965. From the viewpoint of the Johnson administration, in the short term, a robust and successful PDC offered the best way to check the growth of the Left. What is more, the political project of Frei and the PDC seemed to dovetail nicely with the fundamental tenets of modernization theory, the main body of ideas about politics, economics, and society on which the foreign policies of the Kennedy and Johnson administrations drew. Thus, not only did Frei and the PDC stand as an alternative to the immediate challenge of the Marxist Left, they also offered a seemingly viable project for Chile's development in the long term. The partnership, especially as it was viewed by some of the diplomats who worked in Chile through those years, was built not only on the common opposition to the same political adversary but also on a shared vision for the future.

The U.S. embassy in Santiago played a significant and largely underestimated role in the involvement of the United States in Chilean politics in these years. The covert operations carried out by the CIA in the presidential elections of 1964 and 1970 were undoubtedly consequential, and their importance must not be underrated. However, the more consistent but less spectacular action of the embassy between 1964 and 1970 had an equally significant impact on Chilean politics as the CIA's covert actions. During the 1964 presidential race, Joseph John Jova's network of contacts among Chilean politicians allowed him to negotiate—with a great deal of effectiveness—the continuance of Durán's candidacy. Ralph Dungan (who was ambassador from 1964 into 1967) and Edward Korry (who was ambassador from 1967 into 1971) managed to establish very close personal relationships with President Frei and other important PDC officials. These personal relationships greatly facilitated the periodic negotiations over the budget and economic policies on which U.S. aid was contingent. Korry's close friendship with the president and his keen understanding of the character and functioning of Chilean politics made him an ideal broker for the negotiations between the Frei administration and Anaconda over the nationalization of the company's assets in Chile in 1969.

Furthermore, the covert operation carried out by the CIA in the congressional election of March 1969 was mostly conceived and planned by the political staff of the embassy, under Korry's very active leadership. In September and October 1970, while the CIA was seeking to provoke a coup by allying with Chilean assets of a dubious quality, Korry understood better than anyone that any successful move to stop Allende had to be made by Frei, the PDC, or the military as a bloc, and not by hotheads with as little political leverage as Roberto Viaux. Even though Korry wanted a coup as much as Nixon and Kissinger did, he knew the United States could do very little to make it happen if no important Chilean actor moved in that direction of their own will and at their own risk. In this sense, Korry shared the pessimistic, contradictory, and ultimately self-defeating attitude of Frei, some government officials, other PDC politicians, and a few military officers who, fearing for Chile's democracy under a government of the Left, were willing to consider unconstitutional and undemocratic maneuvers to prevent Allende's accession to the presidency.

Nixon's Tactical Shift

Much has been written about Richard Nixon, Henry Kissinger, and the Chilean presidential election of 1970. The covert actions ordered by Nixon against Allende, broadly uncovered in the wake of the Watergate scandal, have elicited widespread condemnation, both in the United States and abroad, and have become a distinctive symbol of the character and style of Nixon's and Kissinger's foreign policy making. Nevertheless, one obvious aspect of this "hostile intent," as one scholar aptly called it, was shared by the two previous Democratic administrations: the intransigent opposition to the possibility of a government headed by the Marxist Left in Chile.[1] Although the strategic approach of the Kennedy and the Johnson administrations toward Chile had a distinct focus on development and took full advantage of the political possibilities offered by Chilean democracy, one cannot but wonder how Lyndon B. Johnson would have reacted toward the events in Chile in 1970 had he been in the White House, and what the United States would have done in case Allende had defeated Frei in the presidential election of 1964. The record of the Democratic administrations of the 1960s, marked by the Bay of Pigs fiasco in 1961, the support given to the military dictatorship established in Brazil in 1964, and the invasion of the Dominican Republic in 1965, anticipated the attitude toward Chile shown by Nixon and Kissinger from 1970 onward.

Still, Nixon's approach to the Chilean electoral process in September and October 1970 departed significantly from his predecessor's, both in intellectual and operational terms. As has been shown, the Johnson administration's overt and covert policies toward Chile during the Frei years made full use of the institutional means provided by the robust Chilean political system. The United States, through its embassy and, to a lesser extent, the CIA station in Santiago, established itself as an informal actor partnering with regular and legitimate participants in the play of Chilean politics. In September and October 1970, Nixon's instructions to, and their implementation by, the CIA repudiated the strategic principles on which U.S. involvement in Chile had stood theretofore. On 15 September 1970, Nixon explicitly ordered that Ambassador Korry be kept in the dark about the CIA operations to be undertaken with extreme urgency, thus taking out of the picture the man and the office on whose shoulders had hitherto rested the most delicate responsibilities regarding U.S. involvement in Chilean politics. In addition, the CIA chose to ignore the warnings of such informed people as Korry and Agustín Edwards against any U.S. complicity with the largely unrealistic plans for a military coup conceived by retired General Roberto Viaux. Korry himself continued to act along the strategic lines he had followed since his arrival in Chile in 1967 and provided political advice to those in the Frei administration, beginning with Frei himself, who wanted to avoid at almost any cost the ascension of Allende to the presidency. He understood, however, that the success of any move against Allende, constitutional or not, hinged on the willingness of Chilean actors with a strong footing in the institutional system—Frei, the PDC, the military—to act forcefully and determinedly. If none of those actors chose to act—and none of them did—the United States could do nothing to alter the course of events according to its own preferences. Nixon and Kissinger did not see things in the same light.

Nixon and Kissinger chose to approach the matter of Allende's election in the most hawkish way as a result of their ignorance about the particulars of Chilean politics. Certainly, the element of urgency introduced to the picture by Allende's victory in the election of 4 September 1970 must not be underestimated. In the context of the Cold War, and considering the strategic and symbolic importance of Latin America for the United States, any president would have perceived another Marxist and revolutionary government in the continent as a substantial threat to the U.S. standing in world politics.

Lyndon B. Johnson's foreign policy record, which includes support for the Brazilian coup in 1964 and the invasion of the Dominican Republic in 1965, suggests that his attitude toward an Allende victory in 1964 or 1970 would not have been benign. In this sense, the comparison between the policies toward Chile of the Johnson and Nixon administrations has the obvious difficulty set by the different realities that both presidents had to confront. While the Johnson administration saw an opportunity to effectively influence political developments in Chile through its support of the Frei campaign in 1964 and its generous provision of aid to the PDC government until 1968, the Nixon administration did not have such a clear-cut choice in the 1970 presidential election and, partly because of that, had to deal with the worst possible result for the interests of the United States in that electoral contest. Consequently, Nixon and Kissinger faced the challenge to U.S. interests posed by the election of Allende with a sense of urgency that Johnson and his foreign policy advisers never experienced.

A sense of urgency, nevertheless, must not necessarily lead to ill-conceived policies or significant changes in strategy and tactics. Ultimately, Nixon chose the described course of action because he and National Security Adviser Henry Kissinger knew and cared little about the particular constitution of the Chilean political system and culture, the character and ways of U.S. involvement in Chile in the previous six years, and the extent to which U.S. actions could bring about specific outcomes in Chilean politics. Nixon and Kissinger seemed to think that forceful, determined, and swift action by the U.S. foreign policy apparatus, in this case represented exclusively by the CIA, sufficed to avoid the dreaded outcome of an avowedly Marxist politician becoming president of Chile, a democratic country, by constitutional means. They were utterly wrong.

One of the most famous lines of Nixon's instructions to Richard Helms on 15 September, "make the economy scream," bespeaks both the characteristic hubris and the lamentable ignorance of the president. Taken at face value, and too many informed people have chosen to do this, the content of the sentence belongs to the language of an imperial ruler. Furthermore, Nixon must have genuinely believed that such a maneuver was feasible. After all, while Nixon was serving as vice president, the CIA had accomplished with seemingly surgical precision the overthrow of Iran's prime minister Mohammad Mossaddegh in 1953 and Guatemala's president Jacobo Arbenz in 1954. It must have seemed only logical for Nixon to assign to the CIA the task of dealing with a challenge perceived as even more urgent and potentially more disruptive than those posed by Mossaddegh's rule and Arbenz's radical program of reform. But was it really possible for the CIA to accomplish Nixon's peremptory orders? What could the CIA have done to bring the complex and relatively modern economy of Chile to its knees in a period of less than forty days?

It is true that a minor panic ensued after Allende's victory in the popular election, but it was a predictable response, fundamentally domestic in nature, to an undoubtedly shocking political development. Moreover, the Frei administration took the necessary emergency measures to deal with such developments, and the initial situation of uncertainty faded away steadily in the course of the following days and weeks. Indeed, as Korry informed the White House and the State Department consistently after the election of 4 September, it was clear that any initiative meant to deny Allende the presidency in those intense days had to come from some significant Chilean political actor or actors. On the contrary, since the electoral process carried the legitimacy given by the constitution and no social unrest had arisen as a result of Allende's victory, any action undertaken by someone outside the established political system was bound to fail miserably. Nixon and Kissinger, out of a sense of urgency and a deep-seated distrust in the more knowledgeable bureaucracies of the State Department, and even the National Security Council, chose to ignore these considerations and sought to block Allende's path to the presidency by resorting to covert actions carried out in alliance with fringe groups with no anchorage whatsoever in the established political system. By making these decisions, Nixon and Kissinger sided with an attempt of subversion of the Chilean political system that could only hurt U.S. interests in Chile, Latin America, and the rest of the world.

The United States and Frei's Revolution in Liberty

If evaluated on the basis of coherence and outcomes, U.S. foreign policy toward Chile between 1964 and 1970 must be considered a failure. Neither the specific covert actions aimed against the electoral success of the Marxist Left nor the abundant resources invested in the Christian Democratic project for development accomplished the basic objective of avoiding a victory of Salvador Allende in the presidential election in 1970. This failure would be later reversed with the military coup that overthrew Allende in 1973 and ushered in a brutal regime with a radical anti-communist discourse that explicitly placed itself on the side of the United States in the Cold War. The Nixon administration's policies toward Allende after 1970—much more in tune with the strategic approach of the Johnson administration, albeit now seeking to oppose the standing government rather than to buttress it—played a role in that reversal. At any rate, Allende's victory in the presidential election of 1970, as well as his fateful three years as president of Chile, demonstrated that no matter how much effort and material resources were devoted by the United States to the cause of defeating the Marxist Left, the final decision rested with the Chilean people, their institutions, and their political representatives. This was proven true again by how things developed during the Allende years, including the 1973 military coup, in which direct U.S. participation has been widely assumed but has yet to be proven by any credible record or testimony.[2]

The strategies and tactics toward Chile of the Johnson and Nixon administrations, however, differed in significant ways, and this must be taken into account by any appraisal of the relations between the two countries during the Frei administration. As has been discussed, after Allende's victory on 4 September 1970, Nixon abandoned the operational principles at the core of the U.S. involvement in Chilean politics in the previous six years, with grave consequences for the future of Chilean politics. A large part of the responsibility for the poisoning of Chilean democracy that resulted from the murder of General René Schneider rests squarely on the shoulders of Nixon, Kissinger and, above all, the CIA—besides, of course, the Chilean extremists who planned and carried out the kidnap attempt that went awry. In fact, the CIA-sponsored murder of General Schneider was absolutely counterproductive for the interests of the United States. The shock provoked in Chile by such senseless action all but ensured Allende's election as president by the Congress, which occurred two days after the shooting of Schneider and the day before his death.

More important, Nixon's outlook on Latin America and Chile since his inauguration in January 1969 differed dramatically from the attitude that underlay the policies of the Kennedy and the Johnson administrations toward the region. The spirit of the Alliance for Progress, already in shambles by the end of the Johnson administration, definitely died with Nixon's arrival in the White House. The U.S. government would no longer provide the lavish economic and political support to Latin American projects of national development such as the one put forward by Eduardo Frei and his Revolution in Liberty. More specifically, the Frei government could no longer rely on the ideological affinity that had underscored its good relationship with the Johnson administration. In 1969, the Nixon administration approved of the negotiated nationalization of Anaconda assets in Chile mostly because the process stood in stark contrast to the way in which the Peruvian military dictatorship had nationalized the International Petroleum Company in 1968 and because Ambassador Korry involved himself directly in the negotiations. However, the Nixon administration did not concede a program loan to the Chilean government in 1969 and did not embrace a political project or a specific candidate in the 1970 electoral process, thus substantially downgrading the close relationship developed between the *oficialista* wing of the PDC and the U.S. foreign policy apparatus over the course of the decade.

Contrary to the pragmatic and largely indifferent attitude of the Nixon administration toward Latin America, the Johnson administration's strategy toward Chile embodied the most optimistic and carefully crafted ideas of the Alliance for Progress. Despite its shortcomings in the short term, that strategy contributed significantly to the implementation of reforms that delineated a distinct, if unfinished, path toward development. The Frei administration, materially, and ideologically backed by the United States, took great steps toward the type of economic and social development promoted by modernization theory and its policy embodiment, the Alliance for Progress. Agrarian reform and rural unionization changed the traditional ways that had prevailed in the countryside for centuries; the "Chileanization" and negotiated nationalization of copper gave the Chilean state a substantial and increasing level of participation in the production and export of the most important staple of the national economy; by contributing to create a better-skilled workforce in the long term, the expansion of primary and secondary education achieved through programs generously subsidized by Alliance for Progress money arguably set the stage for the later modernization of the Chilean economy and its sustained growth in the 1980s and 1990s; important public works (for example, the Lo Prado tunnel that significantly reduced the travel time between Santiago and the port city of Valparaíso; the beginning of the construction of the Santiago subway) and numerous housing projects left a lasting mark on national infrastructure; last but not least, the extraordinary levels of growth and the decrease of the inflation rate between 1964 and 1967, partly the result of an unusually high international price for copper, contributed to a perceivable improvement in the economic conditions of the country and a considerable, if by no means revolutionary, redistribution of income in favor of the urban and rural working classes. One particular economic indicator should suffice to demonstrate the impact of the Revolution in Liberty in the socioeconomic order of the country: while, as a result of the inflationary policies of the Popular Unity government, real wages fell 23 percent between 1970 and 1973, they rose by an average of 8 percent in the years of the Frei administration.[3]

To be sure, some of these policies had little or no chance of survival after 1970. The redistributive spirit of the agrarian reform, taken to the extreme under the Allende government, was swiftly killed by the military regime after 1973. Ultimately, the end of the traditional social and economic order that characterized the countryside until the 1960s would be the result not of the progressive process of agrarian reform under Frei and Allende but of the ruthless implementation of the neoliberal program of the military dictatorship and the rapid opening of the Chilean economy to the world market. The Frei administration's copper policies were swiftly undone by the full nationalization undertaken by the Allende government, which refused to pay proper compensation to the expropriated U.S. companies. The military dictatorship decided to keep the *Gran Minería* in the hands of the state but eventually settled for the payment of compensation to the Anaconda and Kennecott corporations, thus trading a great fiscal cost for the normalization of the country's standing among international suppliers of credits and capitals. The military dictatorship also changed the way in which the state administered public education, transferring responsibility for it to municipalities, and welcomed an increasing participation of private actors in the provision of primary, secondary, and higher education. These later alterations, however, do not diminish the contingent and very noticeable effects of Frei's Revolution in Liberty—probably the most accomplished representation of the spirit of the Alliance for Progress in all of Latin America—even if the ambitious long-term project of development of the PDC could not be carried out in full.

To a large extent, Frei and the PDC were able to deliver on a sizeable part of their 1964 platform because of the economic and political support of the United States. The implemented reforms, moreover, had a significant and in some cases lasting impact on the country. Still, the pace of change was by no means revolutionary. Frei and his following within the PDC understood very well that ambitious social and economic reforms, no matter how progressive in their inspiration, required responsible political management. They also knew that will alone does not bring about success, especially when it comes to economic matters. The success of Frei's Revolution in Liberty depended on the ability of the government to maintain conditions of stability through responsi-

ble and, in some cases unpopular, fiscal policies. This combination of an ambitious reformist drive and a rather orthodox adherence to fiscal prudence,
prevalent in the first half of the Frei administration, yielded positive results; the
pace of the change it brought about, however, could not be as rapid and struc-
turally transformative as the excessive optimism of 1964, fundamentally shared
by the United States, had seemed to announce. The relatively slow pace of social and economic change that resulted from the implementation of the Frei
program—and it must be stressed that it was slow only if evaluated according to
the initial optimism of the PDC in 1964 and compared to the Marxist Left's
vocal promise of revolutionary change—partly explains the sense of unconfor-
mity and failure that took over a large part of the country by the end of the
1960s.

Nevertheless, the polarization of politics and society that began to engulf
Chile by the end of the Frei administration had little to do with the implementation of the original PDC program. The massacres of innocents by the
military in El Salvador in 1966 and by the police in Puerto Montt in 1969
certainly damaged the image of the PDC among workers and the poor, but
neither of those events acquired the character of turning points in the evolution of Chilean politics. The causes of the polarization of Chilean politics lay
within a sociological structure that could not be easily reshaped by the performance of a democratic government, no matter how successful it was. The
Marxist Left had established itself ever more firmly on the grounds of Chilean
politics, fundamentally because their representative parties had a strong following among the middle and, especially, the lower classes and had almost coopted
the organized labor movement. Furthermore, the Left's revolutionary promise,
based on a radically different approach to private property and the relationship
between the state and the national economy, presented the Chilean people with
a seemingly feasible political project, capable of doing away for good with the
economic and social inequalities inherent in a free economy, as the cases of
Cuba and other communist states apparently demonstrated. So powerful and
appealing was the message of the Left for a considerable part of the Chilean
polity that even within the PDC a good number of members promoted an
alliance with the coalition of Communists and Socialists.

In a telling sign of the state and tone of Chile's political affairs by the end
of the 1960s, none other than Radomiro Tomic, the PDC's presidential candidate for 1970, was among the Christian Democrats who believed their party
should form an alliance with the Marxist Left, as this union of forces would
allow for a real transformation in the social and economic structures of the
country. The implication of such an attitude, Tomic's utterances during the

1970 campaign notwithstanding, was that Frei had not really succeeded as president and, worse than that, his ideological refusal to reach an understanding with the Marxist parties was an intellectual and strategic mistake. The revolutionary message of the Chilean Left, in tune with the Cuban Revolution and other communist regimes around the world, possessed a spiritual strength and an ideological consistency that virtually turned it into a spell for many middle- and upper-class politicians and intellectuals. The Left's constituencies would probably not change their preferences in large numbers because of the moderate success of a government committed to gradual change within the boundaries set by what Marxist politicians, including Salvador Allende, considered an inherently insufficient democracy. As a result, the presidential candidate of the Marxist Left obtained in 1970 roughly the same proportion of votes (36.3 percent) as he had obtained in 1964 (38.6 percent).

On the other side of the spectrum, a revitalized Right stood behind the personality and the message of former President Jorge Alessandri, the one man of that ideological sensitivity who enjoyed wide respect among the Chilean people. Unlike 1964, when the crumbling Conservative and Liberal parties had unconditionally sided with the PDC against the Left, toward the end of the Frei administration, the Right adopted a rigid ideological position around the theme of private property that prevented any new tactical alliance with the party of the president. This possibility was further undermined by the radical platform on which Tomic and the PDC decided to run their presidential campaign in 1970. This decision also affected the relationship between the candidate and President Frei and, to a large extent, explains the relatively poor performance of Tomic in the election. Given the procedural rules of Chile's political process, the lack of unity between the anti-Marxist forces gave the Left a chance of success disproportionate to its electoral strength. Until 1970, the system had worked more or less correctly because no government under the Constitution of 1925 had promoted revolutionary change, even though many of them—the Radical governments of the 1940s and the Frei administration—had proposed and carried out ambitious economic and social reforms. In 1970, a candidate riding on an explicitly revolutionary political program reached the highest office of the republic even as he obtained only 36 percent of the votes cast in the presidential election. The Chilean political system and culture, largely identified with the forms and style of liberal democracy and standing on a more or less unaltered state of economic and social stability—even if this was materially insufficient and based on a heavily unequal distribution of income—could not resist the challenge entailed by a revolutionary project whose first and foremost impact was the radical alteration of that stability.

The political forces philosophically opposed to the Marxist Left contributed significantly to the erosion of the civic climate necessary for the survival of democratic institutions. Already in 1964 a few military officers and politicians spoke, albeit casually and unconvincingly, of opposing a possible Allende victory in the presidential election by all conceivable means, including unconstitutional and violent ones. In 1970, not only Viaux and his fanatical followers considered Popular Unity's victory a mortal threat for Chile's institutions. Frei, some of his ministers, and a few active military officers entertained the idea of an institutional crisis or a full-blown military coup that would prevent Allende's accession to the presidency. Ultimately, they did nothing concrete to block Allende's road to power, yet their non-consummated intentions bespoke a mindset dominated by a deep fear and an intransigent rejection of the Marxist Left. This attitude bode ill for the functioning of Chilean democracy under Allende, as it forecast the inability and, in some cases, the unwillingness of the major political forces to delimitate a minimum common ground on which to interact. More ominously, Frei's and his ministers' attitude after the popular election of September 1970 announced their willingness to support an unconstitutional move by the military against Allende. Eduardo Frei, the man who in the wake of the U.S.-supported coup against Guatemala's president Jacobo Arbenz in 1954 had promised his party would always defend "the legal government," supported the military coup in 1973.[4] As did many other Cold War politicians in Chile and abroad, Frei thought Marxism was the gravest threat to the institutions of liberal democracy and, to confront that challenge, unconstitutional and undemocratic measures could be temporarily warranted. The harsh reality of the Pinochet dictatorship proved Frei and other PDC politicians who initially approved of the military coup utterly and cruelly wrong.

The Allende government and the Pinochet dictatorship instantly became symbols of the global Cold War. In addition, the experience of the Chilean road to socialism and the military regime have left a profound imprint on Chilean history and memory. As a result, the Frei government usually has been interpreted and studied as the prelude to the crisis and breakdown of democracy in Chile—rightly so. However, this tragic turn of events was certainly not what most of the subjects of this historical inquiry had in mind, even if some of them were deeply pessimistic as to the future of Chile after Allende's election in 1970. Consequently, their actions deserve a non-teleological appraisal, even if we all know how things eventually turned out. Seen in this light, the

Frei administration and its relationship with the Johnson administration deserve a more prominent place in the history of international politics of the 1960s. The political project of Frei and the PDC represented an original and articulate vision toward development at a time when development was the most pressing political matter for the countries of Latin America and the Third World. Frei's Revolution in Liberty sought to modernize Chile's economy and its social structure, especially in the countryside, by implementing far-reaching reforms, within the boundaries of a capitalist economic order and a democratic political system. Not that it was a unique project. Attempts at social and economic modernization undertaken by contemporary Latin American leaders such as Peru's Fernando Belaúnde and Colombia's Carlos Lleras Restrepo had many points in common with the Revolution in Liberty. Chile's relatively more stable institutions and political history, and its more complex economy, however, made it a better potential stage for substantial change in the short term. In addition, the well-established ideological divide of the Chilean political system, which ran along the lines of the broader ideological confrontation of the Cold War, gave the Frei experiment a high degree of symbolic importance in the context of world politics.

As a progressive political project opposed to both conservative elites and Marxist revolutionaries, Frei's Revolution in Liberty offered one of the most comprehensive projects of modernization of those attempted in Latin America, and particularly in Chile, during the Cold War. It was an unfinished project, and many of its specific policies were reversed by its ideological adversaries in the years of the tragedy of Chilean democracy. However, aided by the United States, it was capable of bringing about significant, if not revolutionary, economic and social change in the course of a few years. This change was materialized without violating the rules of the democratic competition—albeit Frei and some his ministers seriously considered the possibility of a coup in September-October 1970—and while maintaining a situation of institutional and fiscal stability even as the ideological foundations of Chilean politics entered into a frenzied spiral of polarization by the end of the Frei administration. It was also sustained by a government that, in spite of its supposedly distinctive progressive outlook, chose to enforce the rule of law with great determination, following the historic pattern of the Chilean state's violent repression of modes of mobilization perceived as unacceptable challenges to the social order. This strategic decision of the Frei administration, however, did not significantly affect the president's personal standing among the population and was not a significant factor in the result of the election of 1970, in which, it is worth repeating, Salvador Allende obtained a smaller share of the vote than in the election of

1964. True, the Chilean electorate turned its back on Radomiro Tomic in 1970—and he still obtained over a quarter of the popular vote—but arguably that rejection was the result of an ill-conceived campaign that tried too hard to depart from the spirit of the Frei government.

Frei's ideological convictions and his political project for Chilean modernization and development would not have another chance. In the most brutal and saddest irony of Chilean history, the military regime that overthrew Salvador Allende in 1973 turned out to be much more revolutionary and transformative than its predecessors. The dictatorship's modernization of the Chilean economy, successful in some quantitative terms, stood on the brutal suppression of dissent and on adjustment policies promoted by monetarist economists, most of them trained at the University of Chicago, who blatantly and even proudly ignored the immediate and almost catastrophic social consequences they brought about in the mid-1970s. The democratic system that followed the military dictatorship in 1990 was based on a new constitution and a different political culture, devoid of the wide ideological diversity that characterized Chile until 1973. Among other reasons, this change occurred because the most radical force in Chilean politics before the military coup, the Socialist Party, had shed its most extreme views and had embraced, somewhat grudgingly, the inescapable realities of free markets and liberal democracy. The first president of Chile's new democracy was an experienced Christian Democratic politician of the Frei line, Patricio Aylwin—supported, among others, by the Socialist and Radical parties. The most ambitious developmental programs of the old PDC, however, could not be revived, as the Chilean and the world economy had acquired a radically different character. After the tragic experience of Chilean democracy in the 1970s and 1980s, the last decade of the twentieth century was a time for political restraint, moderate expectations, growth-oriented economic policies, and fiscal prudence. It was no longer a time for revolution, not even a Revolution in Liberty.

Notes

Introduction: The United States and Chilean Politics in the Cold War

1. *Qué Pasa*, 28 August 2004.

2. U.S. Congress, Senate, *Alleged Assassination Plots*; U.S. Congress, Senate, *Covert Action in Chile*.

3. *La Tercera*, 29 August 2004. Zaldívar has reiterated this position more recently, conspicuously in 2013, amid the commemoration of the fortieth anniversary of the 1973 military coup.

4. I follow the definition of the term *political culture* provided by political scientists John Booth and Patricia Richard. They describe it as "a learned set of attitudes, norms, expectations and values concerning the political environment that shapes the political behavior of citizens." Booth and Richard, *Latin American Political Culture*, pp. 6–7.

5. Eduardo Frei Montalva was president of Chile between 1964 and 1970. His son, Eduardo Frei Ruiz-Tagle, held the same office between 1994 and 2000. Throughout this work, every mention of the name Eduardo Frei and its variations (Frei, President Frei) refers to the former.

6. On Eduardo Frei Montalva and his government, the best and most comprehensive work is that of Gazmuri, *Eduardo Frei Montalva y su época*. Other works on the Frei administration include Sigmund, *The Overthrow of Allende*, and Fleet, *The Rise and Fall of Chilean Christian Democracy*.

7. The idea of the Cold War in the Third World as a clash between different models of modernization has been proposed by Westad, *The Global Cold War*.

8. Gustafson, *Hostile Intent*; Taffet, *Foreign Aid as Foreign Policy*.

9. Telegram from the U.S. embassy in Chile to the Department of State, 29 March 1968, *Foreign Relations of the United States (FRUS), 1964–1968*, Vol. XXXI, pp. 612–613.

10. On modernization theory and U.S. foreign policy, see Latham, *Modernization as Ideology*, especially pp. 69–108, and *The Right Kind of Revolution*. The best-known historic interpretation of and blueprint for capitalist modernization was proposed by Walt W. Rostow, who would later serve as national security advisor for President Lyndon B Johnson: *The Stages of Economic Growth*.

11. An extensive body of literature, in English and Spanish, has explored and analyzed a number of aspects of the trajectory of Chilean politics in the years of the Frei administration: Gil, *The*

Political System of Chile; Valenzuela, *The Breakdown of Democratic Regimes*; Scully, *Rethinking the Center*; Fermandois, "La época de las visitas" and *Mundo y fin de mundo*; Casals, *El alba de una revolución*; Palieraki, *¡La revolución ya viene!*; and Torres, *La crisis del sistema democrático*.

12. The concept of "empire by invitation" was coined by historian Geir Lundestad in his seminal assessment of the relations between the United States and Western Europe in the wake of World War II, "Empire by Invitation?" Historian Alan Knight has suggested that the structure of the relations between the United States and Latin America fits relatively well into this paradigm: "U.S. Imperialism/Hegemony and Latin American Resistance," p. 36. On the hegemonic character of the U.S. presence in the Americas, see Loveman, *No Higher Law*.

13. Ulianova and Fediakova, "Algunos aspectos de la ayuda financiera del Partido Comunista de la URSS."

14. The theoretical discussion about the concepts of empire, imperialism, and hegemony is extensive and, unfortunately, inconclusive. Authors of such different backgrounds and intellectual sensibilities as Michael Mann and Henry Kissinger understand the concept *empire* in the past two centuries as the establishment and consolidation of an international order with a recognizable unilateral leadership. For Mann, the United States was the imperial power in the post–World War II period; for Kissinger, the United States has historically been the empire in the Americas. Kissinger, *Diplomacy*, p. 21; Mann, *The Sources of Social Power*, pp. 86–128. As useful as they are for a broad understanding of the functioning of international relations, these interpretations fail to account for the particulars of different sets of bilateral, multilateral, or regional relations. A more nuanced understanding of the term *empire* with similarities to the ideas of Kissinger and Mann was earlier proposed by Tony Smith in his book *The Pattern of Imperialism*, pp. 6–7 and 142–143. Other authors, such as Maier, in *Among Empires*, also associate the term *empire* or *imperial power* to the maintenance of an international system with particular characteristics. A similar interpretive framework, but preferring the term *hegemony* over *empire*, is proposed by Ikenberry, *Liberal Leviathan*. A similar view, although less developed theoretically and more critical of U.S. foreign policy, is put forth by Hunt, *The American Ascendancy*. In this work, I have assumed the distinctions between the concepts of empire and hegemony proposed by political scientist Michael Doyle and historian Paul Schroeder. For them, empires exercise effective control over the internal and external decisions of a foreign community, whereas a hegemonic power, as Schroeder puts it, exercises a "clear, acknowledged leadership and superior influence . . . within a community of units not under a single authority." Doyle, *Empires*, p. 12; Schroeder, "From Hegemony to Empire," pp. 63–64.

15. The involvement of the United States in Chilean politics in the years of the Allende government has been the subject of many books in the United States, Chile, and elsewhere. Before the massive declassification of documents on Chile ordered by President Bill Clinton in 1999, several scholars published books on the matter: Petras and Morley, *The United States and Chile*; Jensen, *The Garotte*; and Sigmund, *The United States and Democracy in Chile*. After the 1999 release of documents, several books on the subject were published: Haslam, *The Nixon Administration and Allende's Chile*; Qureshi, *Nixon, Kissinger and Allende*; and Moniz Bandeira, *Fórmula para o caos*. Chilean authors have also written on the involvement of the United States in Chile in the Allende years, all of them from a militantly anti-American point of view: Verdugo, *Allende*; Corvalán Márquez, *La secreta obscenidad de la historia de Chile contemporáneo*; and Basso, *La CIA en Chile*. By far the best books on the foreign relations and international standing of the Allende government, including U.S. involvement in Chile in that period are those of Fermandois, *Chile y el mundo*, and Harmer, *Allende's Chile and the Inter-American Cold War*.

16. Kornbluh, *The Pinochet File;* Gustafson, *Hostile Intent*.

17. Power, *Right-Wing Women in Chile* and "The Engendering of Anticommunism and Fear"; Kirkendall, "Kennedy Men and the Fate of the Alliance for Progress"; Taffet, "Alliance for What?", *Foreign Aid as Foreign Policy,* and "The Making of an Economic Anti-American."

18. The reference to Donoso's work is not gratuitous. Published in 1979, *A House in the Country (Casa de Campo)*, one of the greatest Chilean novels of the twentieth century, has been widely interpreted as a metaphor of Pinochet's Chile.

19. From Embassy Santiago to State Department, "Conversation with Frei," Telegram 1160/1, 25 March 1969, NARA, RG 59, Central Foreign Policy Files, 1967–1969, Political and Defense, Box 1981.

20. Letter from Ralph Dungan to Norman Cousins, *Saturday Review*, 17 February 1966, John F. Kennedy Library, The Personal Papers of Ralph Dungan, Box 14.

21. Bethell and Roxborough, *Latin America between the Second World War and the Cold War;* Schwartzberg, *Democracy and U.S. Policy in Latin America.* On the Cold War and Latin America, see: McPherson, *Intimate Ties, Bitter Struggles;* Grow, *U.S. Presidents and Latin American Interventions;* Brands, *Latin America's Cold War,* and Rabe, *The Killing Zone.*

22. On the growth of the foreign service in the immediate post-WWII era, see Moskin, *American Statecraft,* pp. 454–468; and Kopp, *The Voice of the Foreign Service,* loc. 699.

23. A good treatment of the U.S. motivations to intervene in Central American and Caribbean countries in the first three decades of the twentieth century is found in Atkins, *Latin America in the International Political System,* pp. 88–97. See also Rosenberg, *Financial Missionaries to the World,* and Langley, *The Banana Wars.*

24. The difference between the Central American and Caribbean countries, on the one hand, and the South American countries, on the other, has been aptly noted by Atkins, *Latin America and the Caribbean in the International System,* pp. 33–38. The differences in the relations between the United States and the countries of the two large Latin American regions have been identified and analyzed in terms similar to those proposed in this work by Knight, "U.S. Imperialism/Hegemony," pp. 32, 38–39.

25. On the United States and Western Europe after World War II, see Hogan, *The Marshall Plan,* and Hitchcock, "The Marshall Plan and the Creation of the West." On the particular cases of France and Italy, see Brogi, *A Question of Self-Esteem.*

26. Peterson, *Argentina and the United States,* pp. 450–455; Siekmeier, *The Bolivian Revolution.*

1. The U.S. Embassy in Santiago and the Presidential Election of 1964

1. On the early history of the Christian Democratic Party, see Boizard, *La Democracia Cristiana en Chile.*

2. Memorandum from the President's Special Assistant (Dungan) to the President's Special Assistant for National Security Affairs (Bundy), 18 January 1964, *Foreign Relations of the United States, (FRUS), 1964–1968,* Vol. XXXI, p. 549; Memorandum from the Assistant Secretary for Inter-American Affairs (Mann) to Secretary of State Rusk, 1 May 1964, *FRUS,* Vol. XXXI, *1964–1968,* p. 564.

3. Schoultz, *That Infernal Little Cuban Republic;* Dobbs, *One Minute to Midnight.*

4. On the constitution and actions of the Church Committee, see Johnson, *A Season of Inquiry Revisited.*

5. Jorge Alessandri was elected by Congress in 1958, after he narrowly beat Salvador Allende, the candidate of the Left, in the popular vote. Even though he did not belong to any political party, Alessandri was the undisputed leader of the conservative forces in Chilean politics. His father, Arturo Alessandri Palma, was a towering figure in Chilean politics in the first half of the twentieth century, as a liberal-progressive reformer in his first term as president (1920–1925) and as an implacable enforcer of the constitutional order in his second period in La Moneda (1932–1938).

6. *La Nación,* 7 February 1964.

7. *El Mercurio,* 15 March 1964.

8. From Embassy Santiago to State Department, "Joint Weeka No. 11," Airgram 685, 23 March 1964, NARA, RG 59, Central Foreign Policy Files, 1964–1966, Political and Defense, Box 2025.

9. Carlos Ibáñez del Campo, an army officer with progressive political inclinations, had become president in 1927, after a series of military interventions, and ruled as a de facto dictator until 1931 when massive protests against the government led to his resignation. In 1952, running on a populist platform supported by parties on the Right and the Left, Ibáñez won the presidential election and served the full term until 1958.

10. The most extensive and best recent discussion of the effects of the Naranjazo in the presidential election of 1964 is offered by Casals, *La creación de la amenaza roja*, pp. 290–328. An earlier good assessment is that of Etchepare and Valdés, *El naranjazo*. Other works that treat this episode more or less extensively are: Olavarría Bravo, *Chile entre dos Alessandri*, pp. 110–139; Gil, *The Political System of Chile*, pp. 242–243; Moulian, *Fracturas*, pp. 218–220; Gustafson, *Hostile Intent*, pp. 36–38; and Fermandois, *La revolución inconclusa*, pp. 119–123.

11. From Embassy Santiago to State Department, "Joint Weeka No. 12," Airgram 699, 20 March 1964, NARA, RG 59, Central Foreign Policy Files, 1964–1966, Political and Defense, Box 2025.

12. In the election of deputies of March 1965, the Conservative and Liberal parties combined barely gained 15 percent of the vote and elected only nine deputies of a total of 147. In 1961 they had won 31 percent of the vote and elected forty-five deputies. Urzúa, *Historia política de Chile*, pp. 598, 610, 622, 630–631.

13. From Embassy Santiago to State Department, Telegram 762, 16 March 1964, NARA, RG 59, Central Foreign Policy Files, 1964–1966, Political and Defense, Box 2029.

14. National Intelligence Estimate, Number 94-63, "The Chilean Situation and Prospects," 3 October 1963, paragraphs 11 and 12. Lyndon B. Johnson Presidential Library, Papers of Lyndon B. Johnson, President 1963–1969, National Security File, National Security Estimates, Box 9.

15. *El Mercurio*, 17 March 1964.

16. The decision was taken at an extraordinary meeting of the National Assembly of the Party on 5 April, with 139 delegates voting for keeping Durán in the race and twenty-four for accepting his resignation. *El Mercurio*, 6 April 1964.

17. *El Mercurio*, 21 March 1964.

18. Gustafson, *Hostile Intent*, p. 40.

19. Interview of Joseph John Jova by Charles Stuart Kennedy, 1991, "The Association for Diplomatic Studies and Training Foreign Affairs Oral History Project," accessed 22 April 2019, http://adst.org/oral-history.

20. U.S. Congress. Senate, *Covert Action in Chile*, p. 14.

21. Interview of Robert A. Stevenson, by Charles Stuart Kennedy, 1989, "The Association for Diplomatic Studies and Training Foreign Affairs Oral History Project," accessed 22 April 2019, http://adst.org/oral-history.

22. Ulianova and Fediakova, "Algunos aspectos de la ayuda financiera del Partido Comunista de la URSS," pp. 133–134.

23. Zourek, *Checoslovaquia y el Cono Sur*, p. 152.

24. From Embassy Santiago to State Department, "Allende's Finances," 5 May 1964, Papers of Lyndon Baines Johnson, President 1963–1969, National Security File, Country File, Latin America-Brazil, Box 12. Lyndon B. Johnson Presidential Library.

25. Letter from John McCone to Henry Kissinger, 14 September 1970, CREST: 25-Year Program Archive, Freedom of Information Act Electronic Reading Room, accessed 29 January 2017, www.cia.gov.

26. The President's Intelligence Checklist, 21 March 1964, CREST: 25-Year Program Archive, Freedom of Information Act Electronic Reading Room, accessed 29 January 2017. Juan Lechín was a Bolivian union leader and politician.

27. The President's Intelligence Checklist, 23 April 1964, CREST: 25-Year Program Archive, Freedom of Information Act Electronic Reading Room, accessed 29 January 2017. My italics.

28. On the reformist project of the Radical Party in the 1930s and 1940s, especially its political-cultural dimension, see Barr-Melej, *Reforming Chile*. On the parties of the Right, see Correa, *Con las riendas del poder*; and Pereira, *El Partido Conservador*.

29. Milos, *Frente Popular en Chile*.

30. From Embassy Santiago to State Department, "Joint Weeka No. 12," Airgram 633, 20 March 1964, NARA, RG 59, Central Foreign Policy Files, 1964–1966, Political and Defense, Box 2025.

31. *El Mercurio*, 21 March 1964.

32. From Embassy Santiago to State Department, Telegram 1222, 2 May 1964, NARA, RG 59, Central Foreign Policy Files, 1964–1966, Political and Defense, Box 2027.

33. From Embassy Santiago to State Department, Telegram 1034, 12 May 1964, NARA, RG 59, Central Foreign Policy Files, 1964–1966, Political and Defense, Box 2027.

34. From Embassy Santiago to State Department, "Joint Weeka No. 13," Airgram 715, 26 March 1964, NARA, RG 59, Central Foreign Policy Files, 1964–1966, Political and Defense, Box 2025.

35. From State Department to Embassy Santiago, Telegram 532, 25 March 1965, NARA, RG 59, Central Foreign Policy Files, 1964–1966, Political and Defense, Box 2029.

36. From Embassy Santiago to State Department, Telegram 818, 26 March 1964, NARA, RG 59, Central Foreign Policy Files, 1964–1966, Political and Defense, Box 2029.

37. "Support for the Chilean Presidential Elections of 4 September 1964," Memorandum prepared for the Special Group, 1 April 1964. *FRUS, 1964–1968*, Vol. XXXI, p. 556; Gustafson, *Hostile Intent*, pp. 43–44.

38. From Embassy Santiago to State Department, Telegram 793, 25 March 1964, NARA, RG 59, Central Foreign Policy Files, 1964–1966, Political and Defense, Box 2029. Faivovich's trajectory is a good representation of the ideological contradictions and conflicts that beset the Radical Party in the 1960s and 1970s.

39. Valdivia, *Nacionales y gremialistas*, p. 253.

40. From Embassy Santiago to State Department, Telegram 825, 30 March 1964, NARA, RG 59, Central Foreign Policy Files, 1964–1966, Political and Defense, Box 2029.

41. "Support for the Chilean Presidential Elections of 4 September 1964," Memorandum prepared for the Special Group, 1 April 1964. *FRUS, 1964–1968*, Vol. XXXI, p. 556.

42. *El Mercurio*, 24 April and 1 May, 1964.

43. From Embassy Santiago to State Department, Telegram 821, 27 March 1964, NARA, RG 59, Central Foreign Policy Files, 1964–1966, Political and Defense, Box 2029.

44. *El Mercurio*, 26 March 1964.

45. From Embassy Santiago to State Department, Telegram 811, 25 March 1964, NARA, RG 59, Central Foreign Policy Files, 1964–1966, Political and Defense, Box 2029.

46. From Embassy Santiago to State Department, Telegram 808, 25 March 1964, NARA, RG 59, Central Foreign Policy Files, 1964–1966, Political and Defense, Box 2029; From Embassy Santiago to State Department, Telegram 820, 26 March 1964, NARA, RG 59, Central Foreign Policy Files, 1964–1966, Political and Defense, Box 2029; From Embassy Santiago to State Department, Telegram 828, 31 March 1964, NARA, RG 59, Central Foreign Policy Files, 1964–1966, Political and Defense, Box 2029.

47. From Embassy Santiago to State Department, Telegram 1021, 25 March 1964, NARA, RG 59, Central Foreign Policy Files, 1964–1966, Political and Defense, Box 2027. The amount in dollars has been calculated considering an official exchange rate of 2.3 escudos per dollar. Díaz, Lüders, and Wagner, *La República en Cifras*.

48. From Embassy Santiago to State Department, Telegram 1064, 14 May 1964, NARA, RG 59, Central Foreign Policy Files, 1964–1966, Political and Defense, Box 2027.

49. From Embassy Santiago to State Department, Telegram 1044, 12 May 1964, NARA, RG 59, Central Foreign Policy Files, 1964–1966, Political and Defense, Box 2027.

50. Fermandois, *La revolución inconclusa*, pp. 121–22.

51. From Embassy Santiago to State Department, Telegram 787, 20 March 1964, NARA, RG 59, Central Foreign Policy Files, 1964–1966, Political and Defense, Box 2029.

52. From Embassy Santiago to State Department, Telegram 787, 20 March 1964, NARA, RG 59, Central Foreign Policy Files, 1964–1966, Political and Defense, Box 2029.

53. From Embassy Santiago to State Department, Telegram 981, 2 May 1964, NARA, RG 59, Central Foreign Policy Files, 1964–1966, Political and Defense, Box 2020.

54. "Request for renewal of project [redacted, one word]," Memorandum from William Broe, CIA Chief of Western Hemisphere Division, to Deputy Director for Plans, 20 March 1968. U.S. State Department, Freedom of Information Act (FOIA), Virtual Reading Room, accessed 22 April 2019, foia.state.gov.

55. From Embassy Santiago to State Department, Telegram 981, 2 May 1964, NARA, RG 59, Central Foreign Policy Files, 1964–1966, Political and Defense, Box 2020.

56. From Embassy Santiago to State Department, Telegram 1044, 2 May 1964, NARA, RG 59, Central Foreign Policy Files, 1964–1966, Political and Defense, Box 2027.

57. *El Mercurio*, 11 May 1964. A good account of the negotiations and backroom maneuvers that led to the confirmation of Julio Durán as the candidate of the Radical Party on 10 May, from the perspective of the Chilean press, which ignored many of the details abundantly discussed in the records of the U.S. embassy in Santiago, is provided by Casals, *La creación de la amenaza roja*, pp. 323–28.

58. T. F. Schmidt, "Election Operation in Chile. The 1964 Presidential Race," *Studies in Intelligence: The IC's Journal for the Intelligence Professional*, n.d., Declassified Articles from Studies in Intelligence: The IC's Journal for the Intelligence Professional, Freedom of Information Act Electronic Reading Room, accessed 29 April 2018, www.cia.gov.

59. Salomón Corbalán died in a car accident in 1967. After hearing the news, the embassy rushed to report to the State Department that Luis Corvalán, the secretary general of the Communist Party, had died. A few minutes later the embassy retracted and sent the correct information to Washington. Wishful thinking on the part of the embassy staff or just an innocent mistake? From Embassy Santiago to State Department, Telegram 3115, 11 March 1967, NARA, RG 59, Central Foreign Policy Files, 1967–1969, Political and Defense, Box 1978; From Embassy Santiago to State Department, Telegram 3117, 11 March 1967, NARA, RG 59, Central Foreign Policy Files, 1967–1969, Political and Defense, Box 1978.

60. Manuel Cabieses, "Good Bye Mr. Jova," *El Siglo*, 22 May 1964.

61. *Diario de Sesiones de la Cámara de Diputados*, 3rd Session, 3 June 1964, pp. 196–200. The translation of the excerpt, as are all translations in the book, is mine.

62. *El Siglo*, 7 June 1964.

63. *Diario de Sesiones de la Cámara de Diputados,* 3rd Session, 3 June 1964, pp. 209–211.

64. From Embassy Santiago to State Department, Telegram 1070, 15 May 1964, NARA, RG 59, Central Foreign Policy Files, 1964–1966, Political and Defense, Box 2027.

65. From Embassy Santiago to State Department, Telegram 1084, 19 May 1964, NARA, RG 59, Central Foreign Policy Files, 1964–1966, Political and Defense, Box 2028.

66. In 1968, Communist journalist Eduardo Labarca published a poignant denunciation of U.S. intervention in the 1964 presidential election, including Jova's meddling. Labarca's account did not rely on any verifiable documentary sources and was also framed in the ideological left-wing view of U.S. imperialism toward Latin America. However, the book was not too far off the mark. Labarca, *Chile invadido.*

67. Between 1932 and 1964, there were in Chile seven presidential elections, eight parliamentarian elections, and eleven municipal elections.

68. From Embassy Santiago to State Department, Telegram 1005, 5 May 1964, NARA, RG 59, Central Foreign Policy Files, 1964–1966, Political and Defense, Box 2028.

69. This was the view of Radical politician and businessman Carlos Briceño, who also assured U.S. political officer Frank Ravindal that Radicals would vote for Frei in Congress even if he finished second in the popular election. From Embassy Santiago to State Department, Airgram 833, 6 May 1964, NARA, RG 59, Central Foreign Policy Files, 1964–1966, Political and Defense, Box 2027.

70. In 1958, about 1.25 million people cast their ballots in the presidential election; in 1964, the number of voters had grown to about 2.5 million.

71. The United States did provide Carabineros with abundant anti-riot material between 1963 and 1964 (tear gas, helmets, radio equipment, etc.) and offered training in riot control for Chilean police officers. From USAID Office Santiago to AID Washington, "Monthly Report on the Public Safety Program for Chile," 5 June 1964, NARA, Record Group 286 [RG 286], Records of the Agency for International Development, Office of Public Safety, Latin American Branch, Country File, Box 24; From Embassy Santiago to State Department, Cablegram to AID 1126, 1 June 1964, NARA, RG 286, Office of Public Safety, Latin American Branch, Country File, Box 24.

72. From Embassy Santiago to State Department, "Chile Pre-election Contingency Plan," Airgram 926, 5 June 1964, NARA, RG 59, Central Foreign Policy Files, 1964–1966, Political and Defense, Box 2020.

73. From George C. Denhey Jr., Bureau of Intelligence and Research, Department of State, to the Acting Secretary of State (George Ball), "Pressures for Change Dominate Chilean Presidential Campaign," 1 May 1964, Papers of Lyndon Baines Johnson, President 1963–1969, National Security File, Country File, Latin America-Brazil, Box 12. Lyndon B. Johnson Presidential Library.

74. Bawden, *The Pinochet Generation.*

75. National Intelligence Estimate, Number 94-63, "The Chilean Situation and Prospects," 3 October 1963. Lyndon B. Johnson Presidential Library, Papers of Lyndon B. Johnson, President 1963–1969, National Security File, National Security Estimates, Box 9.

76. From USCINCSO (O'Meara) to Attorney General (Kennedy), 30 April 1964, Lyndon B. Johnson Presidential Library, Papers of Lyndon B. Johnson, President 1963–1969, Confidential File, Box 7.

77. From Embassy Santiago to State Department, "Joint Weeka No. 17," Airgram 803, 24 April 1964, NARA, RG 59, Central Foreign Policy Files, 1964–1966, Political and Defense, Box 2025.

78. Memorandum of conversation, Ralph Richardson—Colonel Oscar Cristi, 27 February 1964, NARA, RG 59, Central Foreign Policy Files, 1964–1966, Political and Defense, Box 2029.

79. From Embassy Santiago to State Department, "Views of Prominent Radical on Political Situation," Airgram 136, 24 August 1964, NARA, RG 59, Central Foreign Policy Files, 1964–1966, Political and Defense, Box 2029.

80. Schmidt, "Election Operation in Chile."

81. From Embassy Santiago to State Department, "Views of Military and Police Officers on Current Political Scene," Airgram 801, 24 April 1964, NARA, RG 59, Central Foreign Policy Files, 1964–1966, Political and Defense, Box 2028.

82. From Embassy Santiago to State Department, "Chile Pre-election Contingency Plan," Airgram 926, 5 June 1964, NARA, RG 59, Central Foreign Policy Files, 1964–1966, Political and Defense, Box 2020.

83. Memorandum from Robert Sayre to McGeorge Bundy, "Chilean Contingency Planning," 31 July 1964, Papers of Lyndon Baines Johnson, President 1963–1969, National Security File, Country File, Latin America-Brazil, Box 12. Lyndon B. Johnson Presidential Library.

84. From Embassy Santiago to State Department, Telegram Action Dept Priority Ten, 2 July 1964, NARA, RG 59, Central Foreign Policy Files, 1964–1966, Political and Defense, Box 2029.

85. Siekmeier, *The Bolivian Revolution.*

86. U.S. Congress. Senate, *Covert Action in Chile,* p. 16–17.

87. From Embassy Santiago to State Department, Airgram 820, 5 May 1964, NARA, RG 59, Central Foreign Policy Files, 1964–1966, Political and Defense, Box 2027.

88. In one of his conversations with Jova, Durán told the U.S. diplomat about an extramarital affair of Senator Bossay with a woman who worked as a telephone operator in Congress. From Embassy Santiago to State Department, Telegram 1044, 2 May 1964, NARA, RG 59, Central Foreign Policy Files, 1964–1966, Political and Defense, Box 2027.

89. From Embassy Santiago to State Department, "Joint Weeka No. 17," Airgram 803, 24 April 1964, NARA, RG 59, Central Foreign Policy Files, 1964–1966, Political and Defense, Box 2025.

2. Time of Hope, 1964–1967

1. On the foreign policy of Lyndon B. Johnson beyond the Vietnam War, including chapters on Latin America, see Brands (editor), *Beyond Vietnam* and Colman, *The Foreign Policy of Lyndon B. Johnson.*

2. Hurtado-Torres, "The U.S. Press and Chile."

3. Memorandum from Gordon Chase to [National Security Advisor McGeorge] Bundy, 18 September 1964, Lyndon B. Johnson Presidential Library, Papers of Lyndon B. Johnson, President 1963–1969, National Security File, Country File, Latin America—Chile, Box 13. Milton was the younger brother of Dwight Eisenhower and, during the latter's tenure as president, he traveled through Latin American as a goodwill ambassador of sorts. His experiences and ideas about the region and its relations with the United States were published in a somewhat influential book in 1963, *The Wine is Bitter.*

4. Interview of Robert A. Stevenson, by Charles Stuart Kennedy, 1989, p. 36, "The Association for Diplomatic Studies and Training Foreign Affairs Oral History Project," accessed 23 April 2019, http://adst.org/oral-history.

5. Rabe, *The Most Dangerous Area in the World,* p. 113.

6. Interview of Aurelius "Aury" Fernandez, by Charles Stuart Kennedy, 1997, p. 18, "The Association for Diplomatic Studies and Training Foreign Affairs Oral History Project," accessed 23 April 2019, http://adst.org/oral-history.

7. From Embassy Santiago to State Department, "Views of Radical Senator Julio Durán," Airgram 5, 9 July 1966, NARA, RG 59, Central Foreign Policy Files, 1964–1966, Political and Defense, Box 2020.

8. From Dungan to Lincoln Gordon [Assistant Secretary of State for Inter-American Affairs], Telegram 1301, 18 April 1966, NARA, RG 59, Central Foreign Policy Files, 1964–1966, Economic, Finance, Box 842.

9. The personal papers of Ralph Dungan, which include his numerous exchanges with U.S. correspondents during his stint in Chile, are located in the John F. Kennedy Presidential Library: The Personal Papers of Ralph Dungan, especially Boxes 13–30.

10. "Project Camelot," Telegram from the Embassy in Santiago to Department of State, 14 June 1965. *FRUS, 1964–1968*, Vol. XXXI, pp. 612–613.

11. Lowe, "The Camelot Affair"; Herman, "Project Camelot"; Soto, *Espía se ofrece*.

12. On the philosophic roots of the PDC's ideology, Castillo Velasco, *Teoría y práctica de la Democracia Cristiana*, pp. 13–93; Boizard, *La Democracia Cristiana en Chile*, pp. 193–213, 281–291; Nocera, *Acuerdos y desacuerdos*, pp. 58–65.

13. The relevant records for his post-1973 activities regarding Chile, including the mentioned slip, are in The Personal Papers of Ralph Dungan, Box 26.

14. *New York Times*, 8 October 2013.

15. The most relevant books on the subject are Latham, *Modernization as Ideology* and *The Right Kind of Revolution*; Engerman et al. (editors), *Staging Growth*; and Gilman, *Mandarins of the Future*.

16. For a more conservative interpretation of communitarianism, see Castillo Velasco, *Los caminos de la revolución*. The left-leaning vision of the term can be found in Silva Solar and Chonchol, *El desarrollo de la nueva sociedad en América Latina*.

17. The almost complete coincidence between the stated goals of the Alliance for Progress and the Christian Democratic program of 1964 has been noted by Yocelevzky, "La Democracia Cristiana chilena," p. 298.

18. The core economic ideas of the PDC program were outlined in 1958 by Ahumada, a CEPAL economist with close ties to Eduardo Frei, in *En vez de la miseria*. On CEPAL thought on Latin American economies and development, see Deves, *El pensamiento latinoamericano en el siglo XX*, pp. 25–33.

19. The best books on the Alliance for Progress, with a good deal of focus on Chile, are Levinson and Onís, *The Alliance that Lost Its Way* and Taffet, *Foreign Aid as Foreign Policy*. For other contemporary presentations and assessments, see Gordon, *A New Deal for Latin America*; and Rogers, *The Twilight Struggle*.

20. Staley, *The Future of Underdeveloped Countries*, pp. 16–17.

21. Agency for International Development, "Chile: Long-Range Assistance Strategy," 20 July 1964, Lyndon B. Johnson Presidential Library, Papers of Lyndon B. Johnson, President 1963–1969, National Security File, Country File, Latin America—Chile, Box 12.

22. Rostow, *The Stages of Economic Growth*. According to Rostow, economic development historically went through five stages: traditional society, transitional stage, take off, drive to maturity, high mass consumption.

23. Almonacid, *La agricultura chilena discriminada*.

24. Agency for International Development, "Chile: Long-Range Assistance Strategy," 20 July 1964, Lyndon B. Johnson Presidential Library, Papers of Lyndon B. Johnson, President 1963–1969, National Security File, Country File, Latin America—Chile, Box 12.

25. "Agreed Note (Rescheduling of Chilean Debt)," 24 February 1966; From Carlos Massad to Pierre Paul-Schweitzer, 8 March 1967, IMF Archives, Western Hemisphere Department Fonds, Immediate Office Sous-Fonds, WHDAI Country Files, Box 48, Chile (1965–1968).

26. Ley 15.564, 11 February 1964, Ley Chile, accessed 23 April 2019, http://bcn.cl/1mnto.

27. Department of State, Agency for International Development, "Chile: FY 1968–1972, Revised," Program Memorandum, June 1966, NARA, Records of the Agency for International Development, RG 286, Office of Public Safety, Latin American Branch, Country File, Box 25.

28. Caputo and Saravia, "The Fiscal and Monetary History of Chile," p. 20.

29. Meller, *Un siglo de economía política chilena*, p. 111.

30. President Ibáñez hired a group of U.S. advisors, the Klein-Saks Mission, to assess and make recommendations on the proper way to contain inflation. The adjustment policies of Ibáñez, as those of Alessandri and, eventually, those of Frei, failed to check the tide of inflation. Couyoumdjian

(editor), *Reformas económicas e instituciones políticas*. See also Sierra, *Tres ensayos de estabilización en Chile*, pp. 51–132.

31. The differences between the stabilization programs of the Ibáñez and Alessandri administrations, on the one hand, and the Frei administration, on the other, are noted by Ffrench-Davis, *Políticas económicas en Chile*, pp. 55–56.

32. From Embassy Santiago to State Department, "Program Loan Negotiations #2," Telegram 703, 30 November 1965, NARA, RG 59, Central Foreign Policy Files, 1964–1966, Economic, Finance, Box 842.

33. From Embassy Santiago to State Department, Telegram 884, 14 January 1966, NARA, RG 59, Formerly Top Secret Central Foreign Policy Files, Box 2.

34. From State Department to Embassy Santiago, Telegram 648, 17 January 1966, NARA, RG 59, Formerly Top Secret Central Foreign Policy Files, Box 2.

35. See chapter 4, "Chilean Copper and U.S. Companies."

36. Memorandum from Walt W. Rostow to the President, 21 December 1966, Lyndon B. Johnson Presidential Library, Papers of Lyndon B. Johnson, President 1963–1969, National Security File, Country File, Latin America—Chile, Box 13.

37. Executive Office of the President, Bureau of the Budget, "Loans for the Government of Chile," Memorandum for the President, 30 November 1966, Lyndon B. Johnson Presidential Library, Papers of Lyndon B. Johnson, President 1963–1969, National Security File, Country File, Latin America—Chile, Box 13.

38. Executive Office of the President, Bureau of the Budget, "Chile Education Sector Loans," Memorandum for the President, 24 June 1967, Lyndon B. Johnson Presidential Library, Papers of Lyndon B. Johnson, President 1963–1969, National Security File, Country File, Latin America—Chile, Box 13.

39. *Diario de Sesiones del Senado*, 13th Session, 13 July 1954, pp. 698–699.

40. Gleijeses, *The Dominican Crisis*; Lowenthal, *The Dominican Intervention*; Rabe, "The Johnson Doctrine"; Woods, "Conflicted Hegemon."

41. Langley, *The Banana Wars*, pp. 111–160.

42. *El Mercurio*, 2 May 1965.

43. Ibid.

44. From Embassy Quito (Harriman) to President and State Department, Telegram 842, 7 May 1965, NARA, RG 59, Central Foreign Policy Files, 1964–1966, Political and Defense, Box 2816.

45. From Embassy Santiago to State Department, "Harriman's Talks with Frei," Telegram 1729, 8 May 1965, NARA, RG 59, Central Foreign Policy Files, 1964–1966, Political and Defense, Box 2816.

46. From Embassy Santiago to State Department, "Harriman's Talks with Frei," Telegram 1729, 8 May 1965, NARA, RG 59, Central Foreign Policy Files, 1964–1966, Political and Defense, Box 2816.

47. *Diario de Sesiones del Senado*, 40th Session, 5 May 1965, p. 2286.

48. *Diario de Sesiones de la Cámara de Diputados*, 40th Session, 5 May 1965, p. 3163.

49. Fermandois, "Chile y la cuestión cubana."

50. *Diario de Sesiones del Senado*, 40th Session, 5 May 1965, p. 2274.

51. Letter from Salvador Allende to Ralph Dungan, John F. Kennedy Library, The Personal Papers of Ralph Dungan, Box 13. The letter is in English.

52. *Diario de Sesiones del Senado*, 40th Session, 5 May 1965, p. 2297.

53. Letter from Ralph Dungan to Salvador Allende, John F. Kennedy Library, The Personal Papers of Ralph Dungan, Box 13.

54. *Diario de Sesiones del Senado*, 40th Session, 5 May 1965, p. 2267.

55. See *Diario de Sesiones del Senado*, 9th Session, 22 June 1954, pp. 427–437; *Diario de Sesiones del Senado*, 23 June 1954, 10th Session, pp. 594–606; *Diario de Sesiones del Senado*, 7th Session, 20 November 1956, pp. 338–347.

56. The debate on the Soviet invasion of Czechoslovakia in 1968, including Salvador Allende's disingenuous condemnation of it, can be found in *Diario de Sesiones del Senado*, 36th Session, 21 August 1968.

57. *Diario de Sesiones de la Cámara de Diputados*, 40th Session, 5 May 1965, p. 3165.

58. Ibid., p. 3166.

59. From Embassy Santiago to State Department, "Memorandum of Conversation with Otto Boye Soto," Airgram 1002, 11 May 1965, NARA, RG 59, Central Foreign Policy Files, 1964–1966, Political and Defense, Box 2026.

60. "Ante el caso de la República Dominicana," *El Diario Ilustrado*, 4 May 1965.

61. *Diario de Sesiones de la Cámara de Diputados*, 40th Session, 5 May 1965, p. 3157.

62. Ibid., p. 3154.

63. Ibid., p. 3158.

64. De embajada en Washington a Ministerio de Relaciones Exteriores (MRREE), Oficio Confidencial 429/16, "La crisis de República Dominicana," 11 May 1965. Archivo Histórico del Ministerio de Relaciones Exteriores (AHMRE).

65. De embajada en Washington a MRREE, Aerograma Confidencial 202, 6 May 1965, AHMRE.

66. De embajada en Washington a MRREE, Cable Confidencial 234, 28 May 1965, AHMRE.

67. *El Mercurio*, 23 May 1965.

68. Hugo Harvey, "La política exterior de Chile," p. 196.

69. A partial list of such instances of repression includes incidents in Iquique (1890 and 1907), Valparaíso (1903), Santiago (1905, 1946, 1957, and 1962), Antofagasta (1906), Punta Arenas (1920), San Gregorio (1921), La Coruña (1925), and Ranquil (1934).

70. Allende's words in *Diario de Sesiones del Senado*, 80th Session, 16 March 1966, p. 4591.

71. From Embassy Santiago to State Department, "Labor Difficulties in the Chilean Copper Mines—An Assessment," Airgram 822, 30 March 1966, NARA, RG 59, Central Foreign Policy Files, 1964–1966, Labor, Box 1287.

72. Gazmuri, *Eduardo Frei Montalva y su época*, T. I, pp. 300–303.

73. The coincidences between Frei's justification of his government's handling of the events in El Salvador and Duhalde's justification of his decisions in 1946, as well as the differences between the PDC leader's words in 1946 and 1966, were noted by Communist Senator Volodia Teitelboim, *Diario de Sesiones del Senado*, 80th Session, 15 March 1966, p. 4580.

74. *El Mercurio*, 15 March 1966.

75. Loveman and Lira, *Las ardientes cenizas del olvido*, p. 268.

3. Time of Trouble, 1967–1969

1. On the agrarian reform, see Tinsman, *Partners in Conflict*; Huerta, *"Otro agro para Chile"*; Fontaine Aldunate, *La tierra y el poder*; and Bellisario "The Chilean Agrarian Transformation."

2. Fermandois, "La época de las visitas."

3. In a March 1967 memorandum for the president, Walt W. Rostow mentioned Turkey and South Korea as successful cases of the Johnson administration's foreign policy and referred to Pakistan, Venezuela, Iran, and Chile as "potential success stories," all of them worth bringing up as examples of the concrete usefulness of foreign aid. From Walt W. Rostow to the President, 6

March 1967, Lyndon B. Johnson Presidential Library, Papers of Lyndon B. Johnson, President 1963–1969, National Security File, Name File, Box 7.

4. From Embassy Santiago to State Department, "Frei Visit Gifts Suggestion," 13 January 1967, Lyndon B. Johnson Presidential Library, Papers of Lyndon B. Johnson, President 1963–1969, National Security File, Country File, Latin America—Chile, Box 12.

5. Various biographic briefs, n. d., Lyndon B. Johnson Presidential Library, Papers of Lyndon B. Johnson, President 1963–1969, National Security File, Country File, Latin America—Chile, Box 12.

6. From Embassy Santiago to State Department, "Information on Frei's Official Party," 11 January 1967; Memorandum, "The Chileans: Knowing and Approaching Them, Topics of Conversation," n. d., Lyndon B. Johnson Presidential Library, Papers of Lyndon B. Johnson, President 1963–1969, National Security File, Country File, Latin America—Chile, Box 12. Bolivia withdrew its ambassador in Santiago in April 1962 in response to the inauguration of a channel that diverted waters of the Lauca River, which runs from Chile toward Bolivia, ordered by President Jorge Alessandri.

7. Memorandum, "Suggested Toast for Use at the President's Dinner for President Frei of Chile," n. d.; Memorandum, "Suggested Introduction to Joint Session of Congress," n. d., Lyndon B. Johnson Presidential Library, Papers of Lyndon B. Johnson, President 1963–1969, National Security File, Country File, Latin America—Chile, Box 12.

8. Memorandum, "The Chileans: Knowing and Approaching Them, Topics of Conversation," n. d., Lyndon B. Johnson Presidential Library, Papers of Lyndon B. Johnson, President 1963–1969, National Security File, Country File, Latin America—Chile, Box 12.

9. See the intervention of Socialist Senator Salomón Corbalán in the session of 28 July 1965. *Diario de Sesiones del Senado*, 28th Session, 28 July 1965, p. 1859.

10. *Diario de Sesiones del Senado*, 67th Session, Extraordinaria, 17 January 1967, pp. 3677–3678.

11. Ibid., 56th Session, 12 January 1967, pp. 3506–3508.

12. "El embajador Korry en el CEP," p. 78; McVety, *Enlightened Aid.*

13. "Review of the Task Force on the Review of African Development Policies and Programs," Washington, 22 July 1966, *FRUS, 1964–1968*, Vol. XXIV, Africa, pp. 334–349.

14. Edward Korry, "The 40 Committee" (unpublished draft), p. 4, John F. Kennedy Library, The Personal Papers of Ralph Dungan, Box. 27.

15. Memorandum from Walt. W. Rostow to the President, 6 April 1967, Lyndon B. Johnson Presidential Library, Papers of Lyndon B. Johnson, President 1963–1969, National Security File, Name File, Box 7.

16. Interview of Joseph John Jova, by Charles Stuart Kennedy, 1991, pp. 51–53, "The Association for Diplomatic Studies and Training Foreign Affairs Oral History Project," accessed 23 April 2019.

17. Letter from Domingo Santa María (Chilean Ambassador in the United States) and Máximo Pacheco (Minister of Education) to President Eduardo Frei Montalva, 6 February 1970, Archivo Casa-Museo Eduardo Frei Montalva [AEFM], Presidencia, Correspondencia, Folder 60.

18. See chapter 5, "The Presidential Candidacy of Radomiro Tomic."

19. Korry, "Los Estados Unidos en Chile y Chile en los Estados Unidos," p. 34.

20. Carta de Claudio Orrego Vicuña a Eduardo Frei Montalva, 5 June 1968, Fundación Frei, Folder 470; Korry, "Los Estados Unidos en Chile," p. 33.

21. From Embassy Santiago to State Department, "Ex-President Alessandri's Views of Actual Politico-Economic Situation in Chile," Airgram 310, 29 December 1967, NARA, RG 59, Central Foreign Policy Files, 1967–1969, Political and Defense, Box 1976.

22. From Embassy Santiago to State Department, Telegram 1871, 21 December 1967, NARA, RG 59, Central Foreign Policy Files, 1967–1969, Political and Defense, Box 1978.

23. From Embassy Santiago to State Department, "Enclosing Memorandum of Conversation: Fitting the President for Pants," Airgram 327, 10 January 1968, NARA, RG 59, Central Foreign Policy Files, 1967–1969, Political and Defense, Box 1981.

24. Backchannel Message from the Ambassador to Chile (Korry) to the Under Secretary of State for Political Affairs (Johnson) and the President's Assistant for National Security Affairs (Kissinger), 9 October 1970, *FRUS, 1969–1976*, Vol. XXI, pp. 348–351.

25. Korry, "The 40 Committee," p. 7.

26. Patricio Guzmán, *Salvador Allende*, documentary film (Chile, 2004).

27. Korry, "Los Estados Unidos en Chile," p. 30.

28. Davis, *The Last Two Years of Salvador Allende*.

29. *New York Times*, 30 January 2003.

30. An account of the events of El Salvador in *Punto Final*, 77, 25 March 1969.

31. "Proposiciones para una Acción Política en el período 1967–1970 de una Vía No Capitalista de Desarrollo," *Política y Espíritu* 303, October 1967.

32. Molina, *El Proceso de Cambio*, pp. 140–142.

33. Ibid., pp. 143–147.

34. *Punto Final*, 77, 25 March 1969.

35. On Sáez's participation in the Alliance for Progress, see *Raúl Sáez*, pp. 27–84.

36. Sigmund, *The Overthrow of Allende*, pp. 65–67; Fleet, *The Rise and Fall of Chilean Christian Democracy*, p. 102–103; Gazmuri, *Eduardo Frei Montalva y su época*, T. II, pp. 669–670, 688–691.

37. From Embassy Santiago to State Department, Telegram 2368, 5 February 1968, NARA, RG 59, Central Foreign Policy Files, 1967–1969, Political and Defense, Box 1976.

38. *Diario de Sesiones del Senado*, 75th Session, 2 April 1968, p. 3160.

39. Ibid., pp. 3173–3174.

40. From Embassy Santiago to State Department, "Rafael Tarud on Wage Bill Crisis," Telegram 2875, 18 March 1968, NARA, RG 59, Central Foreign Policy Files, 1967–1969, Economic, Box 1226.

41. *Diario de Sesiones del Senado*, 75th Session, 2 April 1968, p. 3170.

42. Telegram from the Embassy in Chile to the Department of State, 29 March 1968, *FRUS, 1964–1968*, Vol. XXXI, pp. 612–613.

43. Memorandum from Walt W. Rostow to President Johnson, "$20 Million Program Loan for Chile," 24 July 1968, Lyndon B. Johnson Presidential Library, Papers of Lyndon B. Johnson, President 1963–1969, National Security File, Country File, Latin America—Chile, Box 14.

44. Although the Alliance for Progress contemplated as one of its core goals the consolidation of democracy in Latin America, between 1961 and 1964 several countries had endured military coups against democratically elected governments: Argentina and Peru (1962), the Dominican Republic (1963), and, the most significant of all, Brazil (1964).

45. Eduardo Frei, "The Alliance that Lost Its Way," *Foreign Affairs*, April 1967, pp. 437–448.

46. From President Frei to President Johnson, 28 May 1968, Lyndon B. Johnson Presidential Library, Papers of Lyndon B. Johnson, President 1963–1969, National Security File, Country File, Latin America—Chile, Box 14.

47. On the decisions made by Lyndon B. Johnson regarding escalation of the war, see Logevall, *Choosing War*; on the conflicting domestic and foreign policies of the Johnson administration, see Bernstein, *Guns or Butter*; a comprehensive recent, more positive appraisal of Lyndon B. Johnson's presidency is Woods, *Prisoners of Hope*.

48. Fredrik Logevall, "Why Lyndon Johnson Dropped Out," *New York Times*, 24 March 2018.

49. From Ambassador Korry to Assistant Secretary of State for Inter-American Affairs Covey Olivier, 14 May 1968, Lyndon B. Johnson Presidential Library, Papers of Lyndon B. Johnson, President 1963–1969, National Security File, Country File, Latin America—Chile, Box 14.

50. Brands, "Economic Development and the Contours of U.S. Foreign Policy."

51. Brands, "Richard Nixon and Economic Nationalism in Latin America"; and "The United States and the Peruvian Challenge."

52. From Embassy Santiago to State Department, "Conversation with Frei (HQ—Foreign Policy)," Telegram 1160, 25 March 1969, NARA, RG 59, Central Foreign Policy Files, 1967–1969, Political and Defense, Box 1981.

53. Korry, "The 40 Committee," p. 22–23.

54. De Ministerio de Relaciones Exteriores (MRREE) a embajada en Washington, Oficio Confidencial 81, "Entrevista Embajador Korry con Ministro," 18 October 1968. Archivo Histórico del Ministerio de Relaciones Exteriores (AHMRE).

55. Valdés, *Sueños y memorias*, p. 165.

56. After his tour, Rockefeller produced a report on the region that did not differ much in its content and spirit from the assessments on which the Democratic administrations had relied for their policies. Rockefeller, *The Rockefeller Report on the Americas*.

57. "Report of the Special Latin American Committee on the Consensus of Viña del Mar," *International Legal Materials* 8, no. 5, September 1969, pp. 974–978.

58. Valdés, *Sueños y memorias*, pp. 195.

59. Ibid., pp. 196–197.

60. *Punto Final* 77, 25 March 1969; Loveman and Lira, *Las ardientes cenizas*, pp. 296–298.

61. A critique of Frei's reactions to and repression of protests and other forms of social mobilization during his tenure is offered by Thielemann, "Eduardo Frei Montalva."

62. *Diario de Sesiones del Senado*, 36th Session, 13 March 1969, p. 1830.

63. Ibid., 20 March 1969, p. 1927.

64. *Diario de Sesiones del Senado*, 39th Session, 20 March 1969, p. 1925.

65. Ibid., p. 1937.

66. From Embassy Santiago to State Department, "Repercussions Puerto Montt Clash," Telegram 918, 11 March 1969, NARA, RG 59, Central Foreign Policy Files, 1967–1969, Political and Defense, Box 1980.

67. On the relationship of organizations of squatters and the parties of the Left during the Frei administration, see Espinoza, *Para una historia de los pobres de la ciudad*, pp. 293–296.

68. *Diario de Sesiones del Senado*, 39th Session, 20 March 1969, p. 1978.

69. Gazmuri, *Eduardo Frei Montalva y su época*, T. II, p. 702.

70. Fermandois, *La revolución inconclusa*, pp. 472–475.

71. From Santiago to Washington D.C., 23 September 1969, U.S. State Department, Freedom of Information Act (FOIA), Virtual Reading Room, accessed 27 January 2014.

72. From Embassy Santiago to State Department, Telegram 4471, 24 October 1969, NARA, RG 59, Central Foreign Policy Files, 1967–1969, Political and Defense, Box 1980; De Embajada en Washington a Ministerio de Relaciones Exteriores (MRREE), Télex 988, 21 November 1969. Archivo Histórico del Ministerio de Relaciones Exteriores (AHMRE).

73. Gazmuri, *Eduardo Frei Montalva y su época*, T. II, pp. 710–714.

4. Chilean Copper and U.S. Companies

1. Klubock, *Contested Communities*; Vergara, *Copper Workers*.

2. Moran, *Multinational Corporations*, pp. 21–22.

3. Ibid., pp. 57–118; Fermandois, Bustos, and Schneuer, *Historia Política del Cobre*, pp. 35–100.

4. Fermandois, Bustos, and Schneuer, *Historia Política del Cobre*, pp. 75–100.

5. "Summary of Randall Committee Briefing Paper," n.d., 1964, Records of the Department of State (RG 59), Formerly Top Secret Central Foreign Policy Files, Inco-Tel, Box 2.

6. Briefing Memorandum for the Advisory (Randall) Committee, "American Copper Companies in Chile—Can We Avoid Nationalization?" RG 59, Formerly Top Secret Central Foreign Policy Files, Inco-Tel, Box 2.

7. "Frei sabe lo que el pueblo quiere," pamphlet, 1964, Archivo Alejandro Hales Jamarne, Biblioteca del Congreso Nacional, accessed 24 April 2019, archivohales.bcn.cl.

8. On Anaconda's modernization drive, see Vergara, "Conflicto y modernización en la Gran Minería del Cobre."

9. Moran, *Multinational Corporations*, pp. 127–136.

10. *Diario de Sesiones del Senado*, 46th Session, 8 September 1965, p. 3712.

11. Ibid., p. 3734.

12. Ibid., p. 3804.

13. *Diario de Sesiones del Senado*, 42nd Session, 6 September 1965, p. 3381.

14. Ibid., p. 3387.

15. *Diario de Sesiones del Senado*, 46th Session, 8 September 1965, p. 3697.

16. Ibid. p. 3704.

17. Ibid., p. 3706.

18. Ibid., p. 3702. Right after he finished this sentence, Ibáñez was interrupted by Socialist senator Carlos Altamirano, who interjected: "The injustices are committed by the foreign companies." Ibáñez replied, "I do not share your honor's judgment."

19. *Diario de Sesiones del Senado*, 42nd Session, 6 September 1965, p. 3335.

20. *Diario de Sesiones del Senado*, 57th Session, 12 January 1966, p. 3283–3284.

21. Interview of Jonás Gómez, n.d., "Historia Política Legislativa del Congreso Nacional de Chile," accessed 24 April 2019, http://historiapolitica.bcn.cl.

22. See the argument of Senator Carlos Altamirano, *Diario de Sesiones del Senado*, 42th Session, 6 September 1965, pp. 3442–3443.

23. *Diario de Sesiones del Senado*, 46th Session, 8 September 1965, pp. 3751–3752.

24. Ibid., pp. 3707–3708.

25. Ibid., p. 3760.

26. Ibid., pp. 3767–3768.

27. *El Parlamento chileno* vol. I, p. 584.

28. *Diario de Sesiones del Senado*, 46th Session, 8 September 1965, p. 3758.

29. Ibid., p. 3715. The comparison with other Third World countries, however, had its limits. Senator Ampuero, for instance, accused the Christian Democratic senators, who claimed that other countries offered better terms for foreign investments, of trying to make Chile compete with "the Congo, Peru, Rhodesia, and I don't know what other peoples which have just awoken to civilization or that resign themselves to new forms of dependency." *Diario de Sesiones del Senado*, 46th Session, 8 September 1965, p. 3754.

30. *Diario de Sesiones del Senado*, 46th Session, 8 September 1965, pp. 3752–3753.

31. Ibid., p. 3711.

32. Moran, *Multination Corporations*, pp. 28–37.

33. From McGeorge Bundy to Ralph Dungan, 12 November 1965, Papers of Lyndon Baines Johnson, President, 1963–1969, National Security File, Subject File, Box 8, Lyndon B. Johnson Presidential Library.

34. From Embassy Santiago to State Department (from Harriman to President), Telegram 629, 15 November 1965, NARA, RG 59, Central Foreign Policy Files, 1964–1966, Political and Defense, Box 2817.

35. From State Department (Ball) to Embassy Rio de Janeiro (Solomon), Telegram 42, 18 November 1965, NARA, RG 59, Formerly Top Secret Central Foreign Policy Files, Inco-Tel, Box 2.

36. From Embassy Santiago to State Department, "Text of Announcement of Copper Price Agreement," Airgram 672, 26 January 1966, NARA, RG 59, Formerly Top Secret Central Foreign Policy Files, Inco-Tel, Box 2.

37. *Diario de Sesiones del Senado*, 61st, 62nd, and 63rd sessions, 9 February 1966.

38. Eduardo Simián had in his younger years been a professional soccer player. In fact, he is probably more remembered today because he was the goalkeeper of Universidad de Chile when the team, one of the most popular in the country, won its first national championship in 1940, than because of his extensive career in public service. To this day, Simián is remembered among soccer fans by the nickname he earned because of his outstanding abilities as a goalkeeper: *El Pulpo* (The Octopus).

39. Brands, "Richard Nixon and Economic Nationalism in Latin America" and "The United States and the Peruvian Challenge."

40. From Embassy Santiago to State Department, "Copper," Telegram 1768, 4 May 1969, NARA, RG 59, Central Foreign Policy Files, 1967–1969, Economic, Box 1016.

41. From Embassy Santiago to State Department, "Copper," Telegram 1768, 4 May 1969, NARA, RG 59, Central Foreign Policy Files, 1967–1969, Economic, Box 1016.

42. From President Frei to President Nixon, 4 May 1969, NARA, RG 59, Central Foreign Policy Files, 1967–1969, Economic, Box 1016.

43. From Embassy Santiago to State Department, "Start of Copper Negotiations," Telegram 2228, 2 June 1969, NARA, RG 59, Central Foreign Policy Files, 1967–1969, Economic, Box 1017.

44. In fact, in 1971 all members of Congress voted in favor of the Allende nationalization constitutional amendment.

45. From Embassy Santiago to State Department, "Copper Negotiations #2," Telegram 2256, 3 June 1969, NARA, RG 59, Central Foreign Policy Files, 1967–1969, Economic, Box 1017.

46. From Embassy Santiago to State Department, "Copper Negotiations #2," Telegram 2256, 3 June 1969; From Embassy Santiago to State Department, "Copper Negotiations #4," Telegram 2348, 6 June 1969, NARA, RG 59, Central Foreign Policy Files, 1967–1969, Economic, Box 1017.

47. From Embassy Santiago to State Department, "Copper Negotiations #32," Telegram 2392, 27 June 1969, NARA, RG 59, Central Foreign Policy Files, 1967–1969, Economic, Box 1017.

48. Department of State, Director of Intelligence and Research, Intelligence Note for the Secretary, "Chile: The New Copper Agreement—A Preliminary Political Appraisal," 27 June 1969, NARA, RG 59, Central Foreign Policy Files, 1967–1969, Economic, Box 1017.

49. *Washington Post*, 28 June 1969; *New York Times*, 29 June 1969.

50. From Embassy Santiago to State Department, "Copper Negotiations #33," Telegram 2799, 27 June 1969; From Secretary Rogers to Ambassador Korry, 2 July 1969; From Embassy Santiago to State Department, "Copper," Telegram 2915, 8 July 1969; all in NARA, RG 59, Central Foreign Policy Files, 1967–1969, Economic, Box 1017.

51. From Embassy Santiago to State Department, "Copper Negotiations #33," Telegram 2799, 27 June 1969, NARA, RG 59, Central Foreign Policy Files, 1967–1969, Economic, Box 1017.

52. *El Siglo*, 28 June 1969.

53. From Embassy Santiago to State Department, "Memorandum of Conversation with PN President Sergio Onofre Jarpa," Airgram 194, 19 June 1969, NARA, RG 59, Central Foreign Policy Files, 1967–1969, Economic, Box 1017.

54. From Embassy Santiago to State Department, "Copper Negotiations #34," Telegram 2817, 1 July 1969, NARA, RG 59, Central Foreign Policy Files, 1967–1969, Economic, Box 1017.

55. From Embassy Santiago to State Department, "Copper Negotiations #33," Telegram 2799, 27 June 1969, NARA, RG 59, Central Foreign Policy Files, 1967–1969, Economic, Box 1017.

56. "Chile: Tarea del Pueblo. Programa de Radomiro Tomic," *Política y Espíritu*, no. 317, August 1970, p. 27.

57. Moran, *Multinational Corporations*, pp. 147–152; Fermandois, Bustos, Schneuer, *Historia Política del Cobre*, pp. 123–126.

5. The Presidential Candidacy of Radomiro Tomic

1. Gazmuri, *Eduardo Frei Montalva y su época*, T. II, p. 578.

2. On the outlawing of the Communist Party, see Huneeus, *La Guerra Fría Chilena*; and Garay and Soto, *Gabriel González Videla*.

3. Radomiro Tomic, "El problema del cobre," *Política y Espíritu* (March 1951) and "El cobre: don de la Providencia a Chile y palanca de su desarrollo industrial," *Mensaje* X, no. 97 (March–April 1961; Fermandois, Bustos, and Schneuer, *Historia Política del Cobre*, pp. 43, 95–96.

4. From Embassy Santiago to State Department, "Radomiro Tomic: Some of his Philosophy," Airgram 775, 7 August 1968, NARA, RG 59, Central Foreign Policy Files, 1967–1969, Political and Defense, Box 1978.

5. On Tomic's style, Fermandois, *La revolución inconclusa*, pp. 303–304.

6. From Embassy Santiago to State Department, "Tomic's Views," Telegram 6359, 7 December 1968. Lyndon B. Johnson Presidential Library, Papers of Lyndon B. Johnson, President 1963–1969, National Security File, Country File, Latin America—Chile/Colombia, Box 14.

7. Fermandois, *La revolución inconclusa*, p. 303.

8. From Embassy Santiago to State Department, "Radomiro Tomic: Some of his Philosophy," Airgram 775, 7 August 1968, NARA, RG 59, Central Foreign Policy Files, 1967–1969, Political and Defense, Box 1978.

9. From Embassy Santiago to State Department, "The Chilean Situation: A Personal Assessment," Airgram 283, 1 September 1969, NARA, RG 59, Central Foreign Policy Files, 1967–1969, Political and Defense, Box 1976.

10. From Embassy Santiago to State Department, "PDC Votes to Name Presidential Candidate in August," Telegram 2997, 14 July 1969, NARA, RG 59, Central Foreign Policy Files, 1967–1969, Political and Defense, Box 1978.

11. On the general climate of Chilean politics in the 1960s, see Sigmund, *The Overthrow of Allende*, pp. 14–22; Fermandois, *La revolución inconclusa*, pp. 105–174, 261–280.

12. Rafael Agustín Gumucio is one of the most schismatic politicians in the history of Chilean and probably world politics. In his youth, he was a member of the Conservative Youth and one of the leaders of the faction that left the party in 1938 to found Falange Nacional. Falange Nacional became the PDC in 1957. In 1969, Gumucio would leave the PDC to form another movement further to the left, the Unitarian Popular Action Movement (MAPU). Gumucio and others left MAPU in 1971 to create a new political movement, Christian Left. Gumucio, *Apuntes de medio siglo*.

13. "Proposiciones para una Acción Política en el período 1967–1970 de una Vía No Capitalista de Desarrollo," *Política y Espíritu*, 303, October 1967.

14. From Embassy Santiago to State Department, "Tomic Current Views," Telegram 3729, 19 April 1967, NARA, RG 59, Central Foreign Policy Files, 1967–1969, Political and Defense, Box 1981.

15. Letter from Eduardo Frei to Radomiro Tomic, 13 July 1967. Archivo Casa-Museo Eduardo Frei Montalva [AEFM], Presidencia, Correspondencia enviada por el Presidente Eduardo Frei Montalva a Radomiro Tomic Romero, Folder 462.

16. Letter from Eduardo Frei to Radomiro Tomic, 26 December 1967. AEFM, Presidencia, Correspondencia enviada por el Presidente Eduardo Frei Montalva a Radomiro Tomic Romero, Folder 462.

17. Rodríguez's words have become a widely known and cited symbol of the polarization and intransigence that increasingly characterized Chilean politics in the 1960s. Labarca, *Chile al Rojo*, p. 129.

18. From Embassy Santiago to State Department, "PDC Rebeldes and the Communists: Where There is Love Needs There be Marriage?" Airgram 508, 3 April 1968, NARA, RG 59, Central Foreign Policy Files, 1967–1969, Political and Defense, Box 1977.

19. From Embassy Santiago to State Department, "Enclosing Memorandum of Conversation: 'Fitting the President for Pants'" Airgram 327, 10 January 1968, NARA, RG 59, Central Foreign Policy Files, 1967–1969, Political and Defense, Box 1981.

20. Ibid.

21. From Embassy Santiago to State Department, "Frei Gives Communists Hell," Airgram 339, 13 January 1968, NARA, RG 59, Central Foreign Policy Files, 1967–1969, Political and Defense, Box 1977.

22. From Embassy Santiago to State Department, Telegram 2547, 21 February 1968, NARA, RG 59, Central Foreign Policy Files, 1967–1969, Political and Defense, Box 1977.

23. From Covey T. Oliver (Bureau of Inter-American Affairs) to the Under Secretary, "Ambassador Tomic and Christian Democratic-Communist Popular Front in Chile," Briefing Memorandum, 5 March 1968, NARA, RG 59, Central Foreign Policy Files, 1967–1969, Political and Defense, Box 1981.

24. "Farewell Call by Ambassador Tomic," Memorandum of Conversation: Ambassador Radomiro Tomic, Secretary of State Dean Rusk and Patrick Morris, Country Director, Office of Bolivian-Chilean Affairs. Washington, 19 March 1968, NARA, RG 59, Central Foreign Policy Files, 1967–1969, Political and Defense, Box 1981.

25. Alberto Baltra was a renowned Radical politician who had occupied the post of minister of the economy in the government of Gabriel González Videla. He was elected senator for the provinces of Biobio, Malleco, and Cautín in a by-election held in 1968. In 1971, discontent with the line the PR and the Allende government were taking, Baltra and other prominent Radical figures would leave the party to found a new organization, Partido de la Izquierda Radical (PIR). The PIR joined the Christian Democratic Party, the National Party, and Durán's Radical Democracy in the opposition coalition that confronted Allende's Popular Unity in the congressional elections of 1973.

26. From Embassy Santiago to State Department, "Dialogue: Tomic—The Ambassador. #1," Airgram 580, 11 May 1968, NARA, RG 59, Central Foreign Policy Files, 1967–1969, Political and Defense, Box 1981.

27. *El Siglo*, 25 October 1968.

28. From Embassy Santiago to State Department, Telegram 3449, 30 April 1968, NARA, RG 59, Central Foreign Policy Files, 1967–1969, Political and Defense, Box 1977.

29. Jacques Chonchol had worked in the Cuban agrarian reform in the early years of the Castro regime and belonged in the left-wing of the PDC. In 1969, Chonchol would leave the party, along with Gumucio and other prominent militants, to form MAPU. In the last months of 1969, Chonchol would be the candidate of his party for the Popular Unity nomination, which eventually went to Salvador Allende. For the views of the left-wing of the PDC and specifically those of Chonchol see the book he co-authored with another leader of the *rebelde* faction, Julio Silva Solar, *El desarrollo de la Nueva Sociedad en América Latina*.

30. From Embassy Santiago to State Department, "The President Wears Pants," Telegram 6029, 9 November 1968, NARA, RG 59, Central Foreign Policy Files, 1967–1969, Political and Defense, Box 1981.

31. Bernardo Leighton was another of the founding fathers of Falange Nacional and, later, the PDC. He occupied the position of minister of the interior of the Frei government between 1964 and 1968. Leighton, a man much more given to compromises than Tomic and with a much more agreeable character, was broadly respected in Chilean politics and greatly admired within the PDC, where he was known as *Hermano Bernardo*. As was the case with Tomic, however, his best feature was also his greatest weakness, as he lacked the leadership skills and determination that characterized his contemporaries Frei and Tomic. On 13 September 1973, Leighton, along with twelve other PDC members, signed a letter expressing their condemnation of the military coup that had overthrown Salvador Allende two days earlier, distancing himself from the official party line and, especially, of Frei's position. Exiled by the military regime and living in Rome, in 1975 Leighton survived an attempt on his life, perpetrated by a neo-fascist Italian group and the DINA, the secret police of the Pinochet dictatorship. Boye, *Hermano Bernardo*; Donoso and Dunlop, *Los 13 del 13*, pp. 61–66.

32. From Embassy Santiago to State Department, "Tomic's Views," Telegram 6359, 7 December 1968. Lyndon B. Johnson Presidential Library, Papers of Lyndon B. Johnson, President 1963–1969, National Security File, Country File, Latin America—Chile/Colombia, Box 14.

33. From Embassy Santiago to State Department, "Conversation with Frei (#2 Chilean Politics)," Telegram 1161, 25 March 1969, NARA, RG 59, Central Foreign Policy Files, 1967–1969, Political and Defense, Box 1981. Agustín Edwards was the owner of *El Mercurio* (among other businesses), the most important daily of the country. The Yarur family, for its part, owned several textile industries, one of which is portrayed in the excellent book by Peter Winn, *Weavers of Revolution*.

34. From Embassy Santiago to State Department, "Conversation with Frei (#2 Chilean Politics)," Telegram 1161, 25 March 1969, NARA, RG 59, Central Foreign Policy Files, 1967–1969, Political and Defense, Box 1981.

35. *Ercilla*, 19 March 1969.

36. Letter from Radomiro Tomic to Renán Fuentealba, 2 April 1969. AEFM, Presidencia, Folder 464. The letter was published later by *Ercilla*.

37. From Embassy Santiago to State Department, "Reaction to Tomic Electoral Ultimatum," Telegram 1100, 20 March 1969, NARA, RG 59, Central Foreign Policy Files, 1967–1969, Political and Defense, Box 1978.

38. From Embassy Santiago to State Department, "Conversation with Frei (#2 Chilean Politics)," Telegram 1161, 25 March 1969, NARA, RG 59, Central Foreign Policy Files, 1967–1969, Political and Defense, Box 1981.

39. See chapter 4, "Chilean Copper and U.S. Companies."

40. See for instance, *New York Times*, 29 May and 28 June 1969 and *Washington Post*, 28 June 1969.

41. From Embassy Santiago to State Department, "Radomiro Tomic; Animal, Vegetable or Mineral?" Telegram 2935, 9 July 1969, NARA, RG 59, Central Foreign Policy Files, 1967–1969, Economic, Box 1017. The National Assembly of the Radical Party had decided a few days earlier to expel Julio Durán, Germán Picó, and other members of the right wing of the party, opening the way for an alliance with the parties of the Left. *El Siglo*, 30 June and 1 July 1969.

42. From Embassy Santiago to State Department, "Radomiro Tomic; Animal, Vegetable or Mineral?" Telegram 2935, 9 July 1969, NARA, RG 59, Central Foreign Policy Files, 1967–1969, Economic, Box 1017.

43. See Brands, "Richard Nixon and Economic Nationalism in Latin America" and "The United States and the Peruvian Challenge."

44. From Embassy Santiago to State Department, "More on Tomic and Copper," Telegram 2947, 10 July 1969, NARA, RG 59, Central Foreign Policy Files, 1967–1969, Economic, Box 1017.

45. From Embassy Santiago to State Department, "Tomic and Copper," Telegram 2971, 11 July 1969, NARA, RG 59, Central Foreign Policy Files, 1967–1969, Economic, Box 1017.

46. Letter from Eduardo Frei to Radomiro Tomic, 7 March 1969. AEFM, Presidencia, Correspondencia enviada por el Presidente Eduardo Frei Montalva a Radomiro Tomic Romero, Folder 462.

47. From Embassy Santiago to State Department, "Frei on Copper," Telegram 3185, 25 July 1969, NARA, RG 59, Central Foreign Policy Files, 1967–1969, Economic, Box 1017.

48. In his proclamation speech, Tomic would assert: "The crisis of the minoritarian and capitalist system is reaching the final stages of its disintegration in our land." Radomiro Tomic, "Discurso de proclamación en el Teatro Caupolicán," octubre de 1969, in Donoso (editor) *Tomic*, pp. 357–368.

49. Letter from Eduardo Frei to Radomiro Tomic, 6 August 1969. AEFM, Presidencia, Correspondencia enviada por el Presidente Eduardo Frei Montalva a Radomiro Tomic Romero, Folder 462.

50. Letter from Radomiro Tomic to Eduardo Frei, 9 August 1969. AEFM, Presidencia, Folder 464.

51. Letter from Eduardo Frei to Radomiro Tomic, 13 August 1969. AEFM, Presidencia, Correspondencia enviada por el Presidente Eduardo Frei Montalva a Radomiro Tomic Romero, Folder 462.

52. The programs of the three presidential candidates for the 1970 election are found in *Política y Espíritu*, no. 317, August 1970.

53. Interview of Enrique Krauss, n.d., "Historia Política Legislativa del Congreso Nacional de Chile," accessed 24 April 2019, http://historiapolitica.bcn.cl.

54. From Embassy Santiago to State Department, "Political Situation: PDC President," Airgram 259, 24 October 1972, NARA, RG 59, Central Foreign Policy Files, 1970–1973, Political and Defense, Box 2193.

6. The United States and the Last Two Years of the Frei Administration

1. Sigmund, *The Overthrow of Allende*, pp. 61–67; Gazmuri, *Eduardo Frei Montalva y su época*, T. II, pp. 685–699; Fermandois, *La revolución inconclusa,* pp. 172–175.

2. Sigmund, *The Overthrow of Allende*, pp. 60–61.

3. The resolution of the 22nd Congress of the PS called for the "seizure of power as a strategic objective to be achieved by this generation, with the purpose of establishing a Revolutionary State which will liberate Chile from dependency and economic and cultural backwardness, and which will begin the construction of Socialism." The resolution, supposedly a strategic blueprint for the immediate future, also stated that "revolutionary violence was inevitable and legitimate." The full text of the resolution can be found in Jobet, *El Partido Socialista de Chile*, T. II, p. 130. See also Fermandois, *La revolución inconclusa*, pp. 154–155.

4. Sigmund, *The Overthrow of Allende*, pp. 71–72.

5. On the referred electoral reforms, see Gamboa, "Reformando reglas electorales."

6. According to political scientist Paul E. Sigmund, "Chile was in a perpetual state of electoral fever, and elections became a favorite preoccupation of Chileans at every social and economic level." Sigmund, *The Overthrow of Allende*, p. 16.

7. From Embassy Santiago to State Department, Telegram 681, 20 February 1969, NARA, RG 59, Central Foreign Policy Files, 1967–1969, Political and Defense, Box 1978.

8. From Embassy Santiago to State Department, "Chilean Elections," Telegram 807, 3 March 1969, NARA, RG 59, Central Foreign Policy Files, 1967–1969, Political and Defense, Box 1978.

9. From Embassy Santiago to State Department, Telegram 681, 20 February 1969, NARA, RG 59, Central Foreign Policy Files, 1967–1969, Political and Defense, Box 1978.

10. From Embassy Santiago to State Department, "Chilean Elections," Telegram 807, 3 March 1969, NARA, RG 59, Central Foreign Policy Files, 1967–1969, Political and Defense, Box 1978.

11. Sigmund, *The Overthrow of Allende*, pp. 73–75; Fermandois, *La revolución inconclusa*, pp. 170–171.

12. From Embassy Santiago to State Department, Telegram 681, 20 February 1969, NARA, RG 59, Central Foreign Policy Files, 1967–1969, Political and Defense, Box 1978.

13. From CIA station in Santiago to headquarters, 3 March 1969, U.S. State Department, Freedom of Information Act (FOIA), Virtual Reading Room, accessed 26 April 2019.

14. CIA Memorandum, "Things to Look for in the 2 March 1969 Congressional Election Results in Chile," 26 February 1969, U.S. State Department, Freedom of Information Act (FOIA), Virtual Reading Room, accessed 26 April 1969.

15. From Embassy Santiago to State Department, "Election Hangover Including Frei's views," Telegram 942, 11 March 1969, NARA, RG 59, Central Foreign Policy Files, 1967–1969, Political and Defense, Box 1978.

16. Memorandum for the 303 Committee, "Final Report: March 1969 Chilean Congressional Election," 14 March 1969, Richard Nixon Presidential Library, NSC Files, HAK Office, Country Files, Latin America, Box 128, Folder "Chile Wrap-Up and Post Mortem, March 1971, The President."

17. Luis Corvalán, then secretary general of the Communist Party, has confirmed what was widely assumed at the time: the nomination of Pablo Neruda as the candidate of the PC had the specific purpose of pressuring the rest of the parties of the coalition into finally choosing Allende, the real favorite of the Communists. Luis Corvalán, Oral history interview, Historia Legislativa, Biblioteca del Congreso Nacional, accessed 26 April 2019, historiapolitica.bcn.cl.

18. The Popular Front was a coalition of the Radical, Communist, and Socialist parties whose candidate, Pedro Aguirre Cerda of the PR, won the presidential election of 1938. The coalition broke in 1941, among other reasons because of the PC's support of the 1939 Nazi-Soviet Pact.

19. From Embassy Santiago to State Department, "Elections Again," Telegram 976, 13 March 1969, NARA, RG 59, Central Foreign Policy Files, 1967–1969, Political and Defense, Box 1978. Some people called Hamilton "the Chilean Kennedy." Enrique Krauss, oral history interview, Historia Legislativa, Biblioteca del Congreso Nacional, accessed 26 April 2019, historiapolitica.bcn.cl.

20. *Punto Final*, August 1967.

21. Raúl Ampuero, "Respuesta del Partido Socialista al Comité Central del Partido Comunista," April 1962, in Ampuero, *El socialismo chileno*, pp. 78-94.

22. From Embassy Santiago to State Department, "Conversation with Socialist Leader and Intellectual," Airgram 823, 4 May 1964, NARA, RG 59, Central Foreign Policy Files, 1964–1966, Political and Defense, Box 2027.

23. From Embassy Santiago to State Department, Telegram 1699, 2 July 1964, NARA, RG 59, Central Foreign Policy Files, 1964–1966, Political and Defense, Box 2029.

24. *Última Hora*, 20 July 1967; From Embassy Santiago to State Department, "Ampuero Forms a New Partido Socialista Popular," Airgram 98, 19 August 1967, NARA, RG 59, Central Foreign Policy Files, 1967–1969, Political and Defense, Box 1977.

25. Since USOPO did not join any coalition after 1969—even running its own candidates as an uncomfortable third wheel in the polarized 1973 congressional election—Ampuero's name lost almost all the weight it had carried up to the mid-1960s. He showed up at Allende's house to support the constitutional government on 29 June 1973, when a rebellious colonel unsuccessfully attempted to stage a coup—the Tancazo, a bloody forecast of what would occur a few months later. Despite the political irrelevance on which he had fallen since his ejection from the PS in 1967, Ampuero

was arrested after the 1973 coup. After his release, he went into exile and lived in Rome until 1989, when he returned to Chile and the PS but did not run for or occupy any government office.

26. From Embassy Santiago to State Department, "Chilean Elections," Telegram 807, 3 March 1969, NARA, RG 59, Central Foreign Policy Files, 1967–1969, Political and Defense, Box 1978.

27. From Embassy Santiago to State Department, "Chilean Elections," Telegram 807, 3 March 1969, NARA, RG 59, Central Foreign Policy Files, 1967–1969, Political and Defense, Box 1978.

28. From Embassy Santiago to State Department, "Election Hangover Including Frei's Views," Telegram 942, 11 March 1969, NARA, RG 59, Central Foreign Policy Files, 1967–1969, Political and Defense, Box 1978.

29. Department of State, Meeting of the 303 Committee, Proposed Agenda, 12 July 1968, U.S. State Department, Freedom of Information Act (FOIA), Virtual Reading Room, accessed 26 April 2019.

30. Briefing Paper for the ADDP for the President, 23 January 1969, U.S. State Department, Freedom of Information Act (FOIA), Virtual Reading Room, accessed 26 April 1969.

31. "Request for renewal of project [redacted, one word]," Memorandum from William Broe, CIA Chief of Western Hemisphere Division, to Deputy Director for Plans, 20 March 1968. U.S. State Department, Freedom of Information Act (FOIA), Virtual Reading Room, accessed 26 April 1969, https://foia.state.gov. An excellent account and assessment of the U.S. covert operations in the 1969 congressional elections in Gustafson, Hostile Intent, pp. 53–76.

32. Memorandum for the 303 Committee, "Final Report: March 1969 Chilean Congressional Election," 13 March 1969, U.S. State Department, Freedom of Information Act (FOIA), Virtual Reading Room, accessed 26 April 1969.

33. Memorandum for the 303 Committee, "Final Report: March 1969 Chilean Congressional Election," 14 March 1969, Richard Nixon Presidential Library, NSC Files, HAK Office, Country Files, Latin America, Box 128, Folder "Chile Wrap-Up and Post Mortem, March 1971, The President."

34. Memorandum for the 303 Committee, "Final Report: March 1969 Chilean Congressional Election," 14 March 1969, Richard Nixon Presidential Library, NSC Files, HAK Office, Country Files, Latin America, Box 128, Folder "Chile Wrap-Up and Post Mortem, March 1971, The President."

35. Sigmund, The Overthrow of Allende, pp. 79–80; Gazmuri, Eduardo Frei Montalva y su época, pp. 703–705; Fermandois, La revolución inconclusa, pp. 172–175.

36. Memorandum for the 40 Committee, "Political Action Related to 1970 Presidential Election," March 5, 1970. FRUS, 1969–1976, Vol. XXI, Document 29.

37. From Embassy Santiago to State Department, "Conversation with Senator Rafael Tarud," Airgram 959, 6 November 1968, NARA, RG 59, Central Foreign Policy Files, 1967–1969, Political and Defense, Box 1978.

38. Casals, El alba de una revolución, p. 254.

39. Edwards, Esclavos de la consigna, p. 263.

40. From Embassy Santiago to State Department, "Valdes Building Bridges between US and USSR," Telegram 3861, 23 September 1970, NARA, RG 59, Central Foreign Policy Files, 1970–1973, Political and Defense, Box 2196.

41. A good summary of the polls conducted in 1970 in Navia and Osorio, "Las encuestas de opinión pública en Chile," p. 125.

42. Sigmund, The Overthrow of Allende, pp. 96–97.

43. El Mercurio, 24 July 1970.

7. The United States and the Presidential Election of 1970

1. Several authors emphasize this fact in their assessments of Chilean politics up to the 1973 coup. Alexander, *The Tragedy of Chile*; Sigmund, *The United States and Democracy in Chile*; Fermandois, *Mundo y fin de mundo*, pp. 335–392.

2. There is a considerable body of literature that questions the substance and even the entity of Chilean democracy throughout the twentieth century, mostly on account of its foundation on a highly unequal socioeconomic order and because the state repeatedly resorted to violence against expressions of discontent, usually coming from working class demonstrators. Portales, *Los mitos de la democracia chilena*; Frazier, *Salt in the Sand*; Salazar, *La enervante levedad histórica*. An excellent discussion on the Left's questioning of Chilean democracy can be found in Fermandois, *La revolución inconclusa*, pp. 75–104.

3. Álvarez, "La Unidad Popular y las elecciones presidenciales."

4. Conversely, the overthrow of Allende in 1973 made Western European Communists reconsider their political strategies. Shortly after the 1973 coup, the leader of the Italian Communist Party, Enrico Berlinguer, issued his famous call for a "historic compromise" between Communists and other center-left forces, mainly Christian Democracy, to effectively pursue a path of radical yet feasible reform. Berlinguer, "Imperialismo e coesistenza"; Santoni, "El Partido Comunista Italiano."

5. Nixon, *The Memoirs of Richard Nixon*, p. 490. An excellent discussion on the symbolic as well as the concrete meaning of the metaphor is found in Harmer, "Chile y la Guerra Fría interamericana."

6. Memorandum from Viron P. Vaky of the National Security Council Staff to the President's Assistant for National Security Affairs (Kissinger), "Chilean Election—Another View," 26 June 1970, *FRUS, 1969–1976*, Vol. XXI, Chile, Document 40.

7. Memorandum of Conversation, "Anaconda Requests U.S. Government Financial Assistance for the Alessandri Election Campaign," 10 April 1970, Richard Nixon Presidential Library, NSC Files, HAK Office, Country Files, Latin America, Box 128, Folder "Chile Wrap-Up and Post Mortem, March 1971, The President."

8. Cable from CIA Station in Santiago to Langley, 14 July 1970; Memorandum of conversation (CIA), "Conversation with Mr. Harold S. Geneen, Chairman and President of ITT, on 27 July 1970," 3 August 1970, both in U.S. State Department, Freedom of Information Act (FOIA), Virtual Reading Room, accessed 26 April 2019.

9. Memorandum from John H. Crimmins (Bureau of Inter-American Affairs, ARA) to U. Alexis Johnson, Under Secretary for Political Affairs, "Proposal for Political Action in Chile," 17 March 1970, U.S. State Department, Freedom of Information Act (FOIA), Virtual Reading Room, accessed 26 April 2019.

10. Telegram from the Embassy in Chile to the Department of State, "The Electoral Stakes, the Pot, and the Jockey with the Money," 28 April 1970, *FRUS, 1969–1976*, Vol. XXI, Chile, Document 33.

11. Labarca, *Chile invadido*; Power, "The Engendering of Anticommunism"; Casals, "Chile en la encrucijada."

12. Memorandum for the 40 Committee, "Political Action Related to 1970 Chilean Presidential Election," 22 June 1970, *FRUS, 1969–1976*, Vol. XXI, Chile, Document 38.

13. The last assertion of such conviction is recorded in the report of a conversation between Korry and Frei in the night before the election. Telegram from the Embassy in Chile to the Department of State, "Election Eve Talk with Frei," 4 September 1970, *FRUS, 1969–1976*, Vol. XXI, Chile, Document 61.

14. A good account of an analysis of the decision-making process for the 1970 covert operations is found in Gustafson, *Hostile Intent*, pp. 79–112.

15. From Embassy Santiago to State Department, "Chile: Election Perspectives (Part IV)," Telegram 992, 17 March 1970, NARA, RG 59, Central Foreign Policy Files, 1970–1973, Political and Defense, Box 2195.

16. From Embassy Santiago to State Department, "FMS Tanks and Recoilless Rifles for Chile," Telegram 4696, 7 November 1969, NARA, RG 59, Central Foreign Policy Files, 1967–1969, Political and Defense, Box 1530.

17. From Embassy Santiago to State Department, "General René Schneider Chereau, Commander-in-Chief of Chilean Army: Opinions and Personal Interests," Airgram 377, 9 November 1969, NARA, RG 59, Central Foreign Policy Files, 1967–1969, Political and Defense, Box 1529.

18. From Embassy Santiago to State Department, "General René Schneider Chereau, Commander-in-Chief of Chilean Army: Opinions and Personal Interests," Airgram 377, 9 November 1969, NARA, RG 59, Central Foreign Policy Files, 1967–1969, Political and Defense, Box 1529.

19. *El Mercurio*, 8 May 1970.

20. Fermandois, *La revolución inconclusa*, p. 316.

21. Backchannel from the Ambassador to Chile (Korry) to the Deputy Assistant Secretary of State for Inter-American Affairs (Crimmins), 11 August 1970, *FRUS, 1969–1976*, Vol. XXI, Chile, Document 50.

22. Ibid.

23. Telegram from the Embassy in Chile to the Department of State, "Election Eve Talk with Frei," 4 September 1970, *FRUS, 1969–1976*, Vol. XXI, Chile, Document 61.

24. Cruz-Coke, *Historia Electoral de Chile*, p. 112.

25. This assertion is true in the sense that no other sizable independent country in the world had voted for a candidate running on an explicitly Marxist revolutionary platform. Avowedly Marxist politicians, however, had been elected as heads of government before. In 1953, the leader of the People's Progressive Party (PPP), Chedi Jaggan, was elected prime minister of Guyana, then still under British control. The PPP ran on a platform that promised the construction of socialism in Guyana, and Jagan was an avowedly Marxist politician. His government, however, lasted only four months, and it fell to a coup orchestrated by the British government. Jagan was elected prime minister again when Guyana reached its independence in 1961, but then the political divide that fractured the country had a racial rather than a socioeconomic character. Communist or Marxist parties had also participated in coalition governments in San Marino and Sri Lanka, but these governments did not intend to implement Marxist revolutionary projects. Far more relevant, at least in quantitative terms, was the election of a Communist-led government in the Indian state of Kerala in 1957. Even though the Indian Communist Party trailed the Indian National Congress in the popular vote, it was able to obtain support from members of parliament of other parties and form a government headed by its leader, E. M. S. Namboodiripad. Of course, the Communist-led government had to abide by the Indian constitution, so the establishment of a communist system proper was, indeed, impossible. Nevertheless, the 1957 episode in Kerala is worth considering because of its quantitative importance: over 5,800,000 people cast their votes in the election, over two million of them for the Communist Party; in the Chilean presidential election of 1970, the number of voters did not reach three million. Election Commission of India, "Statistical Report on General Election, 1957 to the Legislative Assembly of Kerala," accessed 11 May 2019, https://eci.gov.in/.

26. Message from the Ambassador to Chile (Korry) to the Central Intelligence Agency, 5 September 1970, *FRUS, 1969–1976*, Vol. XXI, Chile, Document 64.

27. From Embassy Santiago to State Department, "The 1969 Program Loan, the Elections and the US Interest," Telegram 1060, 18 March 1969, NARA, RG 59, Central Foreign Policy Files, 1967–1969, Economic, Box 466.

28. Telegram from the Embassy in Chile to the Department of State, 5 September 1970, *FRUS, 1969–1976*, Vol. XXI, Chile, Document 62.

29. The expansive economic policy implemented in the first months of Allende's presidential term seemed to respond to this notion. In February 1971, Korry reported to Washington: "Just as the Allende government in the political domain has skirted the traditional recipes of other Socialist countries (religious persecution, firing squads, overt censorship, etc.) so too in the economic sphere is it shunning most instruments of Marxist-Leninist planners (rationing and other restrictions, worker discipline, tight control of credits and fiscal deprivation) who believe that capital investment is the imperious priority. Allende is traveling for the moment along quite a different path on which the milestones are a profligate money supply, a tremendous surge in mass consumer liquidity, a reduction of money cost by 25 percent, a flood of credits and worker permissiveness. . . . It is one thing for a Goulart in Brazil or a Peron in Argentina to embark on such a course; it is quite another for the most self-disciplined and Muscovite Communist Party in the hemisphere, with control of all the economic posts of command, to implant such policies." From Embassy in Chile to State Department, "The Honeymoon is Over (Part I of IV)," Telegram 606, 2 February 1970, NARA, RG 59, Central Foreign Policy Files, 1970–1973, Political and Defense, Box 2193.

30. *El Siglo*, 21 August 1968.

31. Raúl Ampuero, "Respuesta del Partido Socialista al Comité Central del Partido Comunista," April 1962, in Ampuero, *El socialismo chileno*, pp. 78–92.

32. *Punto Final* 34, August 1967.

33. Jobet, *El Partido Socialista de Chile*, T. II, p. 130.

34. The views and political ideas of the military are discussed in detail in Valdivia, *El golpe después del golpe*.

35. In a conversation with East German officials in 1966 Allende described himself as performing in Chile the same role Castro had played in Cuba but through other means. Fermandois, *La revolución inconclusa*, p. 231.

8. Eduardo Frei, the U.S. Embassy, and the Election of Salvador Allende

1. The character of the involvement of the United States in the 1970 presidential race and its implications for what happened after Allende's victory is very well treated by Gustafson, *Hostile Intent*, pp. 79–112.

2. Nixon's infamous orders to Director of Central Intelligence Richard Helms in *FRUS, 1969–1976*, Vol. XXI, Chile, Document 93 (Editorial Note).

3. The relevant reports on the covert operations carried out by the CIA between 4 September and 24 October 1970 produced by the U.S. Congress are: Senate, *Alleged Assassination Plots* and Senate, *Covert Action in Chile*. Books that treat these events in detail and mostly from a polemical viewpoint include Jensen, *The Garotte*; Kornbluh, *The Pinochet File*; Verdugo, *Allende*; Corvalán Marquéz, *La secreta obscenidad de la historia de Chile contemporáneo*; and Basso, *La CIA en Chile*. By far the best scholarly work on U.S. covert operations in Chile between 1964 and 1974, including a detailed account of the interlude between the popular election and the runoff in Congress, is the book by Gustafson, *Hostile Intent*.

4. *FRUS, 1969–1976*, Vol. XXI, Chile, 1969–1973.

5. My own essay "El golpe que no fue."

6. *El Mercurio*, 24 July 1970.

7. In 1958, Allende obtained 28.9 percent and Frei 20.7 percent of the vote. It must be noted that the size of the electorate more than doubled between 1958 and 1970. In 1958, 1,250,000

people cast their votes in the presidential election; in 1970, 2.9 million people did so. Cruz-Coke. *Historia Electoral de Chile*, p. 108.

8. Message from the Ambassador to Chile (Korry) to the Central Intelligence Agency, 5 September 1970, *FRUS, 1969–1976*, Vol. XXI, Chile, Document 64.

9. Roberto Viaux was an army general who, in October 1969, was recalled from his position of command after having sent a strongly worded letter to President Frei protesting the low salaries and poor material conditions in which soldiers performed their duties. A few days later Viaux led a mutiny in the Tacna regiment in Santiago. The mutiny caused much concern among Chilean political elites, who were largely unaccustomed to such saber-rattling maneuvers by the military. The movement was quelled rapidly but provoked some relevant changes at the top of the army command structure. Commander in Chief Sergio Castillo was replaced by General René Schneider. Minister of Defense Tulio Marambio was replaced by Sergio Ossa. Viaux was forced to retire, but his prestige among Chilean commissioned and noncommissioned officers remained high. Many thought his excellent standing among soldiers endowed Viaux with a base of support significant enough to become a political leader or, alternatively, a factor to be considered in any possible military intervention in politics.

10. From Embassy Santiago to State Department, "Ex-President Alessandri's Views of Actual Politico-Economic Situation in Chile," Airgram 310, 29 December 1967, NARA, RG 59, Central Foreign Policy Files, 1967–1969, Political and Defense, Box 1976.

11. Intelligence Information Cable (CIA), 6 September 1970, U.S. State Department, Freedom of Information Act (FOIA), Virtual Reading Room, accessed 27 April 2019.

12. Fermandois, *La revolución inconclusa*, p. 318.

13. *El Mercurio*, 7 September 1970.

14. Backchannel Message from the Ambassador to Chile (Korry) to the National Security Council, 7 September 1970, *FRUS, 1969–1976*, Vol. XXI, Chile, Document 65.

15. Backchannel Message from the Ambassador to Chile (Korry) to the National Security Council, 7 September 1970; Central Intelligence Agency Intelligence Information Cable, "Inconclusive Meeting of High Ranking Chilean Military Officers to Discuss the Possibility of a Military Coup Against the Government, *FRUS, 1969–1976*, Vol. XXI, Chile, Documents 65 and 67, respectively.

16. Telegram from the Embassy in Chile to the Department of State, 12 September 1970, *FRUS, 1969–1976*, Vol. XXI, Chile, Document 81. A brief account of this conversation, based on a conversation between the author and Eduardo Frei, can be found in Alexander, *The ABC Presidents*, p. 261.

17. From Embassy Santiago to State Department, "No Hopes for Chile (Part I of II Parts)," Telegram 35378 September 1970, NARA, RG 59, Central Foreign Policy Files, 1970–1973, Political and Defense, Box 2195.

18. Ibid.

19. Telegram from the Embassy in Chile to the Department of State, "One and Only One Hope for Chile," 9 September 1970, *FRUS, 1969–1976*, Vol. XXI, Chile, Document 73.

20. Telegram from the Central Intelligence Agency to the Station in Chile, 9 September 1970, *FRUS, 1969–1976*, Vol. XXI, Chile, Document 72.

21. Telegram from the Embassy in Chile to the Department of State, 10 September 1970, *FRUS, 1969–1976*, Vol. XXI, Chile, Document 75.

22. From Embassy Santiago to State Department, "No Hopes for Chile (Part I of II Parts)," Telegram 3537, 8 September 1970, NARA, RG 59, Central Foreign Policy Files, 1970–1973, Political and Defense, Box 2195.

23. From Embassy Santiago to State Department, "PDC Deputy on Election Scenario," Telegram 3594, 10 September 1970, NARA, RG 59, Central Foreign Policy Files, 1970–1973, Political and Defense, Box 2195.

24. Telegram from the Embassy in Chile to the United States, 12 September 1970, *FRUS, 1969–1976*, Vol. XXI, Chile, Document 80.

25. Backchannel Message from the Ambassador to Chile (Korry) to the 40 Committee, 12 September 1970, *FRUS, 1969–1976*, Vol. XXI, Chile, Document 79.

26. Ibid.

27. Telegram from the Embassy in Chile to the Department of State, 12 September 1970, *FRUS, 1969–1976*, Vol. XXI, Chile, Document 81.

28. Memorandum for the Record, "Discussion of Chilean Political Situation," 14 September 1970, *FRUS, 1969–1976*, Vol. XXI, Chile, Document 89.

29. Backchannel Message from the Ambassador to Chile (Korry) to the President's Assistant for National Security Affairs (Kissinger), 14 September 1970; Backchannel Message from the Ambassador to Chile (Korry) to the 40 Committee, 14 September 1970, *FRUS, 1969–1976*, Vol. XXI, Chile, Documents 83 and 85, respectively.

30. Backchannel Message from the Ambassador to Chile (Korry) to the Under Secretary of State for Political Affairs (Johnson), 16 September 1970, *FRUS, 1969–1976*, Vol. XXI, Chile, Document 96.

31. *El Mercurio*, 17 September 1970.

32. Eyes Only Memorandum, [Agency not identified, no signature], 14 September 1970, U.S. State Department, Freedom of Information Act (FOIA), Virtual Reading Room, accessed 27 April 2019.

33. Backchannel Message from the Ambassador to Chile (Korry), 17 September 1970; Backchannel Message from the Ambassador to Chile (Korry) to the President's Assistant for National Security Affairs (Kissinger), 17 September 1970, *FRUS, 1969–1976*, Vol. XXI, Chile, Documents 101 and 102, respectively.

34. Backchannel Message from the Ambassador to Chile (Korry) to the President's Assistant for National Security Affairs (Kissinger), 17 September 1970, *FRUS, 1969–1976*, Vol. XXI, Chile, Document 102.

35. CIA Cable to Henry Kissinger, 19 September 1970, U.S. State Department, Freedom of Information Act (FOIA), Virtual Reading Room, accessed 27 April 2019.

36. Memorandum from the Station in Chile to the 40 Committee, "Possible Move by Chilean Armed Forces to take over Government with the Knowledge of President Eduardo Frei," 19 September 1970, *FRUS, 1969–1976*, Vol. XXI, Chile, Document 105.

37. CIA Cable to Henry Kissinger and Under Secretary of State for Inter-American Affairs Charles Meyer, 21 September 1970, U.S. State Department, Freedom of Information Act (FOIA), Virtual Reading Room, accessed 27 April 2019.

38. Ibid. Interestingly, a public statement issued by the MIR after Allende's inauguration also identifies Zaldívar, Figueroa, and Rojas as members of a group within the Frei government determined to provoke an institutional crisis and a military coup: *Punto Final*, 10 November 1970. In his rather self-serving memoirs, Patricio Rojas states that Frei and all his ministers rejected the Alessandri formula outright. Rojas, *Tiempos difíciles*, p. 94.

39. Backchannel Message from the Ambassador to Chile (Korry) to the Assistant Secretary of State for Inter-American Affairs (Meyer) and the President's Assistant for National Security Affairs (Kissinger), 21 September, *FRUS, 1969–1976*, Vol. XXI, Chile, Document 108.

40. According to a CIA report, Brazilian President Emilio Garrastazu Medici, one of Nixon's favorites in Latin America, had used the expression to refer to Frei. CIA Memorandum, "Chile—A

Status Report," 21 September 1970, U.S. State Department, Freedom of Information Act (FOIA), Virtual Reading Room, accessed 27 April 2019. The expression had been coined by a Brazilian author, Fabio Vidigal Xavier da Silveira, *Frei, el Kerensky Chileno.*

41. Backchannel Message from the Ambassador to Chile (Korry) to the Assistant Secretary of State for Inter-American Affairs (Meyer) and the President's Assistant for National Security Affairs (Kissinger), 21 September, *FRUS, 1969–1976*, Vol. XXI, Chile, Document 108.

42. *El Mercurio*, 24 September 1970.

43. CIA Cable to Henry Kissinger and Under Secretary of State for Political Affairs, U. Alexis Johnson, 24 September 1970, U.S. State Department, Freedom of Information Act (FOIA), Virtual Reading Room, accessed 27 April 2019.

44. Ibid.

45. From Embassy Santiago to State Department, "PDC Parliamentarian's View of Things to Come: Gloom and Doom," Telegram 3901, 25 September 1970, NARA, RG 59, Central Foreign Policy Files, 1970–1973, Political and Defense, Box 2197.

46. CIA Cable to Henry Kissinger and Under Secretary of State for Political Affairs, U. Alexis Johnson, 26 September 1970, U.S. State Department, Freedom of Information Act (FOIA), Virtual Reading Room, accessed 27 April 2019.

47. Ibid.

48. Backchannel Message from the Ambassador to Chile (Korry) to Henry Kissinger and Under Secretary of State for Political Affairs, U. Alexis Johnson, 25 September 1970, Richard Nixon Presidential Library, Pinochet Files, Box 1, Folder "Chile 14 Sept 70–8 Nov 70."

49. From CIA Headquarters (Langley) to Station in Santiago, 28 September 1970, U.S. State Department, Freedom of Information Act (FOIA), Virtual Reading Room, accessed 27 April 2019.

50. Backchannel Message from the Under Secretary of State for Political Affairs (Johnson) to the Ambassador to Chile (Korry), 30 September 1970, *FRUS, 1969–1976*, Vol. XXI, Chile, Document 128.

51. Backchannel Message from the Ambassador to Chile (Korry) to the Under Secretary of State for Political Affairs (Johnson), 5 October 1970, *FRUS, 1969–1976*, Vol. XXI, Chile, Document 132.

52. On the negotiations toward and contents of the agreement between the PDC and UP, see Hurtado, *Las palabras no se las lleva el viento*, pp. 125–164.

53. From CIA Headquarters (Langley) to Station in Santiago, 23 October 1970, U.S. State Department, Freedom of Information Act (FOIA), Virtual Reading Room, accessed 27 April 2019.

54. Backchannel Message from the Ambassador to Chile (Korry) to the Under Secretary of State for Political Affairs (Johnson) and the President's Assistant for National Security Affairs (Kissinger), 9 October 1970, *FRUS, 1969–1976*, Vol. XXI, Chile, Document 144.

55. Memorandum of Conversation, 15 October 1970; Transcript of a Telephone Conversation between President Nixon and the President's Assistant for National Security Affairs (Kissinger), 15 October 1970, *FRUS, 1969–1976*, Vol. XXI, Chile, Documents 152 and 153, respectively.

56. From CIA Headquarters (Langley) to Station in Santiago, 23 October 1970, U.S. State Department, Freedom of Information Act (FOIA), Virtual Reading Room, accessed 27 April 2019.

57. Schlesinger Jr., *The Imperial Presidency.*

58. Letter from Eduardo Frei Montalva to Henry Kissinger, 28 September 1978, AEFM, Presidencia y Post-Presidencia, Correspondencia, Carpeta 395.

Conclusion

1. Gustafson, *Hostile Intent.*

2. Historian Jonathan Haslam has asserted that the coup was planned by the Chilean military in collusion with the Pentagon. Testimonies from unidentified sources are the only evidence offered by Haslam to back his assertion. Haslam, *The Nixon Administration and Allende's Chile.* The best assessment of the matter is by Tanya Harmer, *Allende's Chile and the Inter-American Cold War,* pp. 220–222.

3. Meller, *Un siglo de economía política chilena,* pp. 109–120.

4. *Diario de Sesiones del Senado,* 13th Session, 13 July 1954, p. 699.

Bibliography

Archives

Archivo Casa-Museo Eduardo Frei Montalva. Santiago, Chile.
Archivo Histórico del Ministerio de Relaciones Exteriores. Santiago, Chile.
International Monetary Fund Archives. Washington D.C.
  Western Hemisphere Department Fonds. WHDAI Country Files.
John F. Kennedy Presidential Library and Museum. Boston, Massachusetts.
  Personal Papers of Ralph Dungan.
Lyndon B. Johnson Presidential Library and Museum. Austin, Texas.
  Personal Papers of Lyndon Baines Johnson, President, 1963–1969.
  Personal Papers of Anthony Solomon.
National Archives and Records Administration II. College Park, Maryland.
  Record Group 59, Records of the Department of State.
  Record Group 286, Records of the Agency for International Development.
  Record Group 306, Records of the United States Information Agency.
Richard Nixon Presidential Library and Museum. Yorba Linda, California.
  NSC Files.
  Pinochet Files.

Online Resources

Historia Política Legislativa del Congreso Nacional de Chile. http://historiapolitica.bcn
  .cl/historia_legislativa#.
U.S. Agency for International Development (USAID), Foreign Aid Explorer. The
  Official Record of U.S. Foreign Aid. Foreign Aid Explorer. https://explorer.usaid
  .gov/index.html.

U.S. State Department, Freedom of Information Act. Virtual Reading Room. https://
foia.state.gov.

Printed Primary Sources

Foreign Relations of the United States
    1964–1968. South and Central America; Mexico, Volume XXXI
    1969–1976. Chile, Volume XXI
U.S. Congress. Senate. Select Committee to Study Governmental Operations with
    Respect to Intelligence Activities. *Alleged Assassination Plots Involving Foreign Leaders.*
    94th Congress, 1st Session, November 20, 1975.
U.S. Congress. Senate. Select Committee to Study Governmental Operations with
    Respect to Intelligence Activities, *Covert Action in Chile, 1963–1973: Staff Report.*
    94th Congress, 1st Session, 1975.
Diario de Sesiones del Senado. Chile, 1964–1970
Diario de Sesiones de la Cámara de Diputados. Chile, 1964–1970

Newspapers and Magazines

Chile

El Mercurio
El Siglo
La Nación
Las Noticias de Última Hora
Ercilla
Punto Final
Mensaje
Política y Espíritu

United States

New York Times
Washington Post

Secondary Sources

"El embajador Korry en el CEP. Entrevista." *Estudios Públicos* 72 (Spring, 1998).
"Report of the Special Latin American Committee on the Consensus of Viña del Mar."
    International Legal Materials 8, no. 5 (September 1969): pp. 974–978.
Ahumada, Jorge. *En vez de la miseria.* Santiago: Editorial del Pacífico, 1958.
Alexander, Robert. *The Tragedy of Chile.* Westport, CT: Greenwood Press, 1978.

——. *The ABC Presidents: Conversations and Correspondence with the Presidents of Argentina, Brazil and Chile.* Westport, CT: Praeger, 1992.

Almonacid, Fabián. *La agricultura chilena discriminada (1910–1960). Una mirada de las políticas estatales y el desarrollo sectorial desde el sur.* Madrid: Consejo Superior de Investigaciones Científicas, 2009.

Álvarez, Rolando. "La Unidad Popular y las elecciones presidenciales de 1970 en Chile: La batalla electoral como vía revolucionaria." *OSAL*, CLACSO XI, no. 28 (November): pp. 219–239.

Ampuero, Raúl. *El socialismo chileno.* Santiago: Tierra Mía, 2002.

Atkins, G. Pope. *Latin America and the Caribbean in the International System.* Boulder, CO: Westview Press, 1999.

Barr-Melej, Patrick. *Reforming Chile: Cultural Politics, Nationalism, and the Rise of the Middle Class.* Chapel Hill: University of North Carolina Press, 2001.

Basso, Carlos. *La CIA en Chile, 1970–1973.* Santiago: Aguilar, 2013.

Bawden, John. *The Pinochet Generation: The Chilean Military in the Twentieth Century.* Tuscaloosa: The University of Alabama Press, 2016.

Bellisario, Antonio. "The Chilean Agrarian Transformation: Agrarian Reform and Capitalist 'Partial' Counter-Agrarian Reform, 1964–1980." *Journal of Agrarian Change* 7 (2007): pp. 1–34.

Berlinguer, Enrico. "Imperialismo e coesistenza alla luce dei fatti cileni." *Rinascita* (28 September 1973).

Bernstein, Irving. *Guns or Butter: The Presidency of Lyndon Johnson.* New York: Oxford University Press, 1996.

Bethell, Leslie and Ian Roxborough. *Latin America between the Second World War and the Cold War, 1944–1948.* Cambridge: Cambridge University Press, 1992.

Boizard, Ricardo. *La Democracia Cristiana en Chile. Un mundo que nace entre dos guerras.* Santiago: Orbe, 1963.

Booth, John, and Patricia Richard. *Latin American Political Culture: Public Opinion and Democracy.* Los Angeles: Sage, 2015.

Boye, Otto. *Hermano Bernardo: 50 años de vida política vistos por Bernardo Leighton.* Santiago: Aconcagua, 1986.

Brands, H. W. (editor). *Beyond Vietnam: The Foreign Policies of Lyndon B. Johnson.* College Station, TX: Texas A & M University Press, 1999.

Brands, Hal. *Latin America's Cold War.* Cambridge: Harvard University Press, 2010.

——. "The United States and the Peruvian Challenge, 1968–1975." *Diplomacy & Statecraft* 21 (2010): pp. 471–490.

——. "Richard Nixon and Economic Nationalism in Latin America: The Problem of Expropriations, 1968–1974." *Diplomacy & Statecraft* 18 (2007): pp. 215–235.

Brogi, Alessandro. *A Question of Self-Esteem: The United States and the Cold War Choices in France and Italy, 1944–1958.* Westport, CT: Greenwood, 2002.

Caputo, Rodrigo, and Diego Saravia. "The Fiscal and Monetary History of Chile 1960–2010." Becker Friedman Institute for Research in Economics, The University of Chicago. Accessed on 14 January 2016. https://bfi.uchicago.edu/initiative/fiscal-studies.

Casals, Marcelo. *El alba de una revolución: La izquierda y el proceso de construcción estratégica de la vía chilena al socialismo, 1956–1970*. Santiago: LOM, 2010.

——. "'Chile en la encrucijada'. Anticomunismo y propaganda en la 'Campaña del Terror' de las elecciones presidenciales de 1964." In *Chile y la Guerra Fría global*, edited by Tanya Harmer and Alfredo Riquelme. Santiago: RIL, 2014, pp. 89–112.

——. *La creación de la amenaza roja: del surgimiento del anticomunismo en Chile a la "campaña del terror" de 1964*. Santiago: LOM, 2016.

Castillo Velasco, Jaime. *Los caminos de la revolución*. Santiago: Editorial del Pacífico, 1972.

——. *Teoría y práctica de la Democracia Cristiana*. Santiago: Editorial del Pacífico, 1973.

Colman, Jonathan. *The Foreign Policy of Lyndon B. Johnson: The United States and the World, 1963–1969*. Edinburgh: Edinburgh University Press, 2010.

Correa, Sofía. *Con las riendas del poder: la derecha chilena en el siglo XX*. Santiago: Sudamericana, 2005.

Corvalán Márquez, Luis. *La secreta obscenidad de la historia de Chile contemporáneo: Lo que dicen los documentos norteamericanos y otras fuentes documentales, 1962–1976*. Santiago: Ceibo Ediciones, 2012.

Couyoumdjian, Juan Pablo (editor). *Reformas económicas e instituciones políticas: la experiencia de la Misión Klein-Saks en Chile*. Santiago: Universidad del Desarrollo, 2011.

Crawley, Andrew. *Somoza and Roosevelt: Good Neighbour Diplomacy in Nicaragua, 1933–1945*. New York: Oxford University Press, 2007.

Cruz-Coke, Ricardo. *Historia Electoral de Chile, 1925–1973*. Santiago: Editorial Jurídica de Chile, 1984.

Dallek, Robert. *Nixon and Kissinger: Partners in Power*. New York: HarperCollins Publishers, 2007.

Davis, Nathaniel. *The Last Two Years of Salvador Allende*. London: Tauris, 1985.

Deves, Eduardo. *El pensamiento latinoamericano en el siglo XX. Tomo II: Desde la CEPAL al neoliberalismo. 1950–1990*. Buenos Aires: Biblos, Centro de Investigaciones Diego Barros Arana.

Díaz, José; Rolf Lüders, and Gert Wagner. *La República en Cifras, Chile 1810–2010. Historical Statistics*. Santiago: Ediciones UC, 2016.

Dobbs, Michael. *One Minute to Midnight: Kennedy, Khrushchev, and Castro on the Brink of Nuclear War*. New York: Vintage, 2009.

Donoso, José. *Casa de campo*. Madrid: Seix Barral, 1978.

Donoso Pacheco, Jorge (editor). *Tomic: Testimonios*. Santiago: Emisión, 1988.

Donoso Pacheco, Jorge, and Grace Dunlop Echeverría. *Los 13 del 13: Los DC contra el golpe*. Santiago: RIL, 2013.

Doyle, Michael. *Empires*. Ithaca: Cornell University Press, 1986.

Edwards, Jorge. *Esclavos de la consigna. Memorias II*. Santiago: Lumen, 2018.

Eisenhower, Milton. *The Wine is Bitter: The United States and Latin America*. Garden City, NY: Doubleday and Company, Inc., 1963.

El Parlamento chileno y el hecho mundial del cobre, vol. I. Santiago: Biblioteca del Congreso Nacional, sección estudios, Andrés Bello, 1972.

Engerman, David et al. (editors). *Staging Growth: Modernization, Development, and the Global Cold War*. Amherst and Boston: University of Massachusetts Press, 2003.

Espinoza, Vicente. *Para una historia de los pobres de la ciudad*. Santiago: Sur, 1988.

Etchepare, Jaime, and Mario Valdés. *El naranjazo y sus repercusiones en la elección presidencial de 1964*. Santiago: Universidad de Chile, Instituto de Ciencias Políticas, 1985.

Fermandois, Joaquín. "Chile y la cuestión cubana, 1959–1964." *Historia* 17 (1982): pp. 113–200.

———. "La época de las visitas: Charles de Gaulle en Chile y Eduardo Frei en Francia, 1964 y 1965." *Mapocho* 52 (Second Semester 2002): pp. 19–37.

———. *Chile y el mundo 1970–1973. La política exterior del gobierno de la Unidad Popular y el sistema internacional*. Santiago: Ediciones Universidad Católica de Chile, 1985.

———. *Mundo y fin de mundo: Chile y la política mundial, 1900–2004*. Santiago: Universidad Católica de Chile, 2004.

———. *La revolución inconclusa. La izquierda chilena y el gobierno de la Unidad Popular*. Santiago: Centro de Estudios Públicos, 2013.

Fermandois, Joaquín; Jimena Bustos, and María José Schneuer. *Historia Política del Cobre, 1945–2008*. Santiago: Centro de Estudios Bicentenario, 2009.

Ffrench-Davis, Ricardo. *Políticas económicas en Chile, 1952–1970*. Santiago: Ediciones Nueva Universidad Católica de Chile, 1972.

Fleet, Michael. *The Rise and Fall of Chilean Christian Democracy*. Princeton, NJ: Princeton University Press, 1985.

Fontaine Aldunate, Arturo. *La tierra y el poder. Reforma agraria en Chile. 1964–1973*. Santiago: Zig Zag, 2001.

Frazier, Lessy Jo. *Salt in the Sand: Memory, Violence, and the Nation-State in Chile, 1890 to the Present*. Durham: Duke University Press, 2007.

Frei, Eduardo. "The Alliance that Lost Its Way." *Foreign Affairs* (April 1967): pp. 437–448.

Gamboa, Ricardo. "Reformando reglas electorales: la cédula única y los pactos electorales en Chile. 1958–1962." *Revista de Ciencia Política* 31, no. 2 (2011): pp. 159–186.

Garay, Cristian, and Ángel Soto. *Gabriel González Videla: "No a los totalitarismos, ya sean rojos, pardos o amarillos. . . ."* Santiago: Centro de Estudios Bicentenario, 2013.

Gazmuri, Cristian. *Eduardo Frei Montalva y su época*, 2 vol. Santiago: Aguilar, 2000.

Gil, Federico. *The Political System of Chile*. Boston: Houghton Mifflin, 1966.

Gilman, Nils. *Mandarins of the Future: Modernization Theory in Cold War America*. Baltimore: Johns Hopkins University Press, 2003.

Gleijeses, Piero. *The Dominican Crisis: The 1965 Constitutional Revolt and American Intervention*. Baltimore: Johns Hopkins University Press, 1978.

Gordon, Lincoln. *A New Deal for Latin America: The Alliance for Progress*. Cambridge: Harvard University Press, 1963.

Grandin, Greg, *The Last Colonial Massacre: Latin America in the Cold War*. Chicago: University of Chicago Press, 2004.

———. *Empire's Workshop: Latin America, the United States and the Rise of the New Imperialism*. New York: Metropolitan Books, 2006.

Grow, Michael, *U.S. Presidents and Latin American Interventions: Pursuing Regime Change in the Cold War*. Lawrence, KS: University Press of Kansas, 2008.

Gumucio, Rafael Agustín. *Apuntes de medio siglo*. Santiago: CESOC, 1994.

Gustafson, Kristian. *Hostile Intent: U.S. Covert Operations in Chile, 1964–1974.* Washington D.C.: Potomac Books, 2007.

Hahnimaki, Jussi. *The Flawed Architect: Henry Kissinger and American Foreign Policy.* New York: Oxford University Press, 2004.

Harmer, Tanya. *Allende's Chile and the Inter-American Cold War.* Chapel Hill: University of North Carolina Press, 2011.

——. "Brazil's Cold War in the Southern Cone, 1970–1975." *Cold War History* 12, no. 4 (2012): pp. 659–681.

——. "Chile y la Guerra Fría interamericana, 1970–1973." In *Chile y la Guerra Fría global,* edited by Tanya Harmer and Alfredo Riquelme. Santiago: RIL, 2014, pp. 193–194.

Harvey, Hugo. "La política exterior de Chile frente a la intervención de Estados Unidos en República Dominicana en 1965." Unpublished PhD diss., Universidad de Santiago de Chile, 2016.

Haslam, Jonathan. *The Nixon Administration and Allende's Chile: A Case of Assisted Suicide.* New York: Verso, 2005.

Herman, Ellen. "Project Camelot and the Career of Cold War Psychology." In *Universities and Empire: Money and Politics in the Social Sciences During the Cold War,* edited by Christopher Simpson. New York: The New Press, 1988, pp. 97–134.

Hitchcock, William. "The Marshall Plan and the Creation of the West." In *The Cambridge History of the Cold War, Vol. 1,* edited by Melvin Leffler and Odd Arne Westad. Cambridge, UK: Cambridge University Press, 2010, pp. 154–174.

Hogan, Michael J. *The Marshall Plan: America, Britain and the Reconstruction of Western Europe, 1947–1952.* Cambridge, UK: Cambridge University Press, 1987.

Huerta, María Antonieta. *"Otro agro para Chile." Historia de la reforma agraria en el proceso social y político.* Santiago: CESOC, 1989.

Huneeus, Carlos. *La Guerra Fría Chilena: Gabriel González Videla y la Ley Maldita.* Santiago: Debate, 2009.

Hunt, Michael. *The American Ascendancy: How the United States Gained and Wielded Global Dominance.* Chapel Hill: University of North Carolina Press, 2007.

Hurtado, Diego. *Las palabras no se las lleva el viento: Lenguajes políticos y democracia durante el gobierno de la Unidad Popular (1970–1973).* Santiago: Centro de Estudios Bicentenario, 2019.

Hurtado-Torres, Sebastián. "The U.S. Press and Chile, 1964–1973: Ideology and U.S. Foreign Policy." *Revista de Historia Iberoamericana* 5, no. 2 (2012): pp. 37–61

——. "El golpe que no fue: Eduardo Frei, la Democracia Cristiana y la elección presidencial de 1970." *Estudios Públicos* 129 (Summer 2013): pp. 105–140.

Ikenberry, G. John. *Liberal Leviathan: The Origins, Crisis and Transformation of the American World Order.* Princeton, NJ: Princeton University Press, 2012.

Jensen, Poul. *The Garotte: The United States and Chile, 1970–1973.* Aarhus, Dinamarca: Aarhus University Press, 1988.

Jobet, Julio César. *El Partido Socialista de Chile. Vol. II.* Santiago: Prensa Latinoamericana, 1971.

Johnson, Loch K. *A Season of Inquiry Revisited: The Church Committee Confronts America's Spy Agencies.* Lawrence, KS: University Press of Kansas, 2015.

Kirkendall, Andrew. "Kennedy Men and the Fate of the Alliance for Progress in LBJ Era Brazil and Chile." *Diplomacy & Statecraft* 18 no. 4 (2007): pp. 745–772.

Kissinger, Henry. *Diplomacy.* New York: Simon & Schuster, 1994.

Klubock, Thomas Miller. *Contested Communities: Class, Gender, and Politics in Chile's El Teniente Copper Mine, 1904–1951.* Durham: Duke University Press, 1998.

Knight, Alan. "U.S. Imperialism/Hegemony and Latin American Resistance." In *Empire and Dissent: The United States and Latin America*, edited by Fred Rosen. Durham and London: Duke University Press, 2008.

Kopp, Harry W. *The Voice of the Foreign Service: A History of the American Foreign Service Association.* Washington D.C.: Foreign Service Books, 2015.

Kornbluh, Peter. *The Pinochet File: A Declassified Dossier on Atrocity and Accountability.* New York: The New Press, 2003.

Korry, Edward. "Los Estados Unidos en Chile y Chile en los Estados Unidos. Una retrospectiva política y económica." *Estudios Públicos* 72 (Spring 1998).

Labarca, Eduardo. *Chile invadido. Reportaje a la intromisión extranjera.* Santiago: Austral, 1968.

——. *Chile al rojo.* Santiago: Editorial de la Universidad Técnica del Estado, 1971.

Langley, Lester. *The Banana Wars: United States Intervention in the Caribbean, 1898–1934.* Wilmington, DE: Scholarly Resources, 2002.

Latham, Michael. *Modernization as Ideology: American Social Science and "Nation Building" in the Kennedy Era.* Chapel Hill: University of North Carolina Press, 2000.

——. *The Right Kind of Revolution: Modernization, Development, and U.S. Foreign Policy from the Cold War to the Present.* Ithaca, NY: Cornell University Press, 2011.

Leonard, Thomas. *Central America and the United States: The Search for Stability.* Athens, GA: University of Georgia Press, 1991.

Levinson, Jerome, and Juan de Onís. *The Alliance that Lost Its Way: A Critical Report on the Alliance for Progress.* Chicago: Quadrangle Books, 1972.

Logevall, Fredrik. *Choosing War: The Lost Chance for Peace and the Escalation of War in Vietnam.* Berkeley: University of California Press, 1999.

Loveman, Brian. *No Higher Law: American Foreign Policy and the Western Hemisphere since 1776.* Chapel Hill: University of North Carolina Press, 2010.

Loveman, Brian and Elizabeth Lira. *Las ardientes cenizas del olvido. Vía chilena de reconciliación política, 1932-1994.* Santiago: LOM, 2000.

Lowe, George. "The Camelot Affair." *Bulletin of the Atomic Scientists: A Journal of Science and Public Affairs* (May 1966): pp. 44–47.

Lowenthal, Abraham. *The Dominican Intervention.* Baltimore: Johns Hopkins University Press, 1972.

Lundestad, Geir, "Empire by Invitation? The United States and Western Europe, 1945–1952." *Journal of Peace Research* 23.3 (1986): pp. 263–277.

Maier, Charles. *Among Empires: American Ascendancy and Its Predecessors.* Cambridge: Harvard University Press, 2009.

Mann, Michael. *The Sources of Social Power. Volume 4: Globalizations, 1945–2011.* New York: Cambridge University Press, 2013.

McPherson, Alan. *Intimate Ties, Bitter Struggles: The United States and Latin America since 1945.* Washington: Potomac Books, 2006.

McVety, Amanda Kay. *Enlightened Aid: U.S. Development as Foreign Policy in Ethiopia.* New York: Oxford University Press, 2012.

Meller, Patricio. *Un siglo de economía política chilena. 1890–1990.* Santiago: Andrés Bello, 1996.

Mihalkanin, Edward, and Warren Keith Neisler, "The Role of the U.S. Ambassador." In *U.S.-Latin American Policymaking: A Reference Handbook,* edited by David Dent. Westport, CT: Greenwood Press, 1995, pp. 307–333.

Molina, Sergio. *El Proceso de Cambio en Chile.* Santiago: Universitaria, 1972.

Moniz Bandeira, Luiz Alberto. *Fórmula para o caos: a derrubada de Salvador Allende, 1970–1973.* Rio de Janeiro: Civilização Brasileira, 2008.

Moran, Theodore. *Multinational Corporations and the Politics of Dependence: Copper in Chile.* Princeton, NJ: Princeton University Press, 1974.

Moskin, J. Robert. *American Statecraft: The Story of the U.S. Foreign Service.* New York: St. Martin's Press, 2013.

Moulian, Tomás. *Fracturas: De Pedro Aguirre Cerda a Salvador Allende, 1938–1973.* Santiago: LOM, 2006.

Navia, Patricio, and Rodrigo Osorio. "Las encuestas de opinión pública en Chile antes de 1973." *Latin American Research Review* 50, no. 1 (2015).

Nixon, Richard. *The Memoirs of Richard Nixon.* London: Arrow, 1979.

Nocera, Raffaele. *Acuerdos y desacuerdos. La DC italiana y el PDC chileno: 1962–1973.* Santiago: FCE Chile, 2015.

Nohlen, Dieter (editor). *Elections in the Americas. A Data Handbook. Vol. 2: South America.* New York: Oxford University Press, 2005.

Olavarría Bravo, Arturo. *Chile entre dos Alessandri. Memorias políticas. Tomo IV.* Santiago: Nascimento, 1965.

——. *Chile bajo la Democracia Cristiana.* 6 vol. Santiago: Nascimento: 1966–1971.

Palieraki, Eugenia. *¡La revolución ya viene! El MIR chileno en los años sesenta.* Santiago: LOM, 2014.

Pereira, Teresa. *El Partido Conservador: 1930–1965, ideas, figuras y actitudes.* Santiago: Vivaria, 1994.

Peterson, Harold J. *Argentina and the United States, 1810–1960.* New York: State University of New York, 1964.

Petras, James, and Morris Morley. *The United States and Chile: Imperialism and the Overthrow of the Allende Government.* New York: Monthly Review Press, 1975.

Portales, Felipe. *Los mitos de la democracia chilena,* 2 vol. Santiago: Catalonia, 2004.

Power, Margaret. *Right-Wing Women in Chile: Feminine Power and the Struggle against Allende, 1964–1973.* University Park, PA: Pennsylvania State University Press, 2002.

——. "The Engendering of Anticommunism and Fear in Chile's 1964 Presidential Election." *Diplomatic History* 32, no. 5 (November 2008): pp. 931–953.

Qureshi, Lubna. *Nixon, Kissinger and Allende: U.S. Involvement in the 1973 Coup in Chile.* Lanham, MD: Lexington Books, 2009.

Rabe, Stephen. *The Most Dangerous Area in the World: John F. Kennedy Confronts Communist Revolution in Latin America.* Chapel Hill, NC: University of North Carolina Press, 1999.

———. "The Johnson Doctrine." *Presidential Studies Quarterly* 36.1 (2006): pp. 48–58.

———. *The Killing Zone: The United States Wages Cold War in Latin America.* New York: Oxford University Press, 2011.

Rockefeller, Nelson. *The Rockefeller Report on the Americas: The Official Report of a United States Presidential Mission.* Chicago: Quadrangle Books, 1969.

Rogers, William D. *The Twilight Struggle: The Alliance for Progress and the Politics of Development in Latin America.* New York: Random House, 1967.

Rojas, Patricio. *Tiempos difíciles: Mi testimonio.* Santiago: Aguilar, 2013.

Ronning, C. Neale, and Albert Vannucci. *Ambassadors in Foreign Policy: The Influence of Individuals on U.S.-Latin American Policy.* Westport, CT: Praeger, 1987.

Roorda, Eric, *The Dictator Next Door: The Good Neighbor Policy and the Trujillo Regime in the Dominican Republic, 1930–1945.* Durham, NC: Duke University Press, 1998.

Rosenberg, Emily, *Financial Missionaries to the World: The Politics and Culture of Dollar Diplomacy, 1900–1930.* Cambridge, MA: Harvard University Press, 1999.

Rostow, Walt W. *The Stages of Economic Growth: A Non-Communist Manifesto.* Cambridge: Cambridge University Press, 1960.

Sáez, Raúl. *Raúl Sáez. Hombre del siglo XX.* Santiago: Dolmen, 1994.

Salazar, Gabriel. *La enervante levedad histórica de la clase política civil: Chile, 1900–1973.* Santiago: Debate, 2015.

Salazar, Gabriel, and Julio Pinto. *Historia contemporánea de Chile I: Estado, legitimidad, ciudadanía.* Santiago: LOM, 1999.

Santoni, Alessandro. "El Partido Comunista Italiano, la lección de Chile y la lógica de los bloques." In *Chile y la Guerra Fría global*, edited by Tanya Harmer and Alfredo Riquelme. Santiago: RIL, 2014, pp. 133–153.

Schlesinger Jr., Arthur. *The Imperial Presidency.* Boston: Houghton Mifflin, 1973.

Schoultz, Lars. *That Infernal Little Cuban Republic: The United States and the Cuban Revolution.* Chapel Hill: University of North Carolina Press, 2009.

Schroeder, Paul. "From Hegemony to Empire: The Fatal Leap." In *Imbalance of Power: US Hegemony and International Order*, edited by I. William Zartman. Boulder, CO and London: Lynne Rienner Publishers, 2009.

Schwartzberg, Steven. *Democracy and U.S. Policy in Latin America during the Truman Years.* Gainesville: University Press of Florida, 2008.

Scully, Timothy. *Rethinking the Center: Party Politics in Nineteenth- and Twentieth-Century Chile.* Stanford: Stanford University Press, 1992.

Siekmeier, James. *The Bolivian Revolution and the United States, 1952 to Present.* University Park, PA: Pennsylvania State University Press, 2011.

Sierra, Enrique. *Tres ensayos de estabilización en Chile.* Santiago: Universitaria, 1967.

Sigmund, Paul. *The Overthrow of Allende and the Politics of Chile, 1964–1976.* Pittsburgh: University of Pittsburgh Press, 1980.

———. *The United States and Democracy in Chile*. Baltimore: Johns Hopkins University Press, 1993.

Silva Solar, Julio, and Jacques Chonchol. *El desarrollo de la nueva sociedad en América Latina: hacia un mundo comunitario*. Santiago: Universitaria, 1965.

Silveira, Fabio Vidigal Xavier da. *Frei, el Kerensky Chileno*. Caracas: Grupo Tradicionalista de Jóvenes Cristianos Venezolanos, 1968.

Smith, Tony. *The Pattern of Imperialism: The United States, Great Britain and the Late-Industrializing World since 1815*. Cambridge and New York: Cambridge University Press, 1984.

Soto, Javiera. *Espía se ofrece: acusaciones de intervencionismo contra Estados Unidos en Chile, 1964–1970*. Santiago: Acto Editores, 2016.

Staley, Eugene. *The Future of Underdeveloped Countries: Political Implications of Economic Development*. New York: Harper & Brothers, 1954.

Taffet, Jeffrey. "The Making of an Economic Anti-American: Eduardo Frei and Chile during the 1960s." In *Anti-Americanism in Latin America and the Caribbean*, edited by Alan McPherson. New York: Berghahn Books, 2006, pp. 113–139.

———. *Foreign Aid as Foreign Policy: The Alliance for Progress in Latin America*. New York: Routledge, 2007.

———. "Alliance for What? United States Development Assistance in Chile during the 1960s." Unpublished PhD diss., Georgetown University, 2001.

Thielemann, Luis. "Eduardo Frei Montalva y la brutalización de la política en Chile." *El Mostrador*, 11 February 2019, accessed 13 May 2019, https://www.elmostrador.cl/noticias/opinion/2019/02/11/eduardo-frei-montalva-y-la-brutalizacion-de-la-politica-en-chile/.

Tinsman, Heidi. *Partners in Conflict: The Politics of Gender, Sexuality, and Labor in the Chilean Agrarian Reform, 1950–1973*. Durham, NC: Duke University Press, 2002.

Torres, Isabel. *La crisis del sistema democrático: Las elecciones presidenciales y los proyectos políticos excluyentes, Chile 1958–1970*. Santiago: Universitaria, 2014.

Ulianova, Olga, and Eugenia Fediakova. "Algunos aspectos de la ayuda financiera del Partido Comunista de la URSS al comunismo chileno durante la Guerra Fría." *Estudios Públicos* 72 (Spring 1998): pp. 113–148.

Urzúa, Germán. *Historia política de Chile y su evolución electoral*. Santiago: Editorial Jurídica de Chile, 1992.

Valdés, Gabriel. *Sueños y memorias*. Santiago: Taurus, 2009.

Valdivia, Verónica. *El golpe después del golpe. Leigh vs. Pinochet, Chile 1960–1980*. Santiago: LOM, 2003.

———. *Nacionales y gremialistas: El "parto" de la nueva derecha política chilena, 1964–1973*. Santiago: LOM, 2008.

Valenzuela, Arturo. *The Breakdown of Democratic Regimes: Chile*. Baltimore: Johns Hopkins University Press, 1978.

Verdugo, Patricia. *Allende: Cómo la Casa Blanca provocó su muerte*. Santiago: Catalonia, 2003.

Vergara, Ángela. "Conflicto y modernización en la Gran Minería del Cobre, 1950–1970." *Historia* 37, II (July-December 2004): pp. 419–436.

———. *Copper Workers, International Business, and Domestic Politics in Cold War Chile.* University Park, PA: Pennsylvania State University Press, 2008.

Westad, Odd Arne. *The Global Cold War: Third World Interventions and the Making of Our Times.* New York: Cambridge University Press, 2005.

Winn, Peter. *Weavers of Revolution: The Yarur Workers and Chile's Road to Socialism.* New York: Oxford University Press, 1986.

Woods, Randall B. "Conflicted Hegemon: LBJ and the Dominican Republic." *Diplomatic History* 32.5 (2008): pp. 749–766.

———. *Prisoners of Hope: Lyndon B. Johnson, the Great Society, and the Limits of Liberalism.* New York: Basic Books, 2016.

Yocelevzky, Ricardo. "La Democracia Cristiana chilena. Trayectoria de un Proyecto." *Revista Mexicana de Sociología* 47, no. 2 (April-June 1985).

Zourek, Michael. *Checoslovaquia y el Cono Sur 1945-1989. Relaciones políticas, económicas y culturales durante la Guerra Fría.* Prague: Universidad Carolina de Praga, Editorial Karolinum, 2014.

Index

CPSIA information can be obtained
at www.ICGtesting.com
Printed in the USA
LVHW091906040220
645826LV00007B/128/J